TOTAL LOSS

Editor: Jack Coote

SHERIDAN HOUSE

This edition published 1992 by
Sheridan House Inc.
145 Palisade Street
Dobbs Ferry, NY 10522

Copyright © Jack Coote 1985
First paperback edition 1992
Reprinted 1993

Library of Congress Cataloging-in-Publication Data
Total loss/editor, Jack Coote.—1st pbk. ed.
    p. cm.
  Originally published: London: A. Coles, 1985.
  Includes index.
  ISBN 0–924486–33–3:$19.95
  1. Yachts and yachting—History.   2. Shipwrecks—History.
  3. Yachts and yachting—Safety measures.   I. Coote, Jack.
  [GV812.T67 1992]   92–6609
  796.1'246–dc20   CIP

Printed in Great Britain

ISBN 0–924486–33–3

DEDICATION
To the friends I have
made through sailing

Contents

Contents

Contents

The Illustrations

The pictorial illustrations are by Trevor Ridley.

The charts are reproduced from sections of Admiralty charts of the appropriate period, with the permission of the Controller of H.M. Stationery Office and of the Hydrographer of the Navy. Tracks have been added by the author.

The sequence of six illustrations on pages 262 and 263, are reproduced from photographs taken by Lieutenant Douglas Perkins of the United States Coast Guard.

Preface

This is not a pessimistic book, for had I thought that by compiling it I would dissuade anyone from setting out in a well found yacht after making proper preparations for a voyage, I would not have begun. Neither do I consider the book to be morbid, since none of the accounts I have included involved the loss of life.

Just as the chances of being involved in an air or rail crash are very small, so a reasonably competent yachtsman can expect to sail for a lifetime without ever facing a situation where he must abandon ship. Nevertheless, it can happen, and perhaps that is why the awful finality of the term 'total loss' holds such a fascination for most of us.

There are many reasons why yachts are lost at sea, some of them obvious and others strange or even unexplained, but it is an interesting fact that most of those who have suffered such a loss are willing, sometimes even eager, to recount their disasters. The accounts they give are often thrilling, and that is one reason for this book; but another is that the willingness to tell their stories springs from a genuine desire to pass on the lessons that can be learned from what they endured.

Acknowledgements

This book could not have been compiled without the cooperation of many people, all of whom I wish to thank in my first sentence, lest I omit to mention any of them later.

The idea for the book was Julian van Hasselt's and he did some preliminary work on it before handing the project over to me. Peter Tangvald had once intended to put together a similar book and he generously told me how far he had got and what difficulties he had met. Early in my preparatory work the late John Scarlett helped greatly by suggesting several fruitful sources from among the members of the Old Gaffers Association. Charles Vilas, editor of *Cruising Club News* in the US, was always ready to help in my search for material and I thank him for his cooperation. Iain McAllister of the Royal Northern and Clyde Yacht Club unearthed the 1894 report of the collision between *Valkyrie II* and *Satanita* and I certainly appreciate the research he did.

I particularly want to thank the people who wrote accounts especially for the book and those who have allowed me to use material that has not been published elsewhere. When I found that the official RORC record of the loss of the Club boat *Griffin* in the 1979 Fastnet was not available, Stuart Quarrie, *Griffin*'s navigator on the race, very kindly wrote an account for me. Henry Irving also promptly responded to my request for his story of the loss of *Strumpet* by fire. Ann Griffin kindly let me have her version of the stranding of *Northern Light*, while Merrill Robson allowed me to use her account of the loss of *Maid of Malham*.

Next, I must thank the editors of those magazines, who, together with the writers concerned, have given me permission to use extracts from their publications. They include: Des Sleightholme, editor of *Yachting Monthly*, and the following authors: Nick Hallam for 'Over in the Atlantic', Malcolm Beilby for 'The Tri that Broke up' and C. Binnings for 'A Chance in a Lifetime'; Dick Johnson, editor of *Yachting World*, and the following authors: Peter Tangvald for 'Hard Chance in a Nutshell', James Houston for 'One Touch of the Button' and Peter Rose for 'Odd Times at Sea'; the editor of *SAIL* and Bob Payne for 'Surviving Hurricane Assault'; the editor of *Yachting* and Bruce Paulsen for 'Four Pumps and Still She Sank' as well as Keith Douglas-Young for 'So Near and Yet—'; David Pardon, editor of *Sea Spray*, and Anthony Lealand for 'Capsize of Rushcutter'.

I found that yacht club journals often contain exciting, well written accounts of incidents experienced by members and for those I have used I must thank the following editors and contributors: the editor of the *Royal Cruising Club Journal* and Alain Catherineau for his part of 'Fastnet Rescue' and Brigadier D. H. Davies (acting on behalf of the late W. H. Tilman) for 'The Loss of Sea Breeze' and 'Mischief's Last Voyage' as well as Robin Gardiner-Hall for 'Disaster in the Mouth of the Elbe'; the editor of the *Journal of the Royal Naval Sailing Association* and George Marshall for 'Whalestrike' as well as Peter Phillips for 'The End of an OSTAR'; the editor of the *Cruising Association Bulletin* and Malcolm Robson for 'The Death of Banba', as well as Dr Douglas Gairdner for 'The Wreck of the Dragon'; the editor of the *Little Ship Club Journal* and Peter Combe for 'The Last Hours of Windstar' and Margaret Wells for 'A Gallant Dutchman'; the editor of the *Old Gaffers Association Newsletter* and Michael Millar for 'A Gaffer's Grave'; the editor of the *Humber Yawl Club Yearbook* and J. S. Robertson for 'Easting Down's Last Cruise'; the editor of *The Silhouette Owner* and Clementina Gordon for 'Bad Luck in Boulogne'; the editor of the *Clyde Cruising Club Journal* and Lionel Miller for 'Oopsie Daisy'; the editor of the *Lowestoft Cruising Club Journal* and George Harrod-Eagles for 'Song – the Final Episode'.

For permission to use excerpts from books, I have to thank Martin Eve of Merlin Press and Frank Mulville for 'Girl Stella's Going' as well as Edward Arnold Ltd and Miss Anne Roberts for 'The Wicked Old Martinet'.

Turning now to the illustrations, I am pleased to record my thanks for the valuable help I was given by Miss M. Perry and Mr M. Hickson of the Hydrographic Department at Taunton, who made it possible for me to locate the charts and select the areas I needed to reproduce from their priceless archives. Trevor Ridley took his usual care to ensure the authenticity of the pictorial illustrations and it was a pleasure to work with him. I also particularly appreciated the trust Lieutenant Douglas Perkins of the US Coast Guard showed by lending me the remarkable series of negatives he took from the deck of the C.G. cutter *Alert*.

Finally, I have to thank my daughter, Janet Harber, and my friend Eric Stone, for reading the first draft of my summary and making several constructive suggestions.

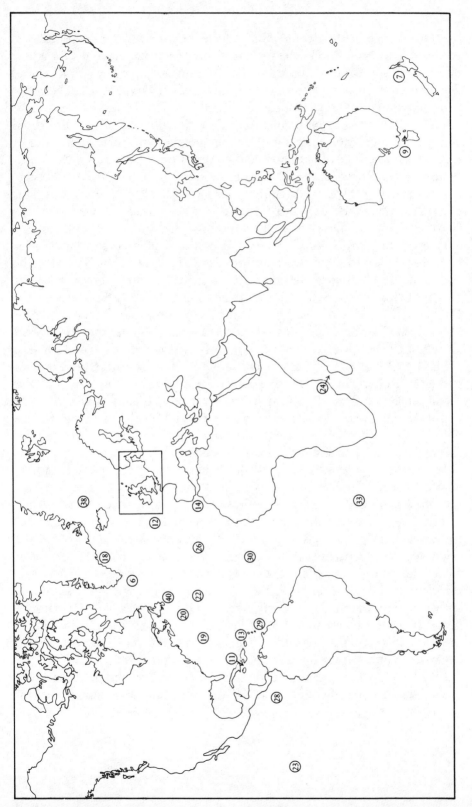

The numbers on these two charts correspond to the chapter numbers, and mark the position at which each yacht was lost.

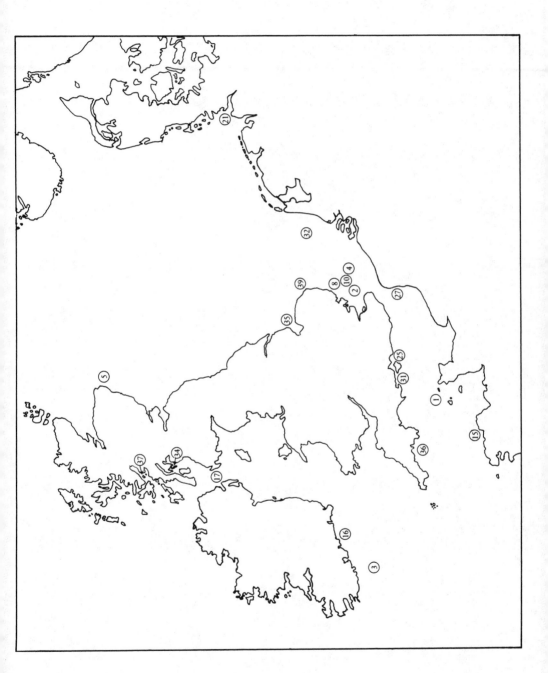

PART I: STRESS OF WEATHER

1: A Disaster

Yacht: *Alektor* (34ft gaff-rigged yawl)
Skipper: W.H.A. Whitworth
Crew: Two un-named undergraduates
Bound from Salcombe, Devon to Guernsey, Channel Islands
Time and date of loss: 1600, April 11th, 1924
Position: approx. 2 miles NW of the Casquets

A surprisingly large number of people have twice experienced the loss of their yachts at sea; W.H.A. Whitworth, Bernard Moitessier, John Nicholls, Malcolm Robson and W.H. Tilman among them. The two accounts by W.H.A. Whitworth of how he came to lose two of his yachts within ten years have been placed first in the book because of Whitworth's stated belief that such reports should be written for the benefit of fellow yachtsmen, and also because the first account, written in 1926, serves to remind us of the tremendous changes that have benefited the cruising yachtsman since the time when to hoist an inverted ensign was a useful way of attracting attention.

As a preface to his first account, Whitworth wrote:

'It is generally agreed that yachts suffer a smaller percentage of total losses than any other class of shipping. The reason is, of course, that the yachtsman, sailing for pleasure, can choose his weather. But the summer of 1924 was one of sudden gales, and by the end of July no less than four yachts had been reported as lost or abandoned. Surely accounts of how these disasters occurred would not only be interesting, but also exceedingly useful. No doubt this does involve a degreee of humiliation for the writers. But we all make mistakes, and I, for one, am willing to pocket my pride and tell the story of *Alektor*'s fate, in the hope that it may induce other unfortunate owners to let us have their yarns in turn.'

Alektor was designed by Dixon Kemp and built in 1882. She was 34ft

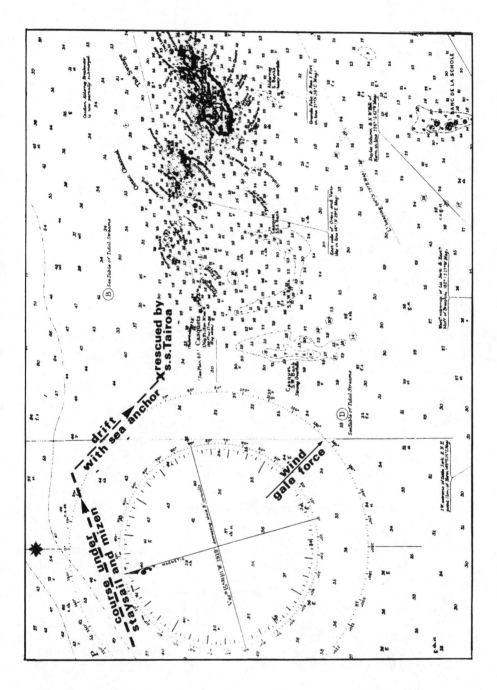

overall with a beam of only 9ft 6in and a draft of 7ft 3in! Her skipper was a university lecturer in mathematics and, with a crew of two undergraduates, they were sailing during the Easter vacation. Having left Portsmouth on a Saturday, they spent two or three days in Salcombe before deciding to cross to Guernsey 'on the following Friday.

——————— " ———————

'High water that Friday morning was at 10 a.m., and we got under way with the first of the ebb. Outside the breeze was light, but it soon freshened to just what we wanted and all day we reeled off five knots, which is quite good for *Alektor*. Our course for Les Hanois Light, Guernsey, was SSE ½E, the distance being 65 miles. We calculated that we should have a fair tide up to St Peter Port during the first five hours of the night from 8 p.m., and hoped thus to make that harbour somewhere about midnight. If we missed our tide or weather conditions were not good, we intended to heave-to for the remainder of the night and go up on the morning's tide.

Until 6.30 p.m. the weather was perfect. It then suddenly began to blow rather more freshly, and to look unpleasant to windward. We hove-to and took in the reef in the mainsail. An hour later we picked up the Les Hanois Light ahead and were looking forward to be soon closing with the land, and incidentally doing an interesting bit of navigation.

But soon after dark there came heavy rain and a great deal more wind; in fact, conditions appeared to be the same as those of the previous evening at Salcombe, and I guessed we were in for a dirty night. The glass, too, had started falling.

Now we had, as explained above, intended to approach St Peter Port in the dark only if the weather conditions were good and we could see what we were doing. Conditions having become the opposite, I decided to heave-to and wait for daylight and improvement in the weather.

This turned out to be a mistake, because the weather did not improve, but got worse instead. Had we gone on, we should have had a difficult piece of navigation to do for the first time under such conditions, but it would not have been impossible. I should like to know whether, in heaving-to, we did the seamanlike thing or not. I think we did, unless our seamanship could be condemned on the score of ignorance in foretelling the weather conditions.

When hove-to she lay N, with Les Hanois SSE – distant about 14 miles. During the night, while hove-to, we increased our offing considerably, so that before daylight came the Hanois Light was obscured by the seas.

At 5.30 a.m. conditions had become much worse, and we held a consultation as to what we had best do. We now lay, as far as I could judge, about 20 miles NNW of Les Hanois. We had either to run for St Peter Port or to increase our offing while we could still sail.

The seas were now such that running before them might become dangerous as we rounded Les Hanois and Cap Martin, or, if the weather continued to get worse, before we got near the land at all. I therefore decided on getting further to sea. We got under way and found we could sail her easily so as to clear the Casquets, our idea being, once clear of them, to run for Cherbourg or heave-to, according to the weather.

Unfortunately, at 6 a.m., the lacing of the mainsail to the gaff gave way. We got the sail down on deck and set the mizen, which is a good-sized serviceable sail. We had not long done this before the jib split in two. By this time we were taking a good deal of water over the bows; getting the remnants of the jib in and setting the staysail was a wet and exhausting business.

Under staysail and mizen we got along very well for a time, but she would not sail anywhere near the wind, which had now backed N of NW, nor would she luff easily to the seas when required. By 8.30 sailing under these conditions became too risky a business and I tried to heave-to. But this she would not do. I could not get her to come up into the wind at all. The sea-anchor was all ready on deck, and the only thing that remained to do was to get it overboard, which was promptly done.

I had ridden to this sea-anchor for some eighteen hours in mid-channel the year before; I had no doubts about being able to ride out a harder blow than this, if we had the necessary room. Nothing was in sight, and I was extremely vague as to exactly how we lay. But I calculated that we must have sea room at least to the extent of twenty miles. It was not, therefore, for some hours that I began to feel anxious about our position. When, however, the weather showed no signs of moderating in the afternoon, the outlook was becoming alarming. I knew we could not have enough room to go on drifting through the night.

At 3.30 p.m., after seven hours' riding to the sea anchor, I informed the crew that we could not be clear of the Casquets, and that I was afraid we were in a bad way. There was nothing more to be done except to hoist a signal of distress. We then sent up the reversed ensign, though I had no expectation of its being seen, owing to the height of the seas, unless some boat happened to stumble right on to us. And this is exactly what did happen only half an hour later.

As she came up my first thought was whether the distress signal could be got down before it was seen! Such was the shock of really being faced with the idea of having to abandon my ship. However, I decided that it was too late, and that if it was pulled down now, it would be an impossible situation to explain!

The steamer proved to be the S.S. *Tairoa* of the Shaw, Savill and Albion Line, a 10,000-ton boat, bound for London from New Zealand round the Horn. She circled right round us, and her captain asked us what we wanted. I could only reply, "To abandon ship." He shouted back, "All right," and came round again. Meanwhile, we were extremely puzzled as to how they proposed to get us on board. We saw them preparing a boat, but thought that getting a boat launched in the seas that were running would be a risky business. As a matter of fact, the boat was only being prepared for emergencies.

The captain handled his huge ship with wonderful skill; he came round to windward of us and then apparently the wind blew her stern round, so that he came down on top of us, with practically no way on, and having us under his lee just about midships.

A line, with a buoy attached, had meanwhile been thrown out to float down to us. We got hold of it and made fast. But though under her lee, the seas were still such as to give *Alektor* a very bad time of it, and before she was again clear her mast had gone.

Having made fast, the next thing was to get on board the *Tairoa*. My crew soon made their way up the pilot's ladder let down to us. But when it came to my turn, I hardly found it so easy. A wooden leg is something of a disadvantage in such circumstances, and with *Alektor* leaping about in the wildest fashion, the chance of being swept off by her mast, when half way up *Tairoa*'s towering iron side, was too great to be pleasant. But the chief difficulty was getting started up the thing at all; pilots' ladders apparently require knowing. They have a central rope as well as the side ropes to which the wooden steps are attached. The natural thing is to hang on to these side ropes; but the secret of success is to pull on the central one. Until I discovered this I found myself unable to get beyond the first rung!

The secret discovered, I was soon on deck, and there right enough were the Casquets and their lighthouse down to leeward. It seemed clear that the hoisting of that ensign had been the right thing.

No sooner had *Tairoa* rescued us than an S.O.S. was received from the S.S. *Buchanness*, a few miles off, asking for a tow. She had a broken shaft, and had apparently been blown from nearer the other side of the Channel, being bound for Barry Dock, and was now like ourselves drifting on to the Casquets.

The captain of the *Tairoa* immediately had the rocket apparatus got ready, and again handled his ship with such skill that a line was got across to the *Buchanness* at the first attempt. But the *Buchanness* people mismanaged things so that the tow rope parted, and as we were now all getting taken so much nearer the rocks, the captain decided he could not risk another attempt. The *Tairoa* had a tremendous amount of windage due to her hull, and there were several smaller vessels in the vicinity which could be handled more easily and safely when tackling such a job. They all failed, however, and we heard by wireless that the *Buchanness* struck the rocks at 1 a.m. just as the weather began to moderate. This piece of news completely laid to rest for the time any remaining doubts we had as to being justified in abandoning *Alektor*.'

—————— ,, ——————

From: *Yachting Monthly*, June 1926

2: Abandoned at sea

Yacht: *Emba* (29ft gaff-rigged cutter)
Skipper: W.H.A. Whitworth
Crew: A schoolboy
On passage from Pin Mill, Suffolk to Holland
Time and date of loss: abandoned 1800, August 10th, 1934
Position: approx. 5 miles NE of the North Foreland

W.H.A. Whitworth's next yacht was the William Atkin designed *Emba*, slightly smaller than *Alektor* and drawing only 5ft. The crew on this occasion was – 'a schoolboy whose experience was limited to having sailed over to Holland with me in a much bigger boat'.

They had left Pin Mill on August 9th.

———————— " ————————

'The weather was fine, with a WSW breeze, rather fresh at times, with a steady glass. That steady glass was to cost me the loss of my ship. Probably it was the cause of some of the other disasters of the following day.

After a pleasant sail up the Wallet nearly to Clacton, we ran back as far as Walton and let go in 1½ fathoms about ¼ mile N of Walton Pier. With the wind off-shore, this proved an excellent anchorage for the night, as well as providing a good starting point for our proposed run across the North Sea next day.

The only reason why we did not start across that afternoon was that I did not feel sure enough of the weather. There was a pleasant one-reef breeze, and, as I have said, a steady glass, reading 30.00. But I am very cautious about the weather, having had quite enough experience of being caught out to last me all my sailing days. I determined, therefore, to wait until next morning, just to see if that glass was going to fall during the night.

Next morning we were up at 4.30 a.m. The wind had held steady all

9

night and was still a one-reef breeze from perhaps a point west of SW, and the glass was still steady.

Yet, for some reason, I felt uncertain. To my crew I said, feeling rather a fool: "Shall we go? I feel doubtful."

"Oh, yes, let's go," he replied, to which I could only answer:

"Well, I see you're one of these fire-eaters; come on then and give me a hand with the anchor."

We sailed by the Goldmer Gat and rounded the Longsand buoy at 8 a.m. Our next point would be the Galloper L.V., but though the glass was as steady as a rock, somehow I still felt doubtful about the weather. The fact that the wind had held all night instead of going down with the sun, combined with a rather yellow sunset, was sufficient to make me anxious. Anyway, I decided not to risk making the banks off the Dutch coast a lee-shore until I was certain that the wind was not going to get any stronger.

Having, then, rounded the Longsand buoy, I brought the ship up to lie close-hauled, and stood down outside the Knock sand with the idea of beating up later on to Margate Roads. It was first-rate sailing, with just the right amount of wind for our single reef, and the sea was slight. The crew kept on exclaiming "I'm enjoying this," and "Isn't this grand?" and seemed a bit puzzled because his skipper did not look quite so enthusiastic.

For I was worried. We had only three more hours of the flood tide, and after that I knew it would be a case of barely holding our own for the next six. By 1 p.m. we could not possibly be near the North Foreland, and what was this wind going to do? I would have given a good deal to see it take off a bit. If it was going to get bad, I had to make sure there was no bank, such as the Galloper, to leeward.

About 9 a.m., what looked like a lightvessel was in sight broad on the starboard bow, about where the Knock would be, our course being S (mag.). At 10 a.m. it was dropping out of sight away on the starboard quarter; we had a very strong tide under us. So the ship was put about on to port tack, and an hour later we were close up to the buoy which marks the south end of the Knock sand, and again tacked ship.

The wind now eased a trifle, and I remarked to my crew that we might yet be able to make a French or Belgian port instead of beating up towards Margate Roads. But the hope of doing this was short-lived.

About noon we sighted the North Foreland, and an hour later I again put the ship on to port tack. Immediately I had done so the wind increased considerably, and I pulled down a second reef and hove-to. I had a look at the glass, but there was still no indication of anything bad coming. The barometer remained at 30.00.

For the next three hours she lay hove-to quite comfortably, but conditions had got worse, as I realized at 4 p.m., when I let the jib draw and with some difficulty (she missed stays twice) got the ship on to the other tack.

The wind now increased rapidly, and blew, as I judged, with force 6. The ship seemed suddenly overpowered, with her lee deck buried. Getting the jib changed and the third reef down in the mainsail (which ought to have been done before, and would have been had the glass shown any sign of falling) would now have been a difficult job. I decided, therefore, to get all sail off her and ride to the sea-anchor, our position being such that we had unlimited sea-room to leeward between the Hinder and Galloper banks.

Until we grappled with the jib, I had little idea how strong the wind was. But jib and mainsail were both stowed without anything carrying away, and the sea-anchor let go.

Emba now rode the seas like a cork. As far as I could see, she had virtually no way on through the water, though she did not by any means ride head to wind and sea.

I have ridden to a sea-anchor before, and my experience of them is that they will not keep a boat head to wind and sea. Nor does it seem to matter.

The seas were now getting rather big, and it was interesting to note how clear it became, the ship being more or less stationary, that their motion was entirely vertical. There was at no time any threat of solid water coming aboard, even though we seemed sometimes to be almost broadside to the seas.

Emba is a boat specially built to meet heavy weather, and I had no anxiety about the seas, however bad the weather should become. That is not to say that our position was one which did not cause me anxiety of a different kind. Bad weather is always an alarming thing when one is seeing it out in a small ship. In this part of the narrow seas it is particularly anxious work, partly on account of traffic and partly because of the various banks. Though I had taken the precaution to see that we had plenty of room to leeward, the southern part of the North Sea is not the place one would choose for unlimited drifting.

The worst thing we had to fear was neither being run down nor drifting over a bank, but the risk of exhaustion. Ten years ago I rode to a sea anchor for 18 hours in the Western Channel, half-way between the Lizard and Ushant. It was quite long enough. How long was this occasion going to be? Down West, too, we had neither banks nor traffic to worry about. On the other hand, we had not half so good a ship.

About 5.30 p.m., taking a look round, I saw a biggish steamer not far away, making for the Straits, and away to the westward there was something under a certain amount of sail. A little later the crew looked out and told me a fishing smack was coming up close astern. I looked out, but could see nothing astern, so climbed up on deck.

To my horror, there was a clumsy-looking smack of some sort within a yard or two of my bows, and coming almost straight at me. I had just time to call my crew up on deck and she was into us, carrying away our bowsprit at the stem-head. For a moment our bows were in contact, and I clambered aboard the smack – not without some difficulty – an example quickly followed by my crew. We thought that at any moment the yacht might be holed and sent to the bottom.

Aboard the smack we found half-a-dozen Frenchmen in a great state of excitement. Their skipper and I could not understand one word spoken by the other. There was the yacht, disabled but still afloat, and with the hull possibly undamaged. With salvage the problem under discussion, sign language proved itself singularly ineffective.

Getting aboard the smack was difficult enough; to regain the yacht, bobbing about like a cork in what was now a rough sea, would have been a dangerous business. But I did not encourage the Frenchmen to make any such attempt. I remembered the fate of Gerbault's *Firecrest*; how, having safely sailed the oceans of the world, she found a watery grave in the Channel when in tow of a steamer.

Nor did I feel too confident in the Frenchmen's ability to get their cumbersome old tub of a smack alongside *Emba* without holing her. Having run her down in the attempt to hail her – if that indeed was their intention – what would they do in an attempt to board her?

Again, it seemed likely that when the weather moderated, salvage by some of the many craft which must sight her would be a more practicable possibility, and it was in this hope that *Emba* was for the time abandoned.

Alas! such hopes were never realized. A small steamer saw her an hour or two later, attempted to tow her, and towed her under. They reported that specially bad seas near the Girdler had filled her cockpit. It is more probable that she had been gradually filling all the time. That night the weather became worse, until it was blowing a full gale, and under such conditions no small yacht could live while being towed through the seas.

Such was the unnecessary end of a splendid little ship. Could she have been saved after the collision?

Looking back from the safety and comfort of an armchair, it seems likely that she could have been. I, her skipper, had no right to leave her just because she was disabled. But riding out bad weather in a small ship in whose hull and gear one has complete confidence because one has fitted her out with such a contingency in mind, is one thing. It is quite another matter to do the same with the ship so disabled that when the weather moderates she can only be sailed to leeward; especially so when the responsibility for the disablement is on the shoulders of another.

Again, she might have been saved had we taken her in tow and then kept the smack moving very slowly head to wind and sea through the night. But whether the Frenchmen would have been willing, or their vessel capable, of doing this, I have no means of discovering.

So that was the end of *Emba*, and I know I shall never have as good a ship again.

Now what of those other disasters? I, for one, should like to hear what my fellow victims have to tell.'

———— ,, ————

From: *Yachting Monthly*, November 1934

3: Fastnet Rescue

Yacht: *Griffin* (Offshore One-Design 34)
Skipper: Neil Graham
Navigator: Stuart Quarrie
Mate: Peter Conway
Crew: Four students from the National Sailing Centre, Cowes
Bound (racing) from Cowes to Plymouth, round the Fastnet Rock
Time and date of loss: approx. 0130, August 14th, 1979
Position: approx. 40 miles SE of the Fastnet Rock

This description of events preceding the loss of *Griffin* was written by her navigator, Stuart Quarrie, and because the subsequent rescue of *Griffin*'s crew from their liferaft was such a remarkable feat of seamanship, I have also included part of Alain Catherineau's account of how he and the crew of *Lorelei* went about it.

——————— " ———————

'We expected a gale during the race – the Met office had forecast one – and we just hoped to be going downwind when it arrived! Rounding Lands End in almost calm conditions we discovered a short in a lighting cable which had drained the batteries – "someone" had turned the isolator to "both" during the night and this meant we couldn't start the engine and only had minimal electrics. It had been impossible to get all the charts we really wanted, owing to a strike in part of the Hydrographic Department. This meant we were short of large-scale charts of Southern Ireland, and those which we had were mainly metric charts but with no colour – very difficult to interpret, especially with a torch.

By the time we got the 0015 forecast on the night of the storm, we already knew we had a blow on our hands. We had progressively gone down from close reaching under spinnaker through No. 2 and No. 3 jibs and reefing the main as the wind came up from just before dusk. As the forecast time

14

approached we were still racing – with Pete and Neil putting the 3rd reef in while I steered. The mouse which we had put in for reefing the 3rd deep reef had come adrift and the operation took about half an hour – by this time we were also down to storm jib.

I asked one of the crew to take the forecast since I was busy, and I could hardly believe it when he said SW/NW 10–11, possibly 12! Unfortunately he had not taken down the time period for the veer to NW, so we didn't know how long the southwesterly would last.

After that forecast we decided to stop racing and I was asked to decide whether to run for shelter or stay at sea. Not knowing the Irish coast and being hampered by lack of some charts I wasn't able to tell that Cork was a possible refuge even in a southwesterly; and, not knowing the time scale for a veer, I didn't want to close the coast. We therefore opted to stay at sea. We reduced sail to storm jib only and found that with a maximum allowed IOR storm jib we surfed and planed in a manner difficult to control, and therefore went to bare poles.

With three crew below and four on deck we then sorted things out and I tried various different helm positions in the hope that we would be able to lash the tiller and all go below. We were quite happy for about 20 to 30 minutes with the helm pushed moderately hard to leeward, until an exceptionally big, unbroken wave rolled the boat. It is worth noting that

those waves which had already broken didn't appear to be dangerous as their crests were mainly foam.

At this stage I was thrown from the boat and my harness hook – which had been clipped to a stanchion base – opened out to leave me "free swimming". This was at about 0130. I first thought of my life insurance – then I miraculously saw a high intensity lifebuoy light 20 or 30 yards away from me, through the water. I swam to it and found the whole boat upside down with the light still in its clip. Neil Graham swam out of the cockpit air-gap and we talked somewhat inanely on the back of this upturned "whale", until another wave finally rocked her upright.

After a head count – with everyone OK – we tried to take stock of the situation. It appeared that the boat was awash to the decks with the cabin almost full to the washboard level, and after a brief attempt at pumping Neil decided – after talking to Pete and me – that it would be prudent to abandon ship in good order, rather than wait for her to start going down.

I must say that at this stage I was in shock to some extent; I had been so sure I was dead just minutes earlier and therefore didn't take as full a part in the decisions as I might have done, but I did agree with Neil.

We launched our Avon eight-man raft with no real difficulty and, taking the yacht's flare pack, abandoned ship into the raft. We couldn't find a sea anchor – whether by stupidity or not we will never know. We arranged ourselves around the raft to try to give it stability. We let off just one parachute flare, more as a gesture than anything else, and settled back to wait for daylight. After about 30 minutes a big wave rolled the liferaft upside down, ejecting two crew as it did so. While righting the raft we lost its canopy, and so after that we were like an open dinghy and up to our armpits in water.

At this stage we realised that one crewman, who had been below, hadn't got an oilskin top on and he was in fact semi-comatose with hypothermia within about 15 to 20 minutes.

After less than half an hour in the open raft we saw the masthead light of *Lorelei*, and the rest of the story belongs to Alain Catherineau . . .'

'We were racing with fifty knots of wind, using the No. 4 jib and with three reefs in the Hood mainsail. At about 0200 (French time), 14th August, were were sailing at 310° at ninety degrees apparent wind, our speed was considerable and below decks there was a constant impression that we were surfing. Thierry, my first mate, was at the helm, taking great pleasure in the almost effortless sailing; the boat was standing up well and quite stable. Towards 0230 we were thirty or forty miles from Fastnet and well on course. After about a mile we set the star-cut; shortly afterwards, with an apparent thirty or thirty-five knots, we replaced this, first with the No. 2

and then with the No. 4. For about an hour we passed many boats, both windward and leeward of us.

Suddenly we were astonished to see a red parachute flare about half a mile downwind. I donned my harness and rushed forward and with the help of Marc and Gerard, the navigator, hauled down the No. 4. I had been prepared for this: the wind was remarkably gusty and our anemometer was recording up to sixty knots. Thierry and I decided to get closer to the red light; with three reefs in the mainsail it was easy for us to steer towards it. After failing on the first try, we finally went about. We were heading roughly south, Thierry still at the helm, when we saw a rocket or a red hand-held flare (I can no longer remember which). We could not see the source of the light, only a red halo that was visible from time to time above the waves. I asked Thierry to stop heading towards the glow and ease off by about thirty degrees; we had no idea what sort of boat we would find. Some hours earlier we had met *Rochelais*, a rusty French trawler from La Rochelle, a most impressive sight. For some reason I thought that the crew in difficulty now was on a fishing boat.

We were very comfortable below deck; however, on deck, we would have lost two or three crewmen had not our harnesses been well-fitted. We were still heading towards the light when we saw two smaller lights above something dark; these were in the same wave and about fifty metres downwind. It was a liferaft. Some way farther on we turned and headed towards the liferaft, our mainsail at three reefs. We came three metres upwind of it, the same distance away from it and at a speed of about three knots. One of my crew threw a rope to the liferaft, but it would not reach. Two of the liferaft's crew hurled themselves towards us in an attempt to catch the hull; instead they fell into the sea and were hauled back by their colleagues.

I decided to take over the helm. I felt it was possible to save these men as long as I was at the helm and an integral part of my boat. I know *Lorelei* (a Sparkman and Stevens designed She 36) very well and can often demand – and get – the impossible. I started the engine and hauled down the mainsail. The engine is a twelve horse-power diesel, but the propeller has automatic variable pitch which gives maximum power very quickly and greater than normal acceleration and deceleration. After seven or eight unsuccessful attempts I finally managed to come about and headed into the wind. During this time we had covered some distance. We were heading south, in total darkness, in search of the red light. Suddenly we saw it. I turned again – an easier job than it had been the first time – and cautiously headed towards the red glow, which lit up the surrounding blackness whenever it became visible. I turned to the north and crossed at about four or five knots. I approached the liferaft and aimed *Lorelei* straight at it when we were about twenty-five metres away. I threw the engine into reverse in the last few metres and thanks to *Lorelei*'s propeller of variable pitch, she drew rapidly to a halt, stopping within a metre of the liferaft.

Thierry and Marc each threw a line to the raft and the crew hauled themselves alongside *Lorelei*. I felt dead. There was some confusion on the liferaft as the crew leaped to catch hold of our ropes or deck. One or two climbed aboard easily; three more remained in our stern on the aluminium toe-rail. I suddenly noticed that the liferaft was drifting away from us with two of the crew still on board. Luckily one of them managed to grasp a rope that had stayed on board and pulled the raft back alongside. A few moments later the liferaft drifted away, empty. The end of the rope had not been made fast. I stopped the motor for safety and some of my crew helped two men climb aboard and three or four more of us at the stern helped the remaining three. The first few castaways were already in the cabin; there were only two left in the sea and we were having difficulty getting them aboard.

I sent the fit members of the liferaft crew to help out on deck. I was holding on to one who had been under the counter with only his head above water. He was one of the few to have a harness and I managed to pass a rope through it and then over the pushpit. In this way I lifted him out of the water. However, the harness slipped over his shoulders and I had to release him into the water again. Philippe was holding him by his T-shirt, the only garment he had. Finally, helped by his fellow English crew members, the castaway was rescued from the waves. He was heavy and it took five or six heaves on the ropes to pull him into the cockpit.

In the cockpit his leg became trapped between two ropes, but we soon released him. The most injured member of the English crew was forward but there was still one more in the sea. I can no longer remember how we finally rescued him. I think that *Lorelei*, crossing the waves, heeled on the right side, sometimes very severely, so that we could grip the last castaway and haul him in a few centimetres. He was stiff with cold and could not help us rescue him. Soon he was in the cockpit surrounded by his rescuers. I realised that there was something wrapped around his head; he was being strangled by a cord on his T-shirt. I pulled at it with all my strength and it finally snapped. He was taken into the cabin.

It was about 0400 by then. An Englishman came out of the cabin and warmly shook my hand in thanks. All seven of his crew were safe; it was a happy moment. Thierry and I were in the stern. We hugged each other fiercely: we had succeeded.'

———————— ,, ————————

From: *Roving Commissions* (Centenary Edition, 1979), published by the Royal Cruising Club

4: The Last Hours of *Windstar*

Yacht: *Windstar* (29 tons bermudan rigged cutter)
Skipper: Captain Bertram Currie
Crew: Peter Combe
Bound from Lowestoft to Cowes
Time and date of loss: approx. 2200, July 29th, 1956
Position: somewhere between the Kentish Knock and Outer
             Gabbard shoals

Windstar was built in Mevagissy in 1937 and had served during the war as an anchor to a barrage balloon; she had just returned from a cruise to Scandinavia, during which she was under the command of a paid skipper, with the owner, Peter Combe, and two others as crew.

For the final passage back to Cowes, there were only two on board; and furthermore Captain Currie was an invalid from recent illness and a diabetic and was only allowed by his doctors – under protest – to make the trip so long as he did not 'overdo it'.

Peter Combe, whose account this is, desribed his skipper as 'A man of astounding imperturbability and apparent nonchalance, with complete disregard for the possibility of hazard, he seemed sublimely and blithely content to sail on indefinitely so long as there seemed to be water under his keel.'

———————— " ————————

'We motored out of the harbour with the jib furled and bent on ready to hoist and the mainsail uncovered, and took the inside passage south from the harbour mouth before heading to sea. At 2200 hours the first gale warning had been broadcast. Neither of us had heard it.

After two miles we had cleared the coastal shallows and set course to southward. "Well, chum," said Bertram, "we're going to be pretty sleepy by the time we get to Cowes. You'd better turn in for a while."

19

The situation then, if not too attractive, presented no cause for anxiety. We knew where we were, the night was clear, and the journey, which should have taken about eighty hours, was well marked and lit all the way. We had enough oil to motor the entire distance, if necessary, and I was confident of being able to hoist the mainsail alone, even if with no great rapidity, if we had a fair wind in daylight.

I did not foresee getting much sleep, as he had said. After we had started I had also some qualms about abetting him in undertaking this tiring run at the end of his holiday; but he was determined to go, and eager to get the boat back to Cowes for the regatta week. There was something of an anticlimax about the run home at the end of the tour, and since leaving Oslo, the nearer we approached England, the colder and wetter and drearier had the weather become. The challenge and amusement of taking the boat home alone did, in fact, enliven what would otherwise have been a rather flat finale.

After sleeping a while I found we were quite a bit to shoreward of our course, due to confusion about lights, and while Bertram took a spell below I ran out to Shipwash Light Vessel from which I had laid the course for a clear run down to Kentish Knock.

At 0700 hours we passed Sunk Light Vessel, the tide having carried us eastwards towards the Thames Estuary, and I laid a new course for Kentish Knock. It was not worth the effort of trying to hoist any sail to hold us steady, as the wind was only a few points off our starboard bow. By now it was as rough as the North Sea passage had been, and even a little more choppy. Apart from the lack of Calor gas it was impossible to do anything in the galley, so we lived that day on some chocolate and biscuits and hard liquor. In any case, I was now feeling far from well, tired, a headache, slightly sick, and sorry that we had let ourselves in for another beating. I had hoped that by the time we reached Dover Bertram would be tired enough to agree to put in there to sleep. As the prospect of a hot, dry lunch in Dover receded I became anxious about Bertram's being able to go on without making himself ill, or taking a bad fall. He had managed to give himself his daily injection of insulin – no mean feat in that weather – but there seemed little chance of his eating his accustomed fill to balance it. By midday the gale was at its height, the seas growing very big, breaking at the tops, and the surface streaked with foam. Visibility grew poorer as the volume of wind-driven spray increased. It was now becoming difficult to steer. Our course fortunately lay into the wind, but we could only hold it spasmodically. There was no question now of a sail holding us steady. We could steer fairly steady about fifteen degrees either side of the wind until a strong gust blew her head away, when she would take a long while to come back up again.

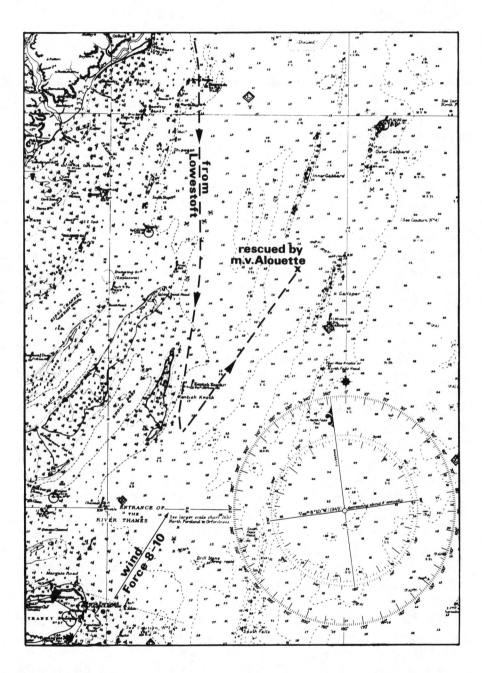

At 1245 hours we passed Kentish Knock Light Vessel very slowly, making possibly two knots had our course been less erratic, and for a moment it looked as though we would be carried down on to her, the tide or the weather taking us still to the eastward. Dover seemed a very long way off. It was now a question of holding our head into the weather and riding out the gale, which was so freakish for the time of year as to seem incapable of lasting. By now it was only possible to hold our head against the wind with the wheel hard over and watching for the ticklish moment when the wind was more or less dead ahead, when, if we were carried off to starboard, it had now become impossible to bring her up again into the wind – the propeller being on the starboard side and the thrust being weaker from that side. Each time she fell away to starboard and kept falling with the weather abeam we now had to wear her right round and start again. Fortunately, we were never badly pooped doing this, but each long lapse to starboard brought us nearer to the Goodwins.

We had the canvas cockpit cover rigged, inside which whichever of us was not steering could shelter from the attentions of the wind, although the water was everywhere coming through it. Whoever was at the wheel, sitting abaft this cover, was obliged to sit up quite high to peer over it – which occasionally seemed a good idea in case one could see anything into which we might be running – getting what cover one could, hunching oneself forward into its lee and steering most of the time by compass. In fact, it became almost impossible to watch the seas ahead, as every time one raised one's head one received at once with uncanny precision a discouraging blast of salt shot in the eyes. In spite of the fact that one shivered more, I then found it more agreeable to steer, as it occupied my mind and distracted it from the disagreeable state of my head and stomach. Facing thus fore and aft with my hands on the wheel, I seemed in a better position to balance. As in the North Sea passage, it was a rather exhilarating sensation, like riding a big high-mettled hunter, as *Windstar* plunged and reared, occasionally taking the seas with a sharp leap like a dolphin. Bertram took one or two crashing falls during the course of the day. In fact, on our return his doctor discovered three fractured ribs.

A day or two before, I had been reading about the forces and symptoms tabled in the Beaufort wind scale, and remarking this to Bertram – shouting conversationally at the top of my lungs – added that, as far as I could see, this bore all the characteristics of a hurricane. "It very likely is," he replied calmly, and we lapsed again into silence for another half-hour or so. We later learned that hurricane Force 10 had, in fact, been registered.

At this period we were still holding our head more or less into the weather and, I think, making some way through the water. We were able, with care, to keep most of the time on the starboard tack and away from the direction of the Goodwins. The engine was well able to keep pumping out any water we were making, and we were riding the seas well, only occasionally shipping a big sea on to the decks at more than a minute's interval which only slightly splashed into the cockpit and drained overboard before the next. My only anxiety was that we should be able to have some indication where to turn westward up channel as soon as possible, to try to make Dover. I had little faith in the good fortune of seeing the East Goodwin Light Vessel on our present course, and hoped that we would see the coast of France before being run on to it. Presumably it would be dark by then and lights visible. The radio D/F receiver was not operative with the engine running, and it was impossible to hold steady into the weather without this.

I was also growing a little anxious about our ability to hold on indefinitely without rest, or something sensible to put inside us, if this wearying, weakening, utterly dreary grind continued without a single glimmer of hopeful change.

But though anxiety had grown, my feeling was chiefly of frustration and impatience, with the apparently indefinite uncomfortable unpleasantness of our situation.

About 1400 hours came a radical change in our situation, though far from welcome. Three things happened almost simultaneously. First, the engine failed. A moment later – and I presume it to have been later, as we swung out of the wind without steerage way though I cannot swear to it – a really big sea broke over our starboard side, and for a while I looked through a pale green world of pouring water, such as one is treated to sometimes in the cinema from uptipped water tanks. I was at the wheel, and held on confidently for the boat to lift, and the sky to reappear, for what seemed some time. When the water stopped I saw the cockpit quite full of it, and Bertram, who had been carried from the starboard side together with the cockpit cover, clear through the cover on the port side, perched between the metal struts, like a bird in a bush, with his behind on the deck. I helped him back, apparently unhurt, and we set about fetching back the lengths of main and jib sheet that were trailing outboard, and cleared away the mess of the cockpit cover.

Although the engine still started and ran, it stalled when we tried to coax it into gear, even astern. While were were still shaken at all this, the jib, which I had earlier doubly secured to keep it quiet in the gale, flung off both its lashings and hoisted itself. Presumably the changed direction of the gale's attack enabled it to get a better purchase. The canvas ran practically to its full and correct height, and promptly blew to bits, with a flapping and crackling most painful to the yachtsman's ear, while I watched fascinated. It would have been madness to try to catch hold of any part of it under those conditions, so we just waited, hoping that it would destroy itself as soon as possible. In doing this it managed to carry away, by the flailing of its sheets and the attached block, the lowest port-side mainstay (a half-inch wire hawser), the for'ard portion of the port side deck rail, together with two stanchions – the next one remaining was bent double over the side as if it had been made of tin – and also the spinnaker boom, which had been secured there.

"There goes the spinnaker boom," I shouted at Bertram as it floated past us, rather as one might point out a porpoise to one's Mum on a trip round the lighthouse in the *Skylark*. He treated this excited comment with the contempt it deserved, there being no possible rejoinder, except perhaps that we probably would not require it this trip. The yacht now, with these first wounds, began to look sorry and unship-shape.

So strong was the gale that she sailed, to my wonder, for ten minutes steady upwind on the few tattered ribbons of jib, but not close enough, so that the seas were dangerously abeam.

"What do we do now?" I said to Bertram after pointing out this interesting phenomenon. "Run before the wind under bare poles," he replied, and I heard the ring of trumpets in his voice. This thrilling phrase, often read in the books of sea adventure which I had devoured as a boy, made me chuckle with surprised delight, yet it seemed quite reasonable. I did not feel disposed to secure the loose stay which was waving about crackling things with the wooden sleeve it wore. Eventually I think it fouled something below the mast and stayed quiet; and I was certainly not eager to try to construct a sea anchor. Later we were told we should have done this, but even had the ship's company been more up to it, the gear easy of access, and conditions more sympathetic to efficient and seamanlike movements, I think it would have been an error. There is something so very helpless about being at the mercy of a sea anchor, and our hull would have taken a worse beating holding into the seas. As it was, we were driven along at an astonishing speed, which we later calculated to have been about six knots. We could thus steer quite well, sustaining less strain on the hull, as we carried along with the weather, sometimes like a surf-board on the crests.

We expected to be badly pooped, but only twice do I remember really big waves breaking in over the stern, which rose wonderfully to each oncoming sea. These did not come in exactly parallel waves, but after a while I found it less tiring and unnerving to steer in the general direction of the weather than to look over my shoulders and try to line up our stern to receive each approaching sea. I am prepared to swear that they varied from thirty to forty foot high at their worst – there are few witnesses to contradict me. One of the advantages of running like this was that we could keep a fairly steady course, which was about north-east, and from where I thought we had been when we turned. We had plenty of sea ahead until we reached the north-west coast of Denmark, or missing it, found ourselves back in Norway – by which time we could only hope that the gale would have blown itself out.

The weather was now less vicious in our faces, but we were fully exposed to the following wind, and I noticed both of us shivered violently all the time we were at the wheel. Earlier in the day I had changed once, but was now quite drenched again. Over blue jean trousers and a thick cotton naval rating's shirt, I wore a sweater and a light ski-ing anorak – chiefly because of its hood which protected my ears – and on top of this an oilskin, more to keep the wind out than the wet. On my feet I had a pair of fleece-lined snow-boots, also completely soaked but nevertheless quite cosy. Strangely enough, the sea and the wind were not very cold; it was only the force of the latter which chilled us, driving right through our backs. We were quite pleased to take a spell below, where everything was now wet and disordered with books, clothes and cushions and other gear all over the floor of the cabin and the saloon. The crew space for'ard was even wetter, and the galley a fine jumble of smashed crockery, tins and pots which had broken loose. When I went below to drag, without much success, at a damp cigarette, and find a little peace, I kept throwing things back off the deck, but eventually gave up. Whoever went below shut the door from the cockpit after him to keep out the splashes, and the man at the wheel was left alone in the water. Occasionally we bailed for each other with biscuit tins – chiefly for the sake of morale. The cockpit was quite isolated, in the watertight sense, from the rest of the craft, but the self-draining part of it had some sort of valve trouble. Having effectively removed the water, it had the habit of belching back as much again with a merry gurgle. We had accordingly settled its hash with a champagne cork some days before. I found the large glass binnacle cover more useful for bailing the cockpit, and developed a handy technique of holding it in the corner with my foot while steering, and after a good roll hoisting it up full of water, with my spare hand. I had already discovered the uselessness of putting a quick temporary lashing on the wheel while I left it for a moment to do anything. She just kicked it off in about three sharp jolts.

At some time after 1500 hours – I do not remember looking at my watch at any time after we started running north-east, the situation became timeless and immediate – I began to check the well when I went below. It was showing a good deal of water, but as I had not had occasion to look into it myself since leaving Oslo, I had no idea what would be considered normal. On a previous occasion, when water had been showing on the lower part of the deck by the galley door on a return trip from Deauville, it caused little alarm as I remember, and this was not yet apparent. This time, however, we could not pump it out with the engine, the drive being off the shaft. I pumped a while by hand, but it was difficult to tell how much difference I was making – if any. I told Bertram that we had a good deal of water inboard, and he was naturally not surprised. I pumped some more, and later, when it seemed to me that the hand pump was achieving very little, I told him this. Later, when he took a spell below himself, and had been through similar motions, he confirmed my fears that we were gradually making water.

The situation then, although we did not discuss it, took on a more doleful aspect. It became colder as the day faded, and we were both quite eager to take a turn below pumping. It seemed to me from the bore and the feel of the pump's action that it might be able to hold the water we were making in various ways above water-level as it filtered down into the bilges; but what was happening below the water-line one could only guess.

At about 1600 hours, while I was at the wheel, I suddenly saw a trawler off to port on a parallel course up weather about three hundred yards, and yelled at the top of my lungs, to Bertram, "Do you want to signal her?" "Oh, I don't think that's necessary," he replied, and disappeared again below.

It seemed to me, since we were alone and helpless, that we might have asked for a tow, or at least through her made our presence known to the outside world, but although I waved wildly with my spare hand I saw no answering sign. In fact, I believe that she would have been unable to turn out of the wind and come to us without getting into difficulties herself. It would have been a good idea to have been wearing a signal to say at least that our engines had failed, and were under no control, if anyone could have noticed and read our tiny signal flags. The only other thing I had seen that afternoon was a large dolphin which came gambolling down the side of a big sea to meet us like a puppy, and apparently quite undismayed by the weather.

It gradually became clear that we were making water much faster than we could pump, if, indeed, the pump was achieving anything. I selfishly took long spells at the pump believing that I could pump a great deal faster than Bertram.

It was strange below, comparatively quiet, comparatively dry and warm, and gave one a strange sense of security, while the movement of the ship itself seemed less violent. It seemed so remote, I kept wondering whether I would open the doors of the cockpit and find Bertram had disappeared over the side without my knowing, and as I looked at them, bolted to keep them shut, it was hard to realise how easily a really big sea coming over the stern could stave in their frail wood like cardboard.

I arranged the cockpit cushions on the deck by the pump, and pumped hard and long with my right arm stiff, rolling my body back and forth, which seemed a less tiring method, for an indefinite period. There was no comparable method possible with the left hand, the pump being hard against the port side of the engine space, but I used my left arm on occasions to save fatigue. I did not fancy having my arms too tired to pump before the rest of my body was too exhausted to care.

I kept thinking petulantly, "This is such an utterly dreary and stupid way to die", as I lay there damply rocking, confronted with a confined prospect of darkly swirling bilgewater and the stink of diesel oil.

Towards 1900 hours I thought of putting on the wireless, which since the engine was no longer working would receive without interference, and enjoyed complete unreality for a while from the unctuous smugness and patronising *bonhomie* of the B.B.C. until the news bulletin. "Unprecedented gales in the Channel," the announcer tritely enunciated – at least we were authenticated. The *Moyana*, returning triumphantly from winning the Torbay to Lisbon race, had sunk in the early morning – 80-mile-an-hour gusts registered in Cornwall. A steamer had capsized with the loss of one life. Out of twenty-four yachts in the Channel Race, only ten had been accounted for. Lifeboats and distress calls all along the Channel. I began to feel proud of ourselves for being afloat. Apples had been flying off the trees in Kent (too bad), and a dozen people had been killed ashore by falling or flying objects. Perhaps we were safer here!

With this happy news I relieved Bertram at the wheel. I asked him if he knew where the distress flares were, and suggested that we should have them handy. He agreed. I also asked him to switch the navigation lights on while he was below, so that we were ready and visible when it got dark, and we started the engine, running it slowly, to keep the batteries charged. It was somehow heartening that Bertram now seemed prepared to admit that we were sinking, and should make the fact known if we met anyone who was interested.

I had hitherto always been sustained by a sort of metaphysical confidence that it was not yet my time to die, believing in a kind of eternal "rhyme and reason" or poetic balance – whereby there was something for me in this short life before my card was full and ready to hand in, even though there might be a lot more balance yet to be made in other existences. Taking account of the futility of my life to date and my lack of conviction for the future, I realised that this confidence in my own purpose and capacity had of late faded. Bertram, who seemed to have lost all zest for life since his son died, and seemed to show little will to live, would have been rather happy, I think, to have gone down in *Windstar* which he loved. It did in fact seem devastatingly right – or at least agreeable to sublime rhyme and reason –

that "finis" should be written here.

As sands ran out and the water in, it occurred to me that this was my last opportunity to make the acquaintance of God Almighty. I felt a natural desire to complain to some eternal authority about the futility of our predicament without knowing where I should address myself; it seemed a perfect opportunity for the Almighty to show His hand and fill me with faith – not faith in deliverance, that would be too much to ask of any deity at first acquaintance; nor could I reasonably hope for the vision of Jesus Christ drawing up alongside in Simon Peter's fishing smack to come striding across the waves to take my hand or pass us a celestial tow; but almost everyone, when age, disease or sorrows strike him, inclines to think there is a God or something very like him. I remember learning these words at school and this rather stark state of affairs seemed well designed to edge me into a cosy state of belief. Perhaps He was waiting for the final moments; in any case, I took a few sharp pulls of the brandy bottle instead, which imparted a more direct, if temporary, glow before I took over the wheel as dusk was falling.

I was quite looking forward to a little more dark, as it would increase the chances of seeing a light, or having ours seen, at greater range. I did not want to burn our few flares until we definitely saw something to show them to, after which I planned to let the pump take a position of secondary importance while I made a distress signal with the masthead light, and kept on making it until something happened.

When we got low enough in the water for the seas to start breaking inboard seriously, and accelerate matters, I could not somehow see us making brave and stirring valedictory gestures to each other. Should I suggest putting a note in a bottle to keep the records straight and say "good-bye" to our friends? We would have to drain a bottle first. Happy thought!

About 2100 hours I suddenly saw for a moment a large vessel bearing green 130 about three miles off, and yelled for the flares. Bertram, after a short argument with the cabin doors, leant out on to the seat with a red tin which had a screw cap on one side, and seemed to take an age to unscrew. He then tried to get out a flare through a small hole, and after a great deal of probing and pulling, produced a piece of rumpled newspaper packing. This went on for some time until he had fished out quite a few newspaper scraps with some difficulty. At last a flare permitted itself to emerge. We then had to discover what to do with them. "They are self-igniting," said Bertram. But how, neither of us knew, hoping faintly they would burst into flames when they understood what we wanted. Neither of us could see very well by this time, yet when I found light and spectacles I could make out the far from striking printing, which said, "Tear off cap, and rub inside smartly against head of flare." This produced absolutely no result, and as it seemed

28

to smack rather of Aladdin's cave I tried it several other ways, even pulling one flare entirely to pieces. Eventually I went to the galley and found a packet of matches which did work, and striking a whole box at a time held the exploding heads against the wretched things. One flare, at length, did give a slight sizzle, and I kept working at in the shelter of the cabin – to absolutely no purpose.

Under the stress of these exercises I remember my language grew unregrettably unparliamentary, and I even spoke quite sharply to Bertram. It was curious though, as we remarked afterwards, that throughout this entire adventure we remained ridiculously polite to each other, if a little curt, without any of the, "For heaven's sake, grab that, you bloody fool" kind of dialogue, usual in such emergencies.

I then soaked a strip of the driest piece of cloth I could find with a can of lighter fuel, and wrapped it round a flare. This also was too damp, and wouldn't burn. I gave up the flares, briefly thinking of starting a bonfire with them somehow on the deck.

Our ship seemed to have disappeared. I went for the Aldis lamp, which I plugged into the masthead light socket at the foot of the mast, there being no other place for it. It didn't work. When I told him, Bertram said, "It worked the other day," and I put the masthead fitting back. No masthead light either. This, anyway, had been suffering from mysterious fits of failure which the electricians had been unable to cure. I checked the other navigation lights. None of them was burning – nor would they.

All this time I was moving very fast about the deck, and below, slipping and bumping in my hurry, and increasing the mess in the galley looking for matches, and in the saloon looking for the lighter fuel, and something to burn. The inside of the yacht was now a terrible mess. Even the bottom boards had been thrown out of the bunks, and the decks were a mad jumble of clothes, cushions, books, charts, and tins and pots of food, two food lockers having burst open to pour their contents into the muddle, and the water was now splashing up out of the bilges as she rolled. In the middle of it all the swinging Tantalus attached to the saloon table ticked happily back and forth with its cargo of bottles, as though nothing were amiss. I took the hint and some more brandy, and found a wet biscuit on the deck.

Looking again for our ship, I eventually found her a little for'ard of our beam. Her lights were now showing clearly and it was getting darker. A little later I realised she was another craft. I could then also see what I took to be the original ship in about the same position as before.

While below I had put on every inside light we had as I passed to show as much of us as we could. And then, to my amazement, when I switched on the stern light it lit – although it had been unshipped by the seas, and had lain banging about the deck at the end of its flex for most of the day. I got up on the deck aft and seized it. With one hand on the back stay I stood holding it as high off the deck as I could, and began to flash S.O.S. in a wide arc between the two ships. The light had flickered out once or twice rather sickeningly, and, not knowing how far above the water the batteries were, I started looking for some other light. Our rubber torch had gone to ground among the rubble on the cabin floor, but Bertram told me where to find an old army pattern map reading and signalling torch in a leather cover, which he had carried in the First World War. With this spare light between my teeth, I went on flashing. It seemed that the smaller vessel was approaching, and at last she quite definitely flashed back to us.

It was a wonderful moment to be in contact at last with someone else in the world. Time and space had returned to focus.

I was now anxious not to lose them. It was strange how, as rescue became more tangible a possibility, and the odds calculable, I became more anxious and impressed with the problems involved. I feared for our battery system and that we might lose each other, playing hide and seek among the troughs of the sea. I kept flashing to her to dispel any doubt they might have about our signals, and to keep our position well in view. The East Gabbard Light Vessel, now visible to them thirteen miles off beyond us, did in fact confuse them for a moment.

Now that they were definitely coming in to us I rested my right arm with the stern light, and kept on flashing with the torch, which had a morse button. As the urgency eased a little, I began to grow ridiculously self-conscious, and wondered if it might not be more professional to send a proper message. I sent our signal letters a few times in between S.O.S.s, so that they could relay our identity in case of mishap.

We found we could steer towards the ship fairly comfortably, and eventually I saw she was a small vessel about 100 tons register coming in quite slowly with a nice big Aldis lamp on the bridge searching amongst the waves for us. I began to realise the difficulties ahead, of getting from a comparatively helpless yacht on to a steamship, in the dark, in a hurricane.

I asked Bertram – who, by this time, had been continuously at the wheel since I started playing with the distress flares – whether he wanted to try to take a tow, or whether I should try to board her as soon as possible, and organise some means of transit for himself. This was my gravest worry, as I did not see how he could be expected to perform any violent gymnastics.

"Yes," he said, "you had better do that."

As she got closer I went below, found my brief-case among the rubble, and put my address book in the pocket of my oilskin, ignoring my passport and wallet which were next to it. This was a completely superstitious gesture. It seemed that I would be lucky to get my body out of it alive; what else could I not dispense with in the circumstances? It seemed to be tempting fate to put anything else in my pockets, but to lose an address book, as I had done before, breaks a great number of human contacts, cutting off some for ever, so I had decided to go and fetch this.

While I was below, Bertram shouted that she was flashing to us. Let her flash, I thought, this is no time for conversation and, in any case, I would probably not be able to understand. I expected her to be a French or Belgian, or even a Dutch coaster, and only hoped that we would understand each other when we got within range for yelling instructions.

She came round very slowly and carefully astern of us. I tried to wave her on in the direction of the weather, since that was the only way we could steer, and shouted to Bertram to hold her there. He replied that he couldn't see. The cabin lights dazzled him, and as all this time he had sat very quiet, I thought he was pretty tired out. I think now, considering this eye trouble, that he was probably suffering from an overdose of insulin as well as everything else. I directed him from the stern as well as I could until the ship came in alongside.

It was the most admirable piece of seamanship. She came in very slowly, carefully and deliberately, in that appalling weather, and laid herself alongside us as though we were a pier on a fine day instead of an erratically bobbing yacht.

They began to throw us lines, and eventually we were close enough for them to land aboard. I cannot exactly remember everything which took place from this moment in fast frenzied succession. I leaped and clawed my way about *Windstar*'s deck as swiftly as I could, trying to secure and make ropes fast. They threw me the heaviest hawsers they had, which made it even more difficult to find anywhere to belay them effectively on such a craft.

It was difficult to see in the dark punctuated by the dazzling glare of her searchlight. They had thrown oil on the water, which covered the hawsers and splashed aboard, so that I slipped and slithered more than ever, and at one moment heard myself sobbing with the effort like a wounded cowboy in an action-packed western – a dramatic exercise in which I had never before believed.

"Put a line round the mast," someone yelled, and I thought vaguely how clever of them to have noticed our ensign and taken the trouble to speak English. I led one hawser round the mast which jammed somewhere before I could get enough rope round and make more than a half-hitch with a bight. I dropped the eye of another round the anchor winch for'ard, and then found that we were moving forward. In fact, the steamship had sternway and was slipping back. We had taken some violent bumps against her side already, but moving forward under the sheer of her bows was even more alarming. I expected to be pounded under at any moment as we both plunged up and down.

31

To complicate matters, two wire stays caught behind her anchor, where they began to saw up and down, making a horrible noise like a mad violin. The bo'sun told me afterwards that I swung myself up and wrenched these free, kicking against her plates, but I really don't remember. I was too preoccupied with the urgency and concern of having made only one line properly fast for'ard, and nothing aft to stop us sliding away like this. Her bow looked very sharp and vicious, glistening black and silver in the dark and wet as she chopped up and down. Imagine being a mouse on the block at Tower Hill, whom a drunken executioner is trying to behead, at night, during a thunderstorm and an earthquake.

We moved apart quite quickly, while I tried to make fast the hawser, which had pulled free of the mast and was now running out over the stern. I got it through the fairlead, but couldn't hold it, nor find anything strong enough to suddenly jump it on to. I considered the binnacle for a moment, but it wasn't stout enough. It would have been useless to damage the boat any more, ripping out stanchions, or stays, or the binnacle, in the hope that it would check our flight. The bar on which the main sheet block ran would have been ideal, but the hawser was too thick to push through it easily as it ran out like a live thing, and the block itself slamming from side to side as we rolled could have removed my fingers very easily. I watched the rope snake away overboard.

We were driven forward and across the steamer's bows while she slid backwards and round our stern until she seemed to be about a hundred yards off or more, over our starboard quarter, and still holding us on the remaining hawser like a badly harpooned whale. Her rope was thus around all the standing rigging from just for'ard of the mast on the port side to just for'ard of the cockpit on the starboard side. As the strain increased it seemed impossible that she could reel us back in, or fail to bring down rigging, boom and mast on top of us. The hawser stood between us in a stiff, straight line. There was a sharp series of vicious cracks, whangs and creaks, and eventually the hawser parted with a snap. I think only two stays had carried away, but I didn't bother to check.

I was now afraid that after the beating we had taken against the steel hull we must be filling with water even faster, and for a while feared that the steamer would or could not return to us again. For an unreasonable moment I even thought perhaps she might be more interested in salvage, and wiggled the stern light at her again in what I hoped was a winsome fashion. As she eventually came in again I made ready multiple loops from the tangle of sheets, made fast at several points to bend her next hawser on to. Bertram, I noticed, had finally left the wheel and was sitting in the cockpit looking rather dazed. "The steering's jammed," he said, and went below to collect ship's papers and one or two valuables. I tried to shift the wheel, and after a hard heave it spun out of my hand like a catherine wheel. Something had either broken or jumped out of gear as we bumped against the steamship. We were now completely helpless.

I stood on the stern again with the stern light in my hand to watch how the ship came in again. As we swung helplessly about I tried, ineffectually, to keep the ensign from flapping in my face, and then caught hold of the jackstaff to put it out and clear it overboard. This suddenly seemed not the thing to do, apart from looking like an unlucky gesture of despair.

As I had plenty of time to indulge in romantic gestures, I went and searched for my knife in the cabin, and then climbed aft again to cut the ensign down, stuff it into the collar of my oilskin like a scarf, and jettison the jackstaff. I wonder if I would have made this quaint gesture had it not been for a nostalgic respect for the white variety of ensign.

As the steamer approached I yelled that we could not now steer to help in any way.

A voice shouted back, "Do you want to come aboard?"

"Yes," I shrieked in amazement.

Apparently they had noticed Bertram sitting at the wheel in an attitude of such unconcern that they were in some doubt that we wished to leave!

A few moments later we struck her side head on, smashing in the stem and carrying away the forestay. As we rocked crazily alongside again I heard them yelling on deck to look out for the mast as it swung over her deck. I managed to secure another hawser around all the winches for'ard, and it then seemed high time to leave.

Bertram was now on deck, wearing a spare cap (we had both lost ours overboard during the day), and seemed ready to abandon ship. I had noticed the previous time, as the two vessels soared up and down alongside like a pair of demented elevators, that her deck rail for'ard came within reach now and again. This time I did not intend to let the opportunity slip, and made my way for'ard to wait until we were scraping alongside again in the same position. For a pessimistic moment I wondered if I still had the strength to pull myself aboard; everything felt numb and weak. I stood for a while trying to take a deep steady breath and relax, hopefully looking at my hands as I flexed my aching fingers. I needn't have worried. When her deck ducked within reach I found myself up and over before I had time to think about making any effort.

As I picked myself off the steel deck I heard someone cry out, "There's one of them aboard," and then repeat it again to the bridge in such a wild tone of voice that I felt for a moment they were going to throw me back! I joined three or four of them by the rail below the bridge and explained at the top of my voice that Bertram could not be expected to do anything violent.

"He's sick," I bellowed, which seemed the simplest formula to inspire a more complicated plan of rescue.

Meanwhile they had thrown several lines down to him, and were shouting at him to tie one round him. Luckily the line I had secured for'ard was well fast and fortunately placed so that *Windstar* towed alongside very nicely as the steamer moved forward just enough to keep her there.

I watched from the dark deck of the steamer and an entirely new viewpoint. I was now safe – so small a phrase and so minute a difference of time and place to denote so vast a change of state – like a spectator watching the brightly lit stage of *Windstar*'s deck from which I had now stepped.

Bertram stood upright with difficulty on the slippery, heaving deck. Luckily the remaining section of portside rail was in front of him as he tried to hold his balance and secure a rope at the same time. Three times the boom swung over and caught him on the back of the neck a sharp blow which looked as though it could fell an ox. He lost his spare cap overboard too, while tying the rope round his middle. He seemed to make, as best he could, a sort of half-hitch with the end which none of us who were watching believed to be really secured. Another line he held in his hand taking a turn around his arm, and we tried to catch his hands as the two decks rose and dipped towards each other. Twice we nearly had his hands, and then as *Windstar* plunged down and away the lines jerked him overboard and he fell between the two hulls.

It was a quite sickening moment, and I think I tried not to see. I know that for some moments I didn't dare to pull on the rope to prove to myself that he was not on the end of it. The bo'sun, who was on the rope with me, deliberately let as much slack go as he could, so that Bertram could either duck below the hulls as they came together or, if not attached, try to secure more line. The gap, however, widened for a moment, and we eased in the line. There was a weight at the end and, expecting any moment to lose our prize, we pulled him aboard in about three heaves, suspended by the middle like a sheep being loaded, and caplessly lacking all the dignity of a captain leaving his sinking ship. When we bundled him over the rail and said, "Thank God – we never thought the rope was fast," he replied at once, "Nonsense – tied it myself," and after he had been dragged across the deck and into the saloon before he could catch his breath he at once began to make quips about knowing how a walnut felt in a cracker, and remarking that he had no need to be a frogman to know what a ship's bottom looked like. He had no right to be capable of either speech or movement at all.

Five minutes later *Windstar*'s mast snapped off about 10 foot above the deck and vanished over the side, but we never went to look at her again. The captain asked Bertram if he should try to tow her, but he told him to let her go. This he did, with great regret.

The ship, we found, called herself M.V. *Alouette* of the General Steamship Navigation Company, and had only been passing because she had been unable to hold her anchorage while sheltering in Margate Roads.

The ship's company were extremely kind and, I think, thoroughly enjoyed the whole business. The captain, Captain F. Baker, a youngish man who had the air of a P. & O. liner captain, and sucked a curved pipe in a stately way, had a great time talking to us. The second night, when we had docked in Harlingen, the crew wanted me to drink with them in the fo'c'sle, which I did with considerable glee, got thoroughly drunk very quickly, and began to relax a bit for the first time.

Our trek across the dykes to Amsterdam, through the kind assistance of the shipping company's agent in Harlingen, was fairly comic, though frustrating to my impatience to get home. We looked like a pair of brigands in our salt-caked clothes. Bertram wore his inflatable blue jacket from which a long rubber nozzle (for inflating) reared itself under his right ear.

We startled two young ladies at the British Consul's office considerably, but were very ably and sympathetically supplied with identity papers, money and air tickets to London at Consular speed.

We made a splendid entry into the reception hall of London Airport, first and alone, being without baggage, except for the tattered ensign I still carried bundled round a small piece of *Windstar* which had been found the morning after, jammed in one of *Alouette*'s hawsers, while the customs officers glared sullenly at our retreating backs. A small party of friends and relations burst into a welcoming sound more like guffaws than the brave and resounding cheers more appropriate to this momentous occasion, but we saw their point.'

———————— ,, ————————

From: *The Little Ship Club Journal*, 1959

5: Oopsie Daisy!

Yacht: *Lazy Daisy* (29ft 6in Catalac catamaran)
Skipper: Lionel Miller
Crew: Bruce Rankin
       Bill Tulloch
       Charlie Tulloch
Bound from Inverness to Kinghorn, Scotland
Time and date of loss: approx. 0530, October 24th, 1980
Position: off Rattray Head, Scotland

Lazy Daisy had left Inverness at 1345 in good weather on a day in late October 1980, bound for Kinghorn on the north bank of the Forth, some 250 miles away.

———————— " ————————

'We quickly settled into a three-hour watchkeeping routine. The weather remained fine and the wind gradually strengthened until we decided to put in a reef just before sunset. The sea was steadily becoming lumpier and all except Bruce began "calling on Hughie" from time to time but without too serious effect on performance. The boat was making excellent progress and we were in good spirits. Mine were improved still more when I caught Bruce retching and attempting to spit to windward (ex marine engineers are not used to being sick, unlike us family sailors).

Bill and I left Charlie and Bruce in charge at 2.00 a.m. and got our heads down for a highly appreciated rest in warm sleeping bags. The noise below was continuous and the boat felt like an old car being driven fast on a rough track but we were tired and pleased to pass the responsibility to the other watch for a bit.

We were roused from our wet sleeping bags by a shout from Bruce: "Your watch." As we came on deck we could see that we were rounding the

36

corner at Kinnards Head and the NE force 6 was giving us a broad reach as we turned south. The sea was a sailing man's dream with big rolling seas swept with silver grey spume under a brilliant cold full moon. Unfortunately our stomachs were unaffected by the beautiful scene and we both moved quickly across to the leeside to be sick. That chore completed we all got busy to dowse the reefed main and open out the roller jib. Bruce, off watch after three hours on the helm, disappeared below to make himself a thick cheese butty and Charlie fastidiously removed his boots and jacket and climbed in the still warm quarter berth. My watchmate, Bill, decided to call the coastguard on V.H.F. to report all's well (a task which my stomach would not allow) and then came back on deck. The boat was handling well as the wind came aft and we had obviously seen the last of beating for a bit as we turned ever further towards the south.

We were making great time and had actually caught the last of the southgoing tide round Buchan Ness over six hours ahead of our planned time. Bruce and Charlie had debated whether to go into Fraserburgh but the look of the harbour entrance in the offshore seas plus the excellent chance of getting round on the favourable tide persuaded them to press on. I was well pleased with the way things were going and handed the helm to Bill for a spell. Lying in the cabin out of the wind I was reasonably warm and comfortable and I wondered whether to get my exposure suit and wellies on, but the thought of going and searching in the forward cabin hanging locker was not appealing. After ten minutes or so the motion altered and I suspected an increase in wind. Out on deck again Bill suggested reducing sail but I wanted to keep the speed up so as to get well clear of the strong tidal area before the tide turned north. I therefore took the helm to assess the situation. We were doing 6–8 knots SE with an apparent wind speed of 25 knots from the north under full jib. The boat was certainly flying along but the heel was not excessive and with the wind so far abaft the beam I felt quite content. The waves were now giving us some fast sleigh rides as we boiled along and despite the darkness and cold at 0530 a.m. we were having a great sail.

Suddenly I found the boat going downhill at an alarming angle, the high flared bows were almost underwater despite their enormous reserves of bouyancy and the hulls vibrated with a deep humming sound as we tore through the water at 12 knots plus. This was unexpected and rather frightening. Bill again looked at me to see if we should reduce sail, but I felt the problem was the size and steepness of the wave rather than the wind forces so I turned the boat so as to present her port quarter to the seas, which did not look any bigger than previously. Down below, Bruce lay awake listening to the crashing and banging of the waves against the hulls. He did not like the sound of our speed as we tore down the waves, and his cheese sandwich was not helping either. Charlie on the other hand was sleeping the sleep of the just – just off watch.

Bill suddenly noticed that the dinghy, which we carry hooked to the aft rail, had come untied at one end. He knelt on the seats and leaned over the rail as he struggled to bring it inboard. I hoped that he could manage to tie it on again successfully as it would be far too cumbersome to have lying around inflated in the cockpit. It was difficult to concentrate on the problem whilst steering because of the need to keep a watch on the waves coming up astern.

Looking round now, all thoughts of the dinghy problem vanished. The wave coming up now was very big, perhaps 30 ft, but the threat of destruction was in the 5 ft high breaking crest which was commencing its avalanche down the long slope towards us.

This was obviously a "survival wave" for our boat with its large open cockpit and lovely big windows. I shouted a warning, and then concentrated on holding the boat on course to take the sea on the quarter, but it was impossible. The stern was smashed round and we were hit almost broadside by many tons of water travelling at 20–30 m.p.h. The enormous thrust of the impact lifted the boat into a vertical position and the press of water under the bridgedeck completed the capsize in a matter of 2–3 seconds.

Below, Charlie awoke in mid air as he flew towards the ceiling. Hitting it, he expected to fall on the floor but instead the floor fell on him followed shortly by a lot of ice-cold sea!

Meanwhile in the other hull Bruce felt a mighty lurch and heard the loudest cacophony it is possible to imagine, as bottles, pans, plates, tools flew across the boat and smashed into the windows over his head. Tonic and lemonade bottles exploded and several knives and forks stuck into the hull after falling the full width of the boat. Bruce thought, "He's been and gone and done it" as the cabin rotated around and things crashed down towards him.

Outside, Bill was flung across the cockpit as the boat accelerated sideways and lifted. He distinctly remembers the blue flash as the batteries shorted out, and then we were both in the water under the boat. I thought "when the boat sinks, we will all drown" and reckoned we had about 15 minutes left. Bill swam under the cockpit seats to the outside but my brain had begun to work again and I realised that the boat might not sink after all.

Inside the boat Charlie picked himself up off the ceiling and made his way forward through the waist-high water and debris whilst his mind grappled with the problem of finding the way out. "Up" was now down and "right" had become left. The normal route out to the cockpit was turn right, up steps on to the bridgedeck and right again. The new route in the cold wet darkness was left, downwards and left again. Pursuing this course he came across Bruce who was attempting to find the door catch. Eventually Bruce found the knob, opened the door an inch or two then pushed it wide as the pressure equalised.

On the other side of the door I had heard Bruce and Charlie talking and swam over to help open the door and to advise them that we might be better off inside the boat rather than outside. They came out and we started to discuss whether to go outside or not, when suddenly the air under the cockpit disappeared into the hull via the open door and the floor of the cockpit came down to push our heads underwater. That curtailed the discussion and we all dived towards the outside.

Bill, of course, had been outside for some minutes and, ever litter conscious, had tidily collected a floating fender and lifebelt and put them into the dinghy which had luckily come unhitched from all its fastenings except the painter and lay bobbing happily at the stern. He had just climbed in when our three heads popped up and we realised that we had all come through our the first test.

Once we had all got in the dinghy and saw that the boat was not going to sink immediately we decided to climb onto the bridgedeck and take the dinghy with us. Unfortunately the dinghy was impossible to untie and none of us had a knife. Luck was on our side again, however, because the painter broke as we climbed out and we soon gathered on the bridge deck with it. The waves occasionally washed through between the hulls but although we had no way of tying on, it was quite easy to stay put and the hulls broke the force of the wind.

Exposure was now the problem, particularly for Charlie who had taken off his windproof jacket and boots when he went to bed. We all huddled together against the windward hull which made a good wind break.

Ashore we could see the lights of civilisation, but we knew that it could be a long time before we were spotted or even missed after our reassuring radio check. Time passed rapidly, although we began to ache from standing in one spot and to shiver from the cold. A grey dawn broke and we could see that though the tide was carrying us north, the wind was pushing us inshore slightly. Another hour and we could see that we were drifting towards a long shallow bay fringed by sand dunes. We decided to beach through the surf in the dinghy as the big waves could have easily rolled and smashed the cat on top of us.

About half a mile off the beach the wreckage began to drag on the bottom and our drift slowed. We launched the dinghy and commenced paddling with our hands downwind towards the breakers. The waves were piling into magnificent combers as they swept in and at first we dreaded the thought of eventually entering them. After almost half an hour of exhausting paddling, however, we were disappointed every time one missed us and we had to paddle some more.

We developed a technique to prevent capsize in the breaking crests. We all threw ourselves sideways towards the breaker as it struck and after a while we were able to judge quite well just how hard to thrust to remain on an even keel. Obviously our second moment of serious danger was imminent and we all wished each other luck every time "the" big one bore down on us. After a while we began to feel a bit stupid at this abortive ritual and so we yelled at the waves to come and get us. Eventually one heard and it impressed us considerably as it mounted and surged towards us. It broke and swept down on us head high in a mass of frothing foam. Bruce and Bill were pushed forward by the impact and the rope Bill was holding broke. Charlie and myself at the front were thrown back by the acceleration and then we were off. The dinghy (just 9 ft long, completely full of water and four grown men) picked up to full speed to match the wave and wriggled like a live thing beneath us. Our heads and shoulders emerged from the foam and we shouted with the exhilaration of surfing at 20 knots in towards deliverance. The surge carried us as though we were an underwater bobsleigh and we covered the 200 yards into the beach in less than half a minute.

Will we buy another multi-hull? Most definitely – a monohull would certainly have been rolled 360° and might have sunk with the loss of all hands.'

—————— ,, ——————

From: *Clyde Cruising Club Journal*, 1981

6: The Last Cruise of the *Joan*

Yacht: *Joan* (22ft 6in yawl-rigged cutter)
Skipper: W.E. Sinclair
Crew: Meredith Jackson
Bound from London – 'towards New York'
Time and date of loss: evening of September 7th, 1927
Position: approx. 350 miles ENE of Belle Isle, Newfoundland

The *Joan* was a small Falmouth Quay Punt, only 22ft 6in overall and 7ft 6in beam, although she did draw 6ft. Rigged as a yawl, she had a self-draining cockpit but no forehatch or skylight – 'so that water found it difficult to get below'. Headroom must have been restricted, since at one time Sinclair used to wear an old bowler hat to save his head from getting hurt.

The voyage to New York started from the Port of London on June 29th, 1927, and as the *Joan* passed the Erith Yacht Club on her way down river a gun boomed out as a salute from the members, who knew the *Joan* and the passages that Sinclair had made in her round Great Britain, to Madeira and to Stockholm.

After sailing north up the coasts of England and Scotland they passed through the Pentland Firth and headed directly into the Atlantic. Reykjavik in Iceland was reached after two weeks, during which they had lain for a while to a sea anchor – normal procedure for the *Joan*. While in Reykjavik they met a young American journalist who later disparagingly accused them in an article of 'lacking rudimentary sea experience'!

The voyage was continued on August 12th and is described by Meredith Jackson:

––––––––––– " –––––––––––

'The wind was fresh northerly, and we were close reefed before leaving the land. Our plan was to pick up Cape Farewell to check our longitude, and then make St John's, Newfoundland. The first part of the passage was wet,

41

cold and wearisome, but fast. The Manual of Seamanship defines Time as "A definite portion of duration," a definition very suitable for the long night watches with the wind coming down from the Arctic. The wind was N or NE and we were only eight days out when we sighted the land. The Greenland mountains had been in sight nearly an hour before we were satisfied that it was land. When we were still some hundred miles off the land there had been most amazing cloud formations. Once I could see a coast in marvellous detail, a high headland backed by snow mountains, with a glacier coming down to the sea, all complete with ice foot and pack. I stared amazed, to watch the whole coast dissolve away. I remember the thrill of my first sight of the Alps, but that was nothing compared with the sight of Greenland – the massed peaks rising to 7,000 ft, and the great ice-field. But then I hold the climbing of mountains to be nearly as good as the sailing of boats; nowhere else in these days can you meet the elemental forces in a decent straight way. Bad weather came along and we saw no more of Greenland, feeling that it was safer to get along the course for Newfoundland.

Life at sea in the *Joan* was strenuous, and as it gets further off it seems very pleasant. There were two kinds of days. When we were sailing the routine was this: breakfast each man got for himself, unless the motion was very bad when we would heave-to, taking half an hour from the morning and the forenoon watches. At one o'clock we generally had boiled potatoes and some kind of meat out of a tin. Tea at four, and another meal, nearly always thick soup or stew, during the second dog watch. The other kind of day occurred when we were hove-to. Then the man on watch could stay below, looking out periodically to see if all was well. After a few days' sailing it was pleasant to heave-to and sleep deeply.

Our stock of food was enormous; I submitted some of my ideas of quantity to a man who had been concerned with Arctic expeditions, and as a result we had 1½ cwt of ship's biscuit and other stores in proportion. The great secret of making several different dishes out of the same chief ingredients is to carry a large stock of flavourings and never use more than one at a time. We had tiller lines rove through blocks and if the wind was not too strong the man on watch at night could indulge in cocoa brewing and still keep the boat on her course.

As for navigation, we carried no patent log, trusting to our estimate of the speed for dead reckoning, and it was fairly accurate. We worked on the old-fashioned morning and noon sights, finding that easier (in the absence of a chart room) than position lines. For time we had a good watch that has been rated. Its rate was not quite constant, but then we always assumed our longitude to be a little doubtful and made landfalls by running down latitude found from noon altitudes. Experts tell me that a chronometer would probably disapprove of the *Joan*'s motion more than the more humble watch, although that does not seem to have happened to Saoirse.

After seeing Greenland we ran into ten days of nearly continuous gale. For most of the time we were hove-to, either on the sea anchor or trys'l. It was not as uncomfortable as it sounds; after a bit you get so used to the motion that you can do almost anything you want to. We used to read and smoke, and I have even made use of a spell of sea anchor work to do some arrears of typing. The really trying part was the lack of exercise of the right kind, and the way in which the wind would simmer down just enough to make it worth getting on sail, and then blow up and make us take it all off again in a very short time. The wind would never blow itself out from the quarter where it started. Nearly all the blows started from SE and finished up NW, causing a vile sea. Spray was liable to come over from nearly any direction, so that it was not wise to go outside without oilskins. In a regular sea the *Joan* kept dry while on a sea anchor, but the cross seas made her wet.

On September 1, we were riding to the sea anchor, feeling that it really was time we had a decent day. The gale seemed to be blowing as hard as wind could blow, and the sea looked as bad as possible, but towards the evening both the wind and the sea increased. I have learned since that it was no ordinary gale. A liner captain told me that "it was not a gale but a hurricane." One liner had to heave-to, some schooners were lost, and several ships damaged. That refers to a region two hundred miles to the south and the previous day, but presumably we were in the track of the storm. Although it was very much worse than I had seen before, it never occurred to me that anything unpleasant might happen. As soon as it was my watch below I turned in and went off to sleep.

I have very little recollection of the manner in which I awoke. It was about 10 p.m. There was a tremendous crash, and I found myself out of my bunk and in a place I could not recognize. Blackness was round me. I thought that it was already Death, and felt petulant because I could still think and yet nothing else happened. Then proper consciousness returned, and I tried to pull open the sliding hatch, only to find that I had my hands through a hole in the torn deck. Sinclair got out of the cabin and told me that the mast had gone. I saw it, floating unpleasantly near the port side. The wreckage had to be cut away before it stove us in, and the foot of water above the floorboards in the cabin had to be returned to the Atlantic. Sinclair did the first job and I did the second. By about one o'clock we had the wreckage cleared and the boat empty of water, but leaking so hard that we had to bale with a bucket until the evening, work that required both of us together at times. The torn deck was plugged with blankets until daylight made it possible to hammer down planking. The following day we started putting the *Joan* together again, caulking, covering the damaged deck with canvas, and nailing strips of lead over holes. Another day's work, and the hull floated with but little leaking. For the first two days we had no dry clothing and no dry bedding, which made work on deck terribly hard. But we had tobacco, tea, and biscuit.

During the first bout of baling I noticed two peculiar things, the one being that the floorboards had fallen out of place, and the other that some coffee grounds and stewed fruit was sticking to the ceiling of the cabin top. The damage to the boat was curious; the mast snapped off about a foot from the deck, carrying away the starboard chainplates and tearing up some eight feet of the starboard covering board and a deck plank. The mizen still stood, but the mizen rigging had strained both quarters, lifting the whole starboard a quarter of an inch, so that the top plank was split. That split took in a great deal of water each time we rolled, and was responsible for making us bale for eighteen hours (the pump being put out of action) before we found the leak and caulked it temporarily with – socks. The explanation would seem to be that the *Joan* went right over until both masts were in the water with the keel in the air, and then righted with such a jerk that the mainmast snapped. The boat was very strongly built, but the strains were so great that heavy iron bolts were bent and twisted. We had tried to secure the mast and wreckage, but it had merely chafed against the sea anchor so that we lost both sets of gear. The damage to the hull was extensive. In addition to the torn deck we had a split rudder, a sprung beam carrying the cabin-top, and strained seams along the top-sides. The seams of much of the deck planking and in the well had opened a little, while sundry pieces of rail, cleats, etc., had been torn away.

The repairs were completed on September 4, just in time to see if the poor old hull would live through a hard blow. With neither sea anchor nor sail set she rode through it, showing that it was only a matter of time before we made land or found a steamer to take us off. Incidentally that confounds the views that a sea anchor should be used to make a boat more comfortable, a good boat being safe if you stow all sail and leave her alone. We had enough material to rig a jury mast out of the bowsprit, and plenty of food. There was enough water for eighty days, if rationed. When that blow was over we hoisted our only possible sail, a big jib set from the stem head to the top of the mizen, and limped away to the south-west.

We had not been able to make the hull quite tight so that we were unable to sail her watch and watch, the man on watch lowering the sail and going below to bale before turning the other man out. Thus it came about that we were both below on the evening of September 7 during the second dog watch. I looked out at the end of the watch and saw the masthead lights of a steamer. We were still to the north of the steamer track, so that it was

44

unexpected luck. There was no doubt about what we should do. The *Joan* was too much smashed up to be worth saving, and it might take weeks to bring her in to land. It was a matter of seconds before Sinclair had found a ship's flare, one of the B.O.T. type, lighting by tearing off a tab and rubbing the exposed surface. None of them would light, until a Primus had been lit and they had been held in the flame! Before the second flare had finished burning we saw the steamer alter her course. We gave her a steady light to steer for and hastily collected our most valuable possessions and put them with the papers and log books into a kit bag. The steamer came close, hailing us to know what we wanted, then circled round and drifted down wind until they could throw us a rope. The rest was rather a muddle. There was nothing for'rd to which the rope could be made properly fast. As we came alongside Sinclair told me to get up the Jacob's ladder that had been lowered. I got up a few feet and turned to get him to hand me the line made fast to the kit bag. The *Joan* had already started to drift astern, and Sinclair had to make a dive for the ladder and not bother about anything else. I climbed over the bulwarks and the sudden transition from a small boat to a big ship sent me reeling across the deck. From the stern we saw the last of the *Joan*. Her steady leak and the open hatch must have sent her to the bottom soon afterwards.

So ended the last cruise of the Joan.'

———————— „ ————————

From: *Yachting Monthly*, December 1927

7: Capsize of *Rushcutter*

Yacht: *Rushcutter* (30ft Harmonic class sloop)
Skipper: Anthony Lealand
Crew: Annette Wilde
Bound from Wellington, New Zealand to Sydney, Australia
Time and date of loss: 0130, April 19th, 1978
Position: 190 miles W of Auckland, New Zealand

Annette Wilde and Anthony Lealand, both from Christchurch, New Zealand, had undertaken to deliver *Rushcutter*, a boat of the Harmonic class, to Sydney for her owner. They had examined her in Wellington and considered it was a reasonable proposition to sail her the 1200 miles across the Tasman Sea.

Anthony Lealand tells the story:

——————— " ———————

'The disaster really started when we spent 10 days stuffing around for a chart, which the Post Office lost, and our beacon battery, already a year on order.

When the new battery arrived, our beacon refused to light its test lamp, but after a day of tests and phone calls to Auckland it was decided that the beacon worked, although the test lamp was at fault. I made a little test unit to take with us for future checks, and this was heat-sealed in polythene bags along with our over-age batteries which still tested "good."

We had stripped our own yacht *Valya* of all her navigational equipment, our sailing necessities, and a good selection of tools, and with this ponderous load of excess baggage we flew to Wellington on April 3, leaving a friend to live in our house, water our cat and feed our plants.

Rushcutter had not been sailed seriously for a year, so we right away had a year's accumulation of rust and stiffness to set to rights. Owner Charles Troup had left us a detailed list of things he knew of to attend to and with

46

what we considered necessary, it was 11 days before we were ready to clear.

We started with a morning's work cleaning out a bilge full of engine oil, dropped by a recently broken oil line. I regarded this as very important for there was no depth to her bilge and it would need only a splash below to have the whole slimy lot swilling around above the cabin sole.

At the masthead I found the reason for the jib halyards needing a winch even to move them. Severe corrosion of the alloy sheaves was bulging the 3/16 in stainless sheave box. To remove the sheaves was difficult for the mast fabricator had bolted the sheave pin in and then welded on mounting flanges, completely blocking the pin's removal.

I did not understand the reason for the severe corrosion until we found the alloy sheave had a bronze bearing. Aluminium in contact with bronze and salt water is severely corroded – a fact well known since 1895 when *Defender*, and America's Cup yacht, was built with bronze hull and aluminium topside plating. She was broken up after six years, so severe was the action.

Our next surprise was to find the available replacements constructed in the same way. Oh well, we greased them well and considered that they would last the two weeks to Australia.

A day at Shelly Bay slipway saw *Rushcutter* fitted with ply deadlights and a spare rudder. The shipwrights and manager took an interest in the work and we were able to get through a long list of minor items, leaving finally with a big handful of assorted nails and a spare sheet of ply for luck.

We had lashed down the liferaft aft in the cockpit. Over this on a board athwartships was our new Sestrel compass. The board was held by headless screws so it could be pulled away should we want to get at the liferaft.

Valya's chronometer seemed to like its new lodgings, and for the first time in its life settled to a steady rate.

We were in some difficulty over our emergency aerial, a 13ft long helical whip we had made in Christchurch. This had been lost in transit, but Ted (Annette's brother) brought it down just in time for our safety inspectors' visit.

Wellington Customs were kind enough to come to the marina to issue our clearance, which made departure easy. It is a nuisance to have to clear from some foul commercial berth with piles a boat length apart.

As we beat out of Wellington we marvelled at the improvement in the mast, now solidly wedged. Her mast, stepped through the deck, had been rubber wedged on our sail some days before, and shook about in a lively manner. Of course the solid wedges now rendered the bendy mast gear inoperative but did mean we no longer had six feet of unstayed mast thrashing about below.

We were perhaps an hour late catching the tide at Sinclair Head, but with full main, a fresh southerly, and an indicated 8 knots, we felt more than happy.

That is till I went below and found all our clothes, bunks and sleeping bags sodden. In the beat out of Wellington the deck joints of the inboard chainplates had obviously hosed water everywhere. It continued to leak even now, running downwind. Murmuring rude words I climbed into the pipe berth, still in my waterproofs, which we were to wear till picked up.

This was my first acquaintance with a pipe berth, and I found it a damn good bunk, even though *Rushcutter*'s were a little narrow.

Annette was tight-lipped about the wet below. She feels that boats with deck leaks just ought not to be allowed. I suppose we were rather spoiled on *Valya* with no deck leaks and a diesel heating stove to dry our gear while off watch.

Rushcutter hustled on, a delight to sail. Occasionally the full quarters would catch on a wave, but she needed no more than a firm hand to bring her back. There was no sign of loss of control.

By now life below was pretty foul. The main hatch was a cunning contrivance of the cabinetmaker's art, for surely no shipwright could have made it. Every slosh that landed on it was delivered below by the hatch's forward slope to dribble across the deckhead, fill galley lockers, soak the charts and eventually wipe out the beacon receiver. What the hell, the sailing was good.

On Sunday *Rushcutter* was changed to cutter rig, using the storm jib as a staysail. The sheet from this ran through roller-bearing blocks to the tiller's windward side and was balanced by a red rubber tube from leeward. She steered herself well, though as the wind drew aft the staysail would have to be backed. Self-steering by this method seems to have a lot in its favour, not least of which is rapidly learning about the balance and steering of the boat. It will not, of course, put you about or hold you on a course with an unbalanced rig while you change sail. But it is very powerful with a breeze in the open sea.

Monday night saw a rising easterly wind which soon had us clearing the deck of lashed-down sails and, for the caution of it, putting the deepest reef in the main. Just as well, for the easterly had us swishing along in perfect control, dodging breaking seas in the confused turmoil that the rapidly rising wind caused. *Rushcutter* sometimes banged solidly up forward, but she had thumped more heavily beating out of Wellington, so we felt no worry.

Charles had mentioned he felt it unwise to let her thump, but to reduce sail when we had such good control seemed a pity.

We had good visibility with a near full moon behind clouds. By the time the moon was setting the wind was dropping, which was just as well for it is less funny to dodge seas in the darkness.

By dawn the wind was light and the seas pleasantly regular. We jilled along quietly that day, doing a lot of sleeping but confident that *Rushcutter* was more boat than she perhaps looked. The cabin was pleasantly dark too, for as the easterly had risen I had whipped out the deadlights and spiked them on with 3 in roofing nails. It seemed a little dramatic and I wondered how I was going to explain the splinters to Charles.

The seas that came rolling in from the south late that day had me thinking we needed even less sail than the deep-reefed main. As the trysail had only a little less area than the main reefed, I hanked on the storm jib. This proved a dubious arrangement. Hanked on the topmast stay, and so having a very long sheet, it vibrated badly, shaking the whole rig, and unless the wind was taken a long way round on the quarter, it would bang from tack to tack with great wrenching thumps.

But now the wind was so strong that we were overpowered and broaching badly on the crests. The storm jib came down, leaving us still overpowered by the yacht's windage alone on the crests but dead and down to 3–4 knots in the troughs. Big seas filled the cockpit. We had never taken serious water from astern into a cockpit before, but, as other commentators have said, in the conditions in which it comes aboard, it is thrown out just as quickly. Which was just as well, for *Rushcutter* had a large cockpit.

By midnight I was worried. The wind was from the south and steady storm force, but seas came from WSW and SE as well. They were about 20 ft high with the top six feet breaking, which it did fairly frequently. *Rushcutter* was piggishly slow to answer in the troughs but a handful on the crests.

Around 1.30 Wednesday morning I asked Annette to send out a Pan call saying that if we did not call up within 24 hours it could be presumed we were in trouble. Unfortunately it was just past the silence period. Indeed the set did not load up well, no doubt as a result of the salt water sloshing over the deck, aerial lead in, and lower backstay insulator.

At 1.40 a.m. as *Rushcutter* slid off the back of a southerly wave, broaching a little to port, from the port beam came a classic breaker. *Rushcutter*, dead in the water, would not turn and to my surprise rolled right over. I came up on her port side, my lifeline taut at water level, to see her floating high and very stable upside-down. My lifeline was short to avoid being flung some distance and injured.

Now as *Rushcutter* settled I was slowly spending more time under water and as my knife had been flung from around my neck, I knew that shortly I would drown. I rapped on the hull for Annette but heard no reply.

Annette was just contemplating a tedious wait for a silence period when *Rushcutter* started pouring the contents of the lockers over her and she saw the whole cabin slowly revolve around her. Water gushed in the gap between the washboards and hatch slide, and perhaps through the ventilator and where the mast was.

She scrabbled at the hatch trying to open it and get out, but the water was soon over her head as she bent to it. Hearing my rapping she saw the water rolling about, and with a quick understanding of the situation blundered back and forth in time with the water, till a good roll built up. *Rushcutter* came up so fast I did not know what happened till I found myself in the cockpit roaring for a knife to release myself from the tangle of sheets, halyards and safety harness. Annette was similarly yelling for me to open the hatch and let her out. In her hand was the carving knife which had jammed the hatch.

We turned to find the mast gone at deck level, about two feet of water below, and the liferaft in its slick fibreglass case surging alongside. It was agreed in an instant not to stuff around getting it on board, for it was a six-man weighing well over 100 lb, and I would have had to go into the water to get a line securely around it. At any instant we expected to be slammed again, and *Rushcutter*'s stability and self-righting were seriously in doubt now she had taken so much water below.

We pulled yards of string from the liferaft, till it popped open and was full in an instant. Annette leapt in gratefully, for although totally in control she had been thoroughly freaked when trapped below. I cut free our water bottles and bag of emergency gear, passing these to Annette who lashed them into the liferaft. One bottle had been holed, and so I left it. There was another below but the boom of a nearby sea had me in the raft in an instant. The line was cut, *Rushcutter* went behind a wave and we did not see her again.

Inside the raft we had to shout to make ourselves heard, for the canopy flogged with an insane rage. Its door, something one would hesitate to fit to a pup tent, could not be closed properly, for the foolish stiff plastic domes just kept popping open.

Then a great crushing roar slammed us into numbness. The raft was very full of water, on its side, and the door torn. By moving our weight inside we righted her and then bailed, using a cut-open gallon water bottle. We had poured its contents into the 5-gallon bottle which was not completely full, purposely so that it would be easy to handle and float.

We had just finished stabbing holes and lashing the door shut when we were hit again. This time the canopy burst open on the opposite side. Again we bailed, stabbed holes and lashed, and again we went over.

This time the raft stayed upside-down. Annette did not know where she was and I was spluttering in the little air under the raft trying to get my arm out of one of the rope handles. Annette decided which way was up and told me to cut the rope. The water-activated light inside the raft must have been obscured by the torn canopy. Without this light we would have been totally lost in the black tangle and drowned blindly.

Diving outside the raft, I did not think of anything tied to that rope. It must have been very dark now for I did not see the raft's waterballast bags whose existence I knew of. Instead I clawed my way on to the bottom, holding handfuls of the rubber, put my feet in the girdling rope and threw myself backwards. Annette slid in as the raft surfaced, awash, and bailed till I could be dragged aboard safely.

At this stage the canopy had pulled away completely from the raft, the glue line having failed.

We were not flipped again, just filled by roaring seas. Perhaps the loss of the canopy contributed to our stability.

Dawn brought us the sight of huge seas marching from the south, and still small steep cross-seas making crests tumble and break. With light we felt out of a minute-to-minute survival situation, and started to make things shipshape. It was then I saw our five gallons of water had gone, cut away by me when I freed my arm.

With our weight at one side of the raft it took up an attitude with the remains of the door side of the canopy across the wind. We, in the lee of this, had tightened up all our belts and buckles and with an aluminised plastic foil blanket around us were reasonably warm.

It was impossible to keep the raft dry; sloshes and occasional big seas came on board, slamming the canopy tube down on us. I had the beacon out, tied to my wrist, and we kept a constant lookout for breaking seas. I folded the aerial at any hint of one, for aerial length is critical for transmission of a signal.

I doubt that we could have survived the night had we been alone, or with anyone else but each other. There were so many occasions when we had to know exactly what the other was doing without even talking or with a few brief words.

We sat in silence, from time to time bailing as seas hit, and licking the salt splashes of the beacon's aerial insulator. From time to time the wind would rise, and in an instant the wavetops would be hissing and breaking.

Around 10 a.m. (a guess, for we had no watch), I saw a vapour trail overhead. Annette, who had lost her glasses, could only just see it. It cheered us greatly.

Lunch was tinned peaches. And I can thoroughly recommend them. Easy to swallow, sweet and wet. Later we tried a lifeboat biscuit. Scientifically designed they may be with no protein and high in calories, but they are such a foul brew, forming a great sticky glob in our mouths, that we gave up eating them.

Early that evening I snapped out of a doze to see a flashing red light above us in the sky. But when I had a red parachute flare in my hand, I could not see it. Surely I had seen it. Perhaps I had seen a star scintillate strongly.

Some time later Annette woke me to point out another flashing red. If she without glasses could see it I was convinced, and I had two parachute flares fired before I realised the plane could be 20–30 miles away as it was fairly low on the horizon.

Annette slept now and I held the beacon as high and as far out as I could, keeping it away from the salty wet canopy which would absorb the signal. Every time the tattered canopy started to shiver with a rise in the wind we both felt a sick apprehension that it would continue to rise, treating us to another night of breaking seas.

Dawn brought considerable cheer to Annette for she recognised a stable Tasman sky. It also brought me water, which I was craving. We had caught a little water in the showers the previous day, about a quarter cup each. Most had been wasted in waiting for the salt to be rinsed off the canopy. Torn and tied as the half left was, it caught water rather well.

Anyway we punctured the first of our six pint tins of water, drank, and then spent about half an hour devising a way of holding the rest so it did not spill. The beacon we lashed to the canopy support tube.

I had been having hallucinations for some time and we decided that I was dehydrated, not because of lack of water but because of all the salt I had drunk while admiring *Rushcutter*'s underwater sections.

We had not drunk much in the last couple of days on *Rushcutter*, for it had really been too rough to bother fixing the innumerable cups of tea I normally fill my day with. So it was with the measured precision of a drunk that I carefully knelt up to listen to a plane sound I heard. I decided it was the wind.

Fish had been bumping under the raft, so we set to trailing a lure and then pulling it in with inviting tugs. From time to time I checked the beacon's output with our tester, finding the needle still flicking high.

I had to put a strong conscious effort into ignoring flaring red and blue blobs which crossed my vision. Even the shiny black raft floor was bad to look at, reflecting a writhing image of the sky.

Annette was still her quiet self, not even very hungry or thirsty. Our next can of peaches was again a winner, but the fishing was not going too well. We could not have eaten the fish had we caught it, for fish is very high in protein, needing lots of water to digest. We were going to just suck the juices out for water.

It was just when the sea around the raft was starting to resemble a marine safari, for there were so many fish, that Annette heard the low throaty roar of a real piston and propeller aeroplane. We could not see him, low though he was, because of the cloud and blinding sun, and after our last waste of flares we were excessively cautious. Then, sighting the Orion, we had smoke and parachute flares ready for his next run.

Leaving us marked with a sonar buoy and smoke candles, the Orion went to fetch a Japanese refrigerated freighter, the *Toyu Maru*, who was 20 miles off.

They were alongside us in an hour and a quarter, crossing very close upwind of us, with a ladder and boarding nets out. The raft leapt over the bow wave, leaving us wishing we had lifejackets for this last bit. I grabbed a thrown monkey's fist and twirled it on to the raft, Annette meanwhile holding her weight central in the raft to stop the floor bulging up and sucking the raft down, which happens when flexible rafts are towed.

Thumping into the ship's side threw me on to the ladder, which I started to climb, my legs hardly able to support my weight. Below me as I climbed I could see Annette climbing too.'

————— ,, —————

From: *Sea Spray*, June 1978

8: The Wicked Old *Martinet*

Vessel: *Martinet* (99 tons ketch-rigged 'boomie' barge)
Skipper: A.W. ('Bob') Roberts
Crew: Jerry Thomason (mate)
      Freddie (third hand)
Bound from Swanscombe, Kent to Norwich, Norfolk
Time and date of loss: abandoned 0830, February 1941
Position: in Hollesey Bay, off Aldeburgh, Suffolk

All the Thames sailing barges that now remain in commission are being sailed as yachts, and because of the great and continuing interest in these remarkable craft, I have included this account by Bob Roberts.

Many sailing barges were lost during World War II, most of them by hitting mines laid in the Thames Estuary; but one barge, the *Martinet*, foundered in rough seas off Aldeburgh in the winter of 1941. Bob Roberts was skipper at the time, and they were bound for Norwich with a cargo of cement intended for use at one or other of the airfields then being hurriedly built in East Anglia.

The trouble really sprang from the fact that sailing craft were not, at that time, permitted to proceed after dark – which in February meant a short sailing day. Consequently, instead of reaching Yarmouth by midnight of the second day out, Roberts had to anchor the already leaking barge off Orfordness in rising wind and sea.

———————— " ————————

'Having got the *Martinet* off to her anchor in the morning I hastened ashore to Gravesend, where I had to clear out of Customs and get my secret documents from the Admiralty office. The mate and third hand were left to batten down the hatches, scrub round and get the barge ready for sea.

We had a new third hand with us this time, a young barge-mate out of the river craft who was waiting to take a berth in a motor ship. He was a good seaman and did his job without having to be told what to do. That is a great thing about men in sail who are any good – they don't need telling when there is a job which obviously wants doing. They just go and do it.

We sailed out of Sea Reach at the crack of dawn and made a splendid run down-Swin and over the Spitway, coming abreast of the Naze in the late afternoon. By this time our lovely west wind had all but disappeared and in its place came a doubtful breeze from further south. There were threatening clouds driving over us and the mate and I discussed the advisability of going into Harwich for the night.

The *Redoubtable*, a big Mistley-owned barge – one of the finest wooden sailing vessels on the coast – went scooting over the Stone Banks under our lee and I had a good mind to follow her. But the tides were such that we should not be able to get out of harbour in the early morning and therefore should fail to make Yarmouth before the next night.

After we had weighed up all the possibilities I let the *Martinet* run on down to Hollesley Bay and anchored under the highest part of the Whiting Sand. That was about five o'clock. I did not like the way the wind was freshening, but it was just one of those chances forced upon us by the wartime anchor-at-night regulation. We could have been in Yarmouth by midnight under pre-war conditions.

I was somewhat alarmed when we came to pump her out before going below for our evening meal. There was a lot of water in her, much more than I had expected. But we sucked her out and then fell-to round the cabin table. While we thus gorged upon the mighty mound of hash the cook had prepared, the mate, who sat next to the bulkhead dividing the cabin from the hold, said that he thought he could hear a lot of water slopping about. We removed a piece of the bulkhead under the mate's bunk and looked into the well. The water was almost on the floor of the hold – and we had sucked the pumps only ten minutes before!

We left the meal half-eaten and hurried up on deck. Both the big pumps aft were got working and the three of us settled down to regular spells, two pumping while one rested. After half an hour of this I went below to see how much was left in her. To my horror there was no difference – if anything, she had more water in her than when we had abandoned our meal and re-started pumping.

It was pitch dark now and there was not much hope of finding where the leak was, especially as the barge was deeply-laden. I had a look round with a torch, but apart from an old leak in the counter (on which a shipwright had spent an entire day recently without making the slightest improvement) I could not find any place bad enough to warrant all this pumping.

There was only one thing left to do – pump all night and get her into some sort of harbour – anywhere – as soon as it was light. In these ominous times all the beaches were mined as a defence against the probable invader and it was not possible to save a vessel in distress by beaching her. She would only be blown to bits if not first sunk by a salvo from the shore batteries. And all the harbours were bolted and barred at night by defence booms and nets. So there was nothing to be done except try and keep her afloat with the pumps until daylight allowed us to make a move.

Eleven o'clock. The pumps were just about holding their own. Then the starboard one choked. Frantically we took it to pieces and lay flat on the deck, the seas breaking over us and washing through our clothes, to reach down the pipe in a desperate attempt to clear it. Each of us had a try in turn but the stoppage was down in the very bowels of the ship. In the end we had to resort to a small pump on the hope of our being able to stick to the ship until daybreak. I was becoming doubtful. In fact it was not very pleasant blundering about below decks up to my knees in water and knowing that, being cement loaded, the ship might take a sudden plunge to her doom.

Each in turn went below and put his personal belongings into kit bags, finally bringing up a stock of hard biscuits, condensed milk, corned beef and the usual items that ship-wrecked mariners endeavour to have beside them. It was no good taking any chances. She might not last until morning.

She sank so low in the water that eventually the tops of the pumps were submerged. It was half-past two. We were wet through and the wind seemed very cold. We could feel sleet driving above the spray. Pumping was no longer of any use – or even possible.

A gloomy trio, we mustered aft under the lee of the wheelhouse. Our prospects were dark indeed. If we took to the lifeboat and lived through the breakers in the bay we were faced with the risk of landing on a steep shingle bank down which the pebbles and stones rushed at amazing speed with each recoiling wave. It was a bad place to try and beach a small boat. And even if we succeeded in getting ashore we should almost certainly be either shot by the soldiers on guard or blown to smithereens by a land-mine.

For two hours we hung on to the side of the wheelhouse, cold, tired and hungry, wondering how long she would last. One more inspection below brought me to a decision. There was so much water in her that she might sink at any moment, though she might wallow in a half-sunken state for many hours, as wooden vessels often do.

We lit a rocket but it misfired, hit the mizzenmast and went straight down into the sea. We tried another and were more successful. It soared skywards in a graceful arc, leaving a trail of sparks behind it. Immediately afterwards we lit a flare so that if anyone on shore had seen our rocket they could then determine the position of our vessel by bearings. It was half-past four. I hoped that the coastguards at Orfordness would see our signals. At least we were advertising the fact that we were in trouble. I felt bound to do that as the lives of the crew depended on my discretion. Whatever risks I like to take myself, I was in no way entitled to gamble with other people's lives.

Our supply of signals was limited, so we waited twenty minutes before we again sent up a rocket and a flare. This we continued to do until about eight o'clock, when the dim streaks of dawn could be seen over the North Sea.

The *Martinet* was practically awash. Only her proud head and shapely counter were above sea level. I estimated, although I could not be certain, that since she had not already gone down she would last several hours more.

It was the third hand who first saw that our salvation was at hand. His keen young eyes spotted something bobbing up and down in the white-capped seas to the eastward. It was the Aldeburgh lifeboat coming to our assistance.

Now that help was near I felt a grim reluctance to leave the ship. I imagined that the old devil in her was laughing at me. Apart from that, the *Martinet* had been my home for practically two years, and I had grown fond of the old vessel in spite of her bad reputation. And although I had decided that the time had come to abandon her, there lingered within me a dim spark of hope that perhaps she might be saved. Common sense told me that her days were about to end, but I could not bring myself to realise it. But there was no holding back now. The lifeboatmen were shouting to us to get ready to jump as they manoeuvred to bring their craft alongside.

It was not an easy matter for the coxswain to take us off the *Martinet*, half-submerged as she was, rolling heavily and with the seas breaking right over her. He brought his boat round in a wide sweep under our port quarter, but at that moment the barge took a wild sheer away from him and the gulf between us was too far to jump.

We hung on while the lifeboat motored down to leeward again and at the second attempt she rose on a sea and almost landed on our deck. As she crashed into our bulwarks Jerry and the third hand slung their kitbags into her and jumped. As she descended into the hollow of the sea I followed them and we all landed in a heap in her cockpit.

The coxswain had come alongside on the tideward side of the barge to make sure of getting us off and he had some difficulty in getting away from the stricken vessel. With three sickening jolts the lifeboat struck the *Martinet* and the seas descended mercilessly on both the rescuers and the rescued. At last the little boat's head was pushed clear and she plunged out to windward.

"Which of you be the captain?" shouted the burly, red-faced coxswain, shrouded in dripping yellow oilskins.

When he had identified me we had a brief conference on the fate of the *Martinet*.

"You 'adn't reckoned on tryin' to save 'er?" asked the coxswain with a forlorn hope of profitable salvage.

I looked over at the *Martinet* and shook my head. Her midship decks were no longer visible above water, even when she rose on a crest, and she had that unnatural, out-of-time motion which spells the doom of a vessel in distress.

"She won't last long now," agreed the coxswain. "She's too far gone. We'd better leave 'er and get you chaps ashore. Go t'hell if you don't look some'ut wet and cold. This 'ere sleet don't 'elp, neither. Where's that there bottle of rum, Horace? Open 'er up. Them biscuits, too."

As we chugged northwards to Aldeburgh, running before the wind and careering giddily down the steep-sided seas, the crew told me their story.

The coastguards at Orfordness had seen our rockets and had telephoned to Aldeburgh. The lifeboat crew were called from their beds at five o'clock in the morning and they hurried down to the beach. There was a heavy sea breaking onshore and there was no hope of getting the biggest lifeboat afloat because an enemy air attack had damaged the slipway the day before.

The only thing they could do was to try and haul off the little "summer" boat, as they called her. This boat was designed for minor rescue operations in fine weather and was hardly fit to be launched in a winter's gale. But these Suffolk men are a hard lot, and although there is no harbour at Aldeburgh to shelter them from onshore winds, they have never failed to go out in answer to a call for help.

Waist deep in the icy water, with the blinding sleet driving almost horizontally, they struggled to get the little cockleshell afloat. Three times men and boat were flung back on to the shingle beach but at the fourth attempt they got her off and drove her out through the breakers.

They deserved that rum.

"Go steady with that bottle, me lads," laughed the coxswain. "Don't forget the shipwrecked mariners."

By the time everyone had had his turn with the bottle it was empty. By a nice piece of judgement there was just enough left in the bottom for the last man, the entire operation taking not more than three or four minutes.

When we arrived off Aldeburgh beach the coxswain told me that there was a boom defence and minefield between us and the shore. He would not be able to beach his boat as he would in the ordinary way. She would have to be brought broadside to the breakers to get in through the narrow gap and round the inner shoal.

"You'll get a wet shirt when she hits," he warned us.

As she struck the beach the seas broke right over our heads and the boat all but capsized. I found myself sprawling in the backwash and some soldiers ran down into the water and dragged me up. Jerry and the third hand were wading ashore, hauling their sodden kitbags after them.

Ten minutes later we were having a hot bath in a water-front hotel. The people on shore had everything ready for us – dry clothes, hot food, hot whisky and cigarettes. They are accustomed to playing host to shipwrecked mariners in Aldeburgh.

After we had eaten I telephoned the Orfordness coastguards and they told me that the *Martinet* was still visible, wallowing half-submerged in a heavy sea. The wind was of gale force and they did not think she would last much longer.

A few hours later she sank. That was the end of the wicked old *Martinet*, last of the "boomie" barges.'

——————— ,, ———————

From: A.W. Roberts, *Coasting Bargemaster* (1949) Edward Arnold & Co.

9: So Near and Yet . . .

Yacht: *Merlan* (43ft Bermudian sloop)
Skipper: W.L. ('Lance') Curtis
Crew: Keith Douglas Young
      Eric Walker
      Brian Shaw
Bound from Georgetown, Tasmania to Geelong, Victoria, Australia
Time and date of loss: 1700, January 16th, 1949
Position: on rocks off Phillip Head, near Melbourne

Merlan had competed and been just beaten into second place in the Sydney–Hobart race of 1948. For the race she had a crew of nine, but only three of them, together with an additional volunteer, were left to sail her back to Geelong. The voyage of 250 miles across the Bass Strait is described by Keith Douglas Young:

———————— " ————————

'We left Georgetown at the mouth of the Tamar River, in Northern Tasmania, at about 1.30 p.m. on Friday, January 14. Not, as events later proved, a particularly auspicious day on which to have sailed. The weather forecast promised a good voyage . . . fine weather with southerly winds veering to southeast, which would give us an easy run to the Heads. According to the radio reports all barometers in Tasmania were rising; and with the weather seemingly assured, we felt no forebodings as we set out under full sail on what should have been a simple and speedy passage of 1½ to two days, for the approximately 250 miles distance.

Fine weather stayed with us for the first day. We made good time with a favourable wind and a gentle swell which set the reef points jigging against the inward curve of the sail. The smooth racing hull of the *Merlan* porpoised forward in a series of powerful lunges while the towering mast described a pattern of arabesques and circles against the sky. It was perfect sailing weather.

The log reading after the first 24 hours showed us to be considerably more than half-way home. However, during the afternoon of the second day our barometer began to fall, slowly at first, but with increasing rapidity as evening approached. At the same time a dirty black scud began to build up in the sky. The almost hourly stream of planes which had been in sight as they sped overhead were lost to view in the rapidly forming cloud-wrack. These planes, in addition to relieving that sense of mid-ocean loneliness and isolation, had served as a good check on navigation. It was comforting, however, to be able to hear them still.

By midnight that night (Saturday) our glass, which had been steady at 30.05, had dropped to a menacing 29.5 and showed signs of falling still further. A good fresh breeze was blowing, but at that time not yet strong enough to cause us any real discomfort or worry. *Merlan*, still under full sail, was giving a good account of herself, although solid water and spray were being hurled aboard in some of the gusts. It was obvious to us that the worst was still to come.

We carried on under these conditions for a further hour or so, when it was decided to take the mainsail off altogether and set the storm trysail. This was accomplished without much difficulty as the wind lulled temporarily while we were shifting sails. Hardly had we made everything secure when it really began to blow. The advance-guard of the gale, as forecast by the rapid and steep fall of the barometer, finally menaced our ship.

Shortly after the gale struck we sighted our first light on the Victorian coast. This was identified as the Cape Woolamai Light. Here it became necessary to change course to the west in order to stand up to the Heads. Our position was confirmed some little time later when the unmistakable 22½-second flash of Cape Schank was sighted in the murky distance.

By this time the wind had veered round to the west. We decided to get away from the land and stand in once more in the morning. With the night pitch black and the coastal lights periodically blacked out in driving rain squalls, it was scarcely a safe risk to approach the land too closely.

There was no rest for any of us that night. Those who tried to snatch a little sleep found it almost impossible to wedge into a bunk securely enough to avoid being pitched out as *Merlan* fell heavily off some of the more precipitous seas. In addition, it had become bitterly cold and all our clothing was thoroughly saturated. It was impossible to prepare any sort of a hot meal or drink. The best we could do was to snatch a handful of biscuits, an orange or an apple and perhaps a bit of chewing gum. I had quite a battle keeping my cigarettes and matches dry, but succeeded by wrapping them securely in a spare oilskin.

It was a thoroughly miserable night. Next morning (Sunday) found us under trysail and jib ploughing through a lumpy grey sea with the wind coming in gusts and sometimes petering out altogether before coming in just as freshly from another quarter.

We were still, at this time, some considerable distance off shore and making slow progress under reduced sail. Again we changed course to make directly for Port Phillip Heads, whereupon the wind began to build up until in a short time it was blowing half a gale directly out of the west. This was rather disheartening, as it meant we had to drive *Merlan* right into the teeth of the wind under trysail, not a particularly efficient sail at the best of times.

By midday the wind had mounted to full gale – about Force 10 or 11 on the Beaufort scale. Some of the gusts we estimated at from 70 to 75 m.p.h., a figure which was later confirmed by Weather Bureau observations made at the time ashore. This state of affairs prevailed for the next few hours, during which we tried to battle our way to the west under the inefficient trysail. Then the wind helped us by backing to the south'ard so that we eventually found ourselves making heavy going against a full sou'westerly gale along the Victorian coast between Cape Schank and the Heads.

Huge seas rolling up Bass Strait were making it difficult and dangerous for those of us who found it necessary to remain on deck. In spite of efforts to ease her over some of the worst of the seas, our decks were being continually swept. There was hardly a moment when the self-bailing cockpit was free of water; for as fast as it could drain the contents of one sea another would pour aboard. Much of this water was finding its way below, where, to add to our troubles, both pumps had gone out of action. Soon the water below reched a level several inches over the floor boards and it became necessary to bail with a bucket, which we continued to do for the ensuing several hours.

In the early afternoon of Sunday it was decided to take in the trysail. Even that small patch of canvas was more than the boat could safely stand. With an almost continuous series of breaking seas hurling themselves feet deep across the decks this was a hell of a job.

Blinded and almost choked by the tumultuous waves, Lance, Brian and I clawed our way forward where, on looking aloft, I was somewhat startled to see the mast trembling and vibrating like a plucked harp string. We returned to the cockpit for a trick at the tiller. At the end of an hour it was time for another spell at the bucket. To our dismay, the water was gaining on us and was now splashing up over the matresses on the bunks. It was now a matter of getting into shelter quickly, or having the boat founder under us.

It was too late to turn back and run for shelter at Flinders or anywhere in the lee of the Schank. Heaving to was likewise out of the question, owing to the size and force of the seas. With the deadness of the sloop occasioned by the terrific weight of water in her, there was always the danger that they would overwhelm us.

Merlan had behaved magnificently in all that we had come through, and any boat less honestly built would, I am convinced, have foundered long before. But there is a limit to what even the best craftsmanship in wood can stand, and it was apparent that *Merlan* was tiring. The bucket bailing was by far the worst of all our previous ordeals. Not only did the bucket become progressively heavier as it was handed up full each time, but the crew handling it had to brace themselves against the unpredictable dips, lurches and wrenches of the yacht.

Meanwhile, under the single jib, we had gradually closed the land until *Merlan* was not more than a mile or two off shore. The height of the seas and the flying spray was such that we could catch only brief glimpses of the nearby coastline. By mid-afternoon we estimated that we could be only a short distance from the Heads. We expected the entrance to be hazardous, but our condition was such by this time that it would have to be attempted in spite of the risks.

At about 4.00 p.m. I wedged myself securely against the boom and strained to catch an identifying glimpse of the shore. At the moment I was about to give up, I caught one brief glimpse of the white shaft of the Lonsdale Lighthouse on the western side of the Heads. This momentary peep was sufficient to give us a bearing, and on checking our position we discovered we were about a mile due south of the Heads. It was a simple matter then to ease our sheets and begin the run for the Heads and what we earnestly hoped would be shelter, safety and rest.

As we drew closer to the entrance we could see the tidal signal flying from the yardarm of the Lonsdale Light. It informed us that the tide was adverse – that it was ebbing. There was no turning back. We would have to try and force our way through. The regular steamer channel in the center of the Rip was a churning, boiling maelstrom in which I am convinced no small boat could possibly have lived. Further to the east lay the dreaded Corsair Rock, unseen in the welter of white water that was the Heads, but still a lurking menace. Our best, in fact our only plan was to carry on as we were – as close as possible to the Lonsdale side.

With gigantic seas sweeping up under our stern as we stormed along on a northerly course, we were picked up and literally hurled ahead at terrific speeds as we skated on the crests of some of the waves. A breaking sea would almost certainly have meant our end; and though many times it did look as though we might be overwhelmed by water hurtling up astern, none broke upon us.

The next greatest danger was the possibility of a broach, and this actually happened during our hazardous dash through the Heads. I found myself grabbing for grip on something as *Merlan* was picked up by a monster sea charging up astern and hurled ahead at a speed we estimated to be in the vicinity of 15 m.p.h. As the yacht began to slide down the almost perpendicular slope of the wave to the great bulk of water which had forced its way below all ran to the nose of the boat. This, of course, left the helmsman with no control and we had a ticklish minute before the yacht was brought back on her course. But this single broach, as it turned out later, had been sufficient to bring us within the orbit of the Lonsdale reef, quite lost to view beneath the boiling surge. Next moment we struck the reef! It was a mortal blow for *Merlan*. That much was obvious after the first shock. I was standing at the foot of the hatch with a just-filled bucket which I was about to hand up to Brian. To the accompaniment of a horrible grinding sound I was pitched the full length of the cabin, where I picked myself up, dazed and shaken, with the bucket still in my hand. The dreadful tearing, rending, crunching sound as the yacht drove on the rocks is something quite impossible to convey.

Picking myself up I began to fight my way to the hatch and escape – through an indescribable confusion of sodden sails and clothing, charts and navigation instruments, mattresses and tins of food which had been flung out of burst lockers. My one thought, I suppose naturally enough, was to get on deck.

Just as I reached the foot of the hatch (about five seconds after the initial shock) *Merlan* struck again. Once more I was hurled the length of the cabin, to end up even more bruised and battered at the foot of the mast. A second time I clawed my way through the hatch just in time to see and feel a really terrific sea lift the *Merlan* bodily and hurl her forward on to the reef. Brian, who had apparently secured a firm grip on something substantial, seemed to be all right. Eric, tightly lashed in the cockpit, had likewise emerged unscathed, though the heavy bronze fitting at the rudder head had snapped completely off, leaving him with the now useless tiller in his hands.

But we did appear to have one casualty. At the moment of impact Lance had been flung violently against the dog-house at the after end of the cabin and his face was a mass of blood which poured from a nasty gash near the bridge of his nose. The effect was pretty ghastly. Apart from the shaking up and a few bruises and scratches, I seemed to be in working order.

The jib had blown itself out at the moment we struck. After a moment Brian and Lance went forward to lower it. However, they found the halyard in such a tangled mess that they were forced to abandon the attempt. In the meantime I had returned below, where I managed to retrieve four life jackets. We put them on. Well we did, for beyond doubt those life jackets saved our lives in the struggle which was to come shortly afterwards.

Within minutes, a large crowd of holidaymakers had begun to gather on the shore about half a mile away. There was, of course, absolutely nothing they could do, but we must have provided them with an interesting spectacle. The keeper of the Lonsdale Light had witnessed the entire happening and had telephoned at once for the lifeboat stationed at Queenscliff.

Before long the lifeboat appeared, but because of the tremendous sea running, the adverse tide and the treacherous currents and tide-rips it could not be brought close to the wreck. At that moment things never looked more hopeless. We held a bit of a conference to decide what our best course of action might be and whether we might, by our own efforts, save ourselves. It was clear to us that so long as the gale prevailed there was absolutely no hope of a boat approaching us. It seemed, therefore, that we would have to take to the water and try to make for the lifeboat cruising up and down about a quarter of a mile away in the lee of the reef.

It was now about 5.00 p.m., and since the tide appeared to be at low water slack we determined to make our effort before darkness set in.

On the cabin top was a small plywood dinghy. Though none too optimistic about its chances of supporting the four of us in the waters swirling and boiling over the reef, we did hope that it might perhaps carry us some of the way. It did – about six feet. We had barely left the stricken *Merlan* when our cockleshell dinghy was swamped and we were left struggling in the powerful, sucking tide-rip.

Within seconds the seas had taken complete control and we had been swept dozens of yards apart. The same gigantic wave which had engulfed our tiny dinghy seemed, once it had us firmly in its grasp, to sweep each one of us in a totally different direction. Then began what was really a nightmare struggle before the eyes of some hundreds of people.

We had swamped in one of the labyrinthine channels of the reef, a channel though which a vast volume of water was swirling at a terrific pace. I began swimming as desperately as possible, but like the others, was entirely at the mercy of the currents.

The most fortunate of the four, I managed to crawl through a mass of slimy kelp on to a more solid portion of the reef. Actually I crawled part of the way on to the reef three times only to be washed off by seas sweeping across. But on the fourth attempt I contrived to hang on. Clinging grimly to the reef for a few minutes to catch my breath I recovered some strength. Then began a staggering walk to the leeward side where I knew I would once more have to take to the sea for a swim to the lifeboat. Before doing so I turned to see how my shipmates might be faring.

I was elated to see Brian dragging himself on to the reef, but was quite alarmed to see Eric and Lance, supported solely by their life jackets, being swept out past the wreck into a position which seemed fatal. Then, as I watched, Eric was swept by a wave into a favourable current and began to approach the reef. He began to struggle once more and by dint of furious efforts was at last able to clamber on to the water-swept rocks. Somewhat later, Lance, nearly spent, made it also.

By this time a group of Queenscliff fishermen had succeeded in launching a dinghy and by a marvellous combination of seamanship and courage had brought the boat right up to the reef from which we had expected to have to make another swim to the waiting lifeboat. One error in judgment, one unpredictable sea sweeping aboard their dinghy, and they too would have been struggling for their lives.

It was a comparatively simple matter to pile into the dinghy, a solidly-built 15-footer, but there was still the dangerous quarter-mile pull to the waiting lifeboat. The seas had not abated, and with eight men aboard even a 15-foot dinghy is somewhat crowded. But our rescuers displayed faultless seamanship; we got a line to the lifeboat and were hauled alongside. In a matter of moments we were wrapped in coats and blankets and a man-sized pannikin of rum was thrust upon each of us. First aid was applied to our cuts and scratches received on the boat and more especially from the jagged rocks on the reef. And so we were rescued.'

———————— „ ————————

From: *Yachting*, October 1950

10: Loss of an Un-named Five Tonner

Yacht: Name not given
Skipper: Anonymous
Crew: Skipper's brother
        Skipper's father
Bound from Pin Mill, Suffolk to Dover
Time and date of loss: approx. 2100, August 17th, 1924
Position: 5 miles SE of Shipwash Light-vessel

When he wrote this account of the loss of his little ship in the North Sea, the author was unwilling to give either his name or that of the yacht, but the story is none the less interesting for that.

———————— " ————————

'Not knowing what lay in store for her, the game little cutter sailed from Pin Mill down the Orwell on August 17, 1924, with a cargo of too much optimism and too little experience, and was in consequence lost at sea. But having, I hope, learnt something from my mistakes on that occasion, I am handing on the yarn to other yachtsmen for what it is worth.

For obvious reasons I will not give her name, suffice it that she was a pretty little 5-tonner, then the apple of my eye. I was barely more than an "infant" in the eyes of the law then, and she was my first sea-going vessel.

She was clinker-built at Southend in 1904, and had a fine, weatherly hull, straight stem, good sheer, and a very pretty counter, 24 ft overall, with a beam of 8 ft she drew about 3 ft 9 in of water. With her black topsides and gold line, varnished teak rail, and white coach-roof and coamings, Yankee-fashion, she really looked a pretty little lady. She was snugly-rigged as a cutter, with tanned canvas and a Wykeham-Martin jib. On the whole she handled fairly well, though she was extremely lively in a sea, and her bluff bows would stop her dead going to wind'ard in anything of a popple, while the large open well was always a source of danger in bad weather. The crew on this occasion consisted of my father and my young brother.

On the morning in question we turned out about 3 a.m. and ran down the Orwell on the last of the ebb before a pleasant nor'westerly breeze. The glass, if rather low, had been steady for the last four days, and wiseacres ashore the previous evening had prophesied "fine weather over the weekend, at any rate."

As dawn broke, the depressing rain cleared off. It was a nasty, high dawn, angry and red, but I trusted to the still steady glass, ignoring the import of a paternal warning, which was mistake number one. So we sailed out past Landguard Point and the old familiar buoys, across to the Sunk Sand Head; intending to sail up the Black Deep, get through the Fisherman's Gat over the Long Sand just before high-water, and make for the Gull Stream, arriving off the Foreland at about half-ebb and so carrying our tide through to Dover.

So much for our plans. Now for the actual facts. In the first place, the wind backed to about west, and we had to beat up the Black Deep. Here we found a nasty popple coming down with the flood running against the wind, and a good deal of water started coming aboard. This made it necessary to get the pump to work, for the little ship was working somewhat, and the hot summer had opened up her top-sides. It was then that we made a somewhat disconcerting discovery. For the pump, after spurting feebly once or twice, would produce nothing but a coughing sound and a little air. Investigation with a spanner indicated the cause – a match-end stuck in the valves. The pump was cleared and reassembled, only to fail again for the same reason, and the process of taking down had to be repeated. This was certainly far from pleasant, as the weather was looking threatening and the pump might be wanted badly before the day was out. Attempts to arrange a trap proved almost useless, as it became increasingly obvious that the people to whom we had previously chartered the boat had the old idea of clearing up below by sweeping all the litter into the bilge. As the motion was now becoming too violent to be able to hold a spanner on the pump, we had to give up the struggle and rely on such bailing as we could do with a bucket.

By this time we were about half way up the Black Deep, had already one reef in and the staysail stowed, and were really needing a second reef down. But with the flood still sweeping us up into the Thames, I reckoned that as the glass had as yet shown no signs of falling, and if the wind backed no further we should soon be able to lay our course for the Gull Stream, we were justified in carrying on. A few more miles and we should be getting the shelter of the Foreland. And, anyway, we were bound west. So off the entrance to the Fisherman's Gat we hove down our second reef, and then found our way cautiously through the Long Sand with the aid of the lead.

Needless to say, there was a most unpleasant short sea in the shoal water, but we consoled ourselves with thoughts of shelter ahead. And in any case, there was the Long Sand uncovering under our lee between us and Harwich, and a foul wind into the Thames, so that it was too late to think of returning. But the glass had now begun to fall, the sky was overcast, and the wind increasing hard, with blinding, stinging squalls of rain. Every sea was breaking, and the dinghy towing very erratically, though she was a splendid little sea-boat and made fast with two new warps from the quarters of the yacht. But as soon as the water deepened and we dared stop threshing to wind'ard, we hove-to and took in the last reef, and then set her at it again. There was nothing for it but to drive her and hope for the best, for the glass was going down with a run, the wind had freshened to half a gale, backing into the sou'west, and as soon as the ebb began, we should be swept down and on to the Kentish Knock. At all costs we must clear that, so we kept her at it, and prayed that nothing would part. I thanked heaven that the running gear was new and the standing rigging sound, whilst her mast was a beautiful new spar. But the sails were old and really past it, and every moment I expected to see the mainsail burst.

The sea now seemed really wicked for a small boat, and here we lost our dinghy. A huge sea, breaking under the yacht, fell upon her satellite. The painters snapped like pack-threads, she was spun round and round like a cork, crushed flat, and reappeared bottom-up some cable's length astern. Things were now looking serious.

The time was as near as I can remember about 12 noon, and it was soon quite obvious that we could not carry on much longer as we were going, for the sea was now too high and too steep, and we were constantly being swept, which made things pretty unpleasant. The mate (my young brother) was suffering agonies as a result of trying to lie down in the cabin to rest. As the saloon was in the most indescribable state of chaos, this was hardly surprising. Every movable article had burst from its fastenings and was cavorting wildly around in about six inches of water. Locker doors had burst open and disgorged their contents, racks had shed their medley of odd gear, and the fog-horn was solemnly pounding the charts to pulp; while every book in our small library had left its place and was swimming around in the general maelstrom on the floor. Cushions and blankets alike floated about, and to add flavour to the melange, the colza can had broken adrift in the foc's'le and poured its aromatic beastliness into the bilge.

The visibility was very bad, though through occasional breaks in the rain squalls we could make out the sails of one or two fishermen, apparently in the direction of the Edinburgh Channel. But we were sagging away to loo'ard, the ebb was sweeping us down, and we then made out the buoys on the southern side of the Knock. So as it would have been suicidal to drive the little vessel any more, and I thought that we now had room enough to clear the sand, we hove-to on the starboard tack and prepared for the gale to blow itself out. In the first place, we endeavoured to clear the ship of water. This was no easy matter, as the violent motion of the yacht made it almost impossible to empty a bucket over the side before the contents had spilled themselves into the bilge. But it presently became clear that even hove-to under storm jib and close reefed mainsail, we were still carrying too much sail, as although we were almost becalmed in the trough, we were on our beam ends on the crest of every sea, and I was fearful of the balast shifting. So now, if ever, was the time to try out our beautiful new sea-anchor, large enough by all the rules of the game to be able to hold a seven-tonner at least. Unfortunately I had not had time in the general rush of fitting out to provide oil-bags, which omission I had meant to remedy at Dover. I had confidence, however, that the sea-anchor would hold her, that she would ride quiet enough, and that with sufficient sea-room for safety, we could get below for a comfortable (?) meal. So much for theory!

In practice, the sea-anchor was rigged on a good new springy warp of some twenty fathoms, and paid out slowly over the weather bow. We tried to roll up the jib, which flew to blazes the moment the sheet was started. The mainsail, however, we stowed safely, and awaited results.

I will not say that my confidence was misplaced, for I still believe that it was an excellent sea-anchor. But I will say that I was dismayed at what happened. For an incredibly short space of time she lay quiet enough, until a huge breaking sea smote her fairly on the bow and threw her over almost on her beam ends in the trough. She righted at once, but lay broached to, rolling to an alarming extent, shipping a lot of broken water and resolutely refusing to budge from that really dangerous position. We hoisted the peak of the mainsail, but she wouldn't shift. We tried to row her round with the rudder, and again with one of the dinghy oars, but all to no purpose.

At last I hit upon a desperate remedy, which constituted big mistake number two. I endeavoured to run the sea anchor warp through the iron traveller on the bowsprit, so that by subsequently hauling on the outhaul I might get the additional leverage of the bowsprit (which was a stout spar, very well staved), to bring her head to sea. But in the hurry of the moment I made no provision for chafe, the iron parted the warp, and having no tripping line on the sea-anchor, it was "good-bye, fare ye well" as far as that was concerned.

Somehow she had to be brought up to meet the seas, and that quickly. So, being in shoal water, we let go the anchor, not thinking that it would hold, but hoping that as she dredged it along, the drag would be sufficient to bring her head up. I have since been told that this is a dodge practised by the Dutchmen. But in this case it proved of no effect, as she towed the anchor and twenty fathoms of chain without a sign of looking up in the right direction. This being the case, we determined that the only thing to do was to run for it, as the wind had backed right round into the sou'west. We should then hope to get a little shelter from Orfordness perhaps, and if the weather moderated, be able to make Lowestoft or Yarmouth. But as we should possibly need our anchor in the event of reaching port in safety, we were loath to lose it, so all hands had to turn to and get it aboard. Having no windlass, it was not an easy job, as we could only get an inch or two at a time as she fell into the trough, while we clawed at the cable till the blood spurted from our finger nails. But we got it aboard at last, the last few fathoms easily enough, hoisted the reefed staysail, and put her before it. In this wise we ran past the Kentish Knock Lightship, between her and the watch buoy, and I shall never forget the picture she made plunging deep into the steep seas and then throwing her streaming bows on high, to the accompaniment of the weird and mournful dirge of her fog-horn. With not a sign of a soul on board, she looked the last word in humid desolation.

From this point we shaped a course as much to the nor'ard as we dared crossing the seas, and paid out the end of the main sheet astern (having lost our kedge warp with the sea-anchor), to divide the seas. It really had a surprising effect, as the most threatening seas would divide on the warp, and breaking, cream away under the counter without doing any harm. To make matters more cheerful, the rain cleared off and the sun shone in a blue sky, while above our heads, low, ragged clouds of fleecy white went scudding by. We also discovered a packet of toffee in an only slightly moist condition, on which we fed ravenously. While as we ran on into deeper water, the sea was not quite so steep, though still running very high and breaking continuously. As we were before the wind and the sun was shining, the temperature rose somewhat, and the slower movement of the ship made life more tolerable again. Wherefore I was confident that we should yet be able to save the ship, and the general outlook was far more cheerful. So that I for one sang blithely at the helm to the accompaniment of the wind in the rigging and the roaring of the sea. Thus we ran on for some hours, until the sun was low in the sky, and the tide was about to turn. And then our troubles began anew.

The most vital problem was that, according to my dead reckoning, we were now about to reach the northernmost limit of my charts. For being bound down Channel, I had no charts northward of Orfordness. We had sighted nothing since passing the Knock some hours ago, and couldn't be certain of our position. If I were right, the Shipwash should be appearing on the port bow; but it wasn't. The bottom was falling out of the barometer, and we were frankly beginning to feel the strain. The gale was still as violent as ever, and when the tide turned, the sea would of course become much worse again. Also, with all the optimism in the world, we could not but realize that with the most northerly course we could steer, we should miss the land off Lowestoft by from five to ten miles. And whereas one doesn't particularly mind drowning oneself, when it comes to risking the greater part of one's family it is rather a different proposition. We knew almost nothing of the sands under our lee, and of course the slightest touch in the darkness would be quite enough to finish us off. So that when a Norwegian tramp came up astern obviously bound to the nor'ard, we ran up a couple of dishcloths rolled into a ball with another below as a square flag, on the ensign halliards, and awaited results.

For some time the tramp, which was a ship in ballast of some 2,500 tons, held on her course. But at length she saw our signal and bore down upon us. We learnt afterwards that they had spotted us some time before, but had thought we were a buoy adrift.

She eased down under our lee, and we hailed her with a megaphone. First we enquired our position, and found that the Shipwash bore about NW, distant 5 miles. So that we were not too far out in our reckoning, for from the elevation of their bridge they were able to see the lightship quite clearly, while we were too low to be able to see it in that sea. But this did not solve the problem of our lack of a chart. It was then that I determined upon a risky expedient, namely, to tow from the end of his bridge within the shelter of his lee side. For I thought that if he could but give us a pluck in towards the land and through the sands off Lowestoft, we should there get a certain amount of shelter, and might possibly be able to get into Yarmouth when he cast us off. Her skipper agreed to do this, and when I asked him what it would cost, for I was not insured and could not face a heavy salvage bill, his reply proved typical of the whole nature of the man we were soon to know well. "It will cost you nothing," he shrieked, and we ran down under her stern, as far to loo'ard as possible to heave a line. And that is where big mistake number three was made. What we should have done, of course, was to run on and let him come up to wind'ard to pick us up. It was a costly lesson!

Events then followed with lightning-like rapidity. A handline came whirling down from the bridge, and with it we hauled aboard a hawser, which we quickly made fast round the bitts. But before the steamship could get way on again, being in ballast and broadside on, she was down on top of us like an express train, and we being becalmed and helpless in the lee of her huge hull, in the twinkling of an eye we were sucked in under her stern and swept across her propeller aperture. There we stuck like a stick across a sluice, and with every sea one blade of her propeller caught us a glancing blow. As her stern descended, the swelling of the quarters aft washed us almost clear, and prevented a direct blow, but it was a hectic time. With about twelve foot rise and fall on every sea breaking under her stern, and the rolling in the trough, rubbing strake, bulwarks and rail on the port side were ground away; the bowsprit was shattered, blocks came tumbling down from aloft, and each glancing blow of the propeller was gradually scoring away through the plank landings. Frantic efforts to shift us for'ard or aft failed, and our position on top of the screw made it impossible for us to get away on the steamship. Then came a more direct blow from the propeller which seemed to start something, and the mate declared that she was making water fast.

When it was quite clear that no efforts would save her, we reluctantly decided to abandon her while there was yet time. For the first direct blow would send her to the bottom at once. So by means of a Jacob's ladder, one by one we reached the tramp's deck, the climb something of an effort, one moment hanging far out over the ditch and the next crashing back against the ship's side. Finally, as I was about to leave, and was dashing below to try to save my log, she got the first, and only, *direct* blow from the propeller. In a flash the whole port side was cut away from keelson to deck, the blade slicing up like a hot knife through butter, and the waters of the North Sea closed round my sea boots as I sprang for the end of the ladder. With the whole of one side cut away and 3½ tons of iron ballast aboard, she went down like a loaded cane. But she did not leave her skipper without a gesture of farewell. For in making her last plunge, she gave me a handshake that I was to remember for many months to come. Part of her rigging caught my left hand as she went down, and split the thumb away, leaving it hanging by the muscle alone.'

—————— ,, ——————

From: *Yachting Monthly*, November 1928

11: Surviving Hurricane Assault

Yacht: *Island Princess* (48ft Bermudian ketch)
Skipper: Barry 'Finbar' Gittelman
Crew: Michael Munroe
      Bob Harvey
      Matthew 'Doc' St Clair
Bound from Marathon, Florida to Belize, Central America
Time and date of loss: 0415, August 6th, 1980
Position: approx. 40 miles S of Santiago de Cuba

This account of the loss of the ketch *Island Princess* is based on the comments of her skipper and crew, linked together by *SAIL* reporter, Bob Payne.

——————— " ———————

Island Princess was being sailed from Florida to Belize by a delivery company based on Key West. The yacht was a strongly built wooden ship with two-inch planking that had been refastened prior to the trip. Both masts had been removed and checked, all standing rigging replaced and the engine put in 'top running order'; so that Gittelman could say:

> 'She was in just about perfect condition. And as far as equipment goes, I would say we had a full complement of the very best safety gear available.'

Among that gear was a four to six man Givens Buoy Liferaft with a water-ballasted stabilization chamber.

The skipper and two of the three-man crew were experienced offshore sailors, but the fourth man, 'Doc' St Clair, was making his first deep-water passage. However, *Island Princess* had two characteristics that were to

74

prove fatal to her. Her internal ballast was in the form of lead pigs and her companionway hatch was offset to starboard, which meant that if she were knocked down to starboard that hatch remained under water for a long time.

Gittelman and his crew had given thought to the possibility of encountering a hurricane, and they had chosen the much longer route round the eastern end of Cuba instead of heading directly across the Gulf of Mexico and down the Yucatán channel because the former route offered more chances of shelter in hurricane holes.

Island Princess left Marathon on July 27th, but the first word they had of Hurrican Allen was on Sunday August 2nd, when WWV weather reported that a low had developed into a tropical storm, had officially become a hurricane and was moving west on a course that would probably take it south of Jamaica.

Bob Harvey remembers hearing a report on the fourth that said the storm would pass south of Jamaica and had been downgraded. Those aboard *Island Princess* heaved sighs of relief. What they didn't know was that at that very time Allen was taking a jog that would put them directly in its path. Nor did they know that it had been downgraded from Category 5 only to Category 4. Being caught in a Category 4 rather than a Category 5 hurricane would be rather like being hit by a train that has slowed to 60 miles an hour. As it turned out, the hurricane was soon to be upgraded again. Munroe said:

'At 1000 on the fifth we sighted a grey wall of clouds. But we weren't worried, because from the reports we'd been getting we thought it must have been a local depression.'

As the wind and seas increased they decided to put a reef in the main, but by the time they were through reefing it they knew they didn't want the main at all. Slowly they began to suspect the truth. What they were experiencing was the front edge of a hurricane.

'My thoughts at that point were that the hurricane was still probably going to pass south of us,' said Gittelman. 'I reasoned that the best thing to do was turn to the north; first, because we wanted to avoid the centre, but just as importantly, if we did get into it and were dismasted or anything like that we would be driven down on the north coast of Jamaica. And the north coast of Jamaica is a rockpile.'

By sunset the wind had reached 50 knots out of the northeast and was building fast. The seas were ten to fifteen feet high. The *Island Princess* with her engine turning over slowly in forward, was close reaching under a tiny forestaysail.

Gittelman was at the wheel; Harvey and Munroe sat with him in the cockpit. They all wore life jackets and safety harnesses. In the dark, Harvey had rigged safety lines all over the boat so that there would always be something to clip on to, and he had crisscrossed the cockpit with heavier lines so that if the boat was knocked down no one would have far to fall before he could grab hold of something.

St Clair was below in his bunk, seasick.

Just before 2200 Harvey went below to listen to the weather report. When he came back he said things sounded bad and were going to get worse. The wind was already blowing over 100 knots.

At midnight the forestaysail blew away.

'Even then I don't recall being particularly worried,' Gittelman recalls. 'Even under bare poles she felt stable and the engine was driving her to windward controllably. I told myself that it was blowing like stink, but I'd seen it bad before, and we could get through this. We just had to grit our teeth and do it.

When the wind got up to somewhere around 125–130 knots, the boat was still stable. The seas were ugly, but they weren't that high, maybe twenty to twenty-five feet, because the wind was blowing the tops off them. The boat would rise up and be stable at the top; then she'd come back down and rise again. We were real happy with her. I was just hanging on, gritting my teeth, pretty well all consumed with driving the boat. I had little else on my mind.

Then it got up to somewhere around 150 knots – I'm guessing at this point – and I'm saying to myself: Jesus, I had no idea it could get this bad. But it can't get any worse, so all we have to do is hang in there.'

And then it did get worse.

About 0300 Gittelman began to have doubts. The boat didn't feel stable any more. In fact, all thirty tons of her were being lifted off the crests and thrown sideways into the troughs. Gittelman thought it was time to try trailing warps.

Clipping into the safety lines, Munroe and Harvey crawled forward – taking about ten minutes to get from the cockpit to the rope locker – and dragged all the anchor lines aft. They streamed them over the stern, along with all their chain and a 45-pound anchor. How long that took they have no idea. 'Nobody was stopping to make log entries,' Gittelman said.

'It took me about two or three minutes to realize it just wasn't going to work,' Gittelman said. 'She was doing 8 knots and was broaching, rolling her sides under. She was squirrelly as hell, and we were getting pooped. So in a relatively smooth patch we brought her back up into the wind and dragged all the lines back aboard.'

How they managed such a mammoth task under those conditions, even they are not sure.

'All I know is that anybody who says he can't do something never had it standing between him and survival,' said Harvey.

'She did all right for another half-hour, but then things got worse,' Gittelman commented. 'And at that point I couldn't tell how much. It was beyond my comprehension. I've been twenty years going to sea, and I just couldn't imagine these things were possible.'

When they were first knocked down, St Clair was still below and, inexperienced sailor that he was, still not sure how bad things were. Half an hour earlier Harvey had come below and told him to get into his foul-weather gear, life jacket and safety harness because the boat looked as though she might not have long to live.

'He didn't sound like he was kidding,' St Clair recalls, 'so I got up.'

When St Clair was dressed he got on the VHF and started calling for anybody who might be listening. He told them who they were and their approximate position, and that they were experiencing hurricane-force winds and didn't know how much longer they were going to be afloat. He did that for four or five minutes but got no response.

'Then I told myself it couldn't be that bad or they would have called me. So I lay down again. About the time I got stretched out good the boat suddenly slammed over and everything on the starboard side fell straight down. I was standing on the port side of the cabinhouse watching a two-foot-high geyser of water coming in the porthole. I couldn't believe it. I had to touch that geyser to convince myself it was there. As soon as I was convinced I knew it was time to get my fanny on deck.'

On the way out he grabbed two things: his good-luck hat and a rigging knife on a lanyard, which he slipped round his neck. As he bolted through the companionway he mockingly chided the rest of the crew for the mess they had made of the inside of the boat.

Then he looked around at what was outside and almost went into shock.

In the orange glow of a sky lit with sheet lightning, he saw the boat lying on its side with water halfway up the cockpit. Gittelman was hanging off the boom gallows, screaming something to Munroe and Harvey, who, covered with lines, were on the high side of the mizzen, with their feet dangling down into the cockpit. Water, glowing orange from the lightning, moved horizontally through the air. Waves struck the boat from all directions. The noise of the wind had gone beyond loudness; it was simply a 'dull white sound'.

In the next twenty minutes the *Island Princess* was knocked down three more times. The crew would be swept over the side to the end of their safety harnesses; then they would drag themselves back aboard, only to be swept over once again. They were constantly swallowing sea water. Water was coming in the boat's engine air intake, her portholes and her companionway.

On the fourth knockdown – which was to starboard – her ballast shifted, putting the companionway under for good. Three or four minutes later the glow from a submerged but still burning deck light was all that marked the spot where she had slipped beneath the waves.

'When Finbar yelled for us to abandon ship,' said St Clair, 'I suddenly realized that this was no movie, so I kicked the raft free and fired the bottle to inflate it.'

The raft inflated upside down. St Clair and Munroe scrambled onto its upturned bottom and fought desperately to push it away from the boat, which was flailing at it with the wildly rolling mizzen mast. St Clair thinks that may have been when he broke his ribs; but he isn't sure as he wasn't aware of the pain until several hours later.

Meanwhile, Harvey and Gittelman were fighting desperate battles of their own. For what almost proved too long, Harvey couldn't get to the end of his safety harness to unclip himself from the sinking boat. He finally had to unclip from his end, and – attached to nothing – leap for the raft from the mizzen. Only a finger-tips grab by Munroe prevented him from being swept away. Gittelman, it seemed to St Clair and Munroe, who watched him from the overturned raft, had decided to go down with the ship.

'I'm not sure what possessed me,' Gittelman said. 'But I just sat at the wheel and tried to steer the boat. It was already under water, everybody else was on the raft. I was clipped to the raft's painter. But I tried to drive.'

Perhaps the boat slipping beneath him finally convinced the skipper to abandon the helm and jump for the raft.

'As soon as I climbed onto the bottom of the raft I realized that something was tangled with it and that the boat was pulling it down. I needed a knife, but couldn't get to mine because it was inside my foul-weather gear. So I shouted for a knife and before the words were out of my mouth, Doc slapped his into my hand. The blade was already open.'

'I'd lost my good-luck hat in the first five minutes,' said St Clair, 'but that knife saved our asses.'

Once the raft was free of the boat a wave crest immediately flipped it right side up and the ballast chamber filled. Everyone scrambled through the opening in the canopy.

Gittelman's order to abandon came at approximately 0415 on Wednesday August 6. By comparing weather service advisories with the *Island Princess*'s position, which was between Port Antonio, Jamaica and the extreme south coast of Cuba, it appears that the four men took to the raft in 175-knot winds.

They had no way of estimating the wind strength, but they do remember that the wind-driven spray sounded like buckshot hitting the canopy and that the thirty-foot seas were cresting and breaking on them from all directions.

'Every time one of those thirty-footers decided to collapse on us it would fill the raft with water and drive it so deep that my ears popped,' said St Clair. 'At that point we would have to push down with our feet and up with our hands to make an air space at the top of the canopy. We were constantly up to our necks in water, and there were even fish swimming around inside the raft. The only thing that helped us to realize we were still alive was a little light glowing at the top of the canopy.'

It was around this time that Gittelman, who is slightly claustrophobic said: 'To hell with this; I'm going outside where I can breathe.' The others made sure he didn't go.

Despite the buffeting they were taking and despite their skipper's claustrophobia, the crew felt that once in the life-raft they had it made. Harvey said:

'Once the ballast chamber filled, which didn't seem to take any time at all, the raft settled right down. You'd feel it pitch over when we were hit by a wave, but as soon as the pressure came off it would come back up again. It was like being in a womb. We were floating around in there, sometimes with our feet off the bottom. We didn't feel comfortable, but we did feel secure.'

Soon after they had entered the raft, the roaring and frothing suddenly ceased. The seas stopped breaking, the wind subsided, and in the darkness overhead the men could see broken patches of sky.

They were in the eye of the hurricane.

Gittelman said:

'We could hear the roar recede into the distance, and then there were five or ten minutes of perfect silence while we just sat there staring at each other.'

St Clair can still remember how the others' faces looked drawn, tight, and with eyes that were big and glistening, and he is sure that his face looked the same. He also remembers saying: 'Finbar; this is another fine mess you've gotten me into!'

Fifteen minutes later the storm was upon them again. They described its approach as sounding like that of a thousand freight trains: 'But we don't know what it looked like; nobody volunteered to look out.'

At about 0600 the sky started getting light, but St Clair remembers:

'I didn't want it to, because I was afraid of what we would see. But I finally pulled down one corner of the Velcro – and wished I hadn't. Waves were collapsing on top of waves that were collapsing on top of waves. Everything was grey and white and screaming. It was insanity.'

But then they discovered a new problem. Munroe had begun to throw up blood. Later, Gittelman – seasick for the first time in his life – would follow.

St Clair had charge of the survival kit, in which he found a knife, six ten-ounce cans of water, two cans of candy and other survival rations, a fish line and hook, a first-aid kit, a whistle, six hand-held flares, eight small pen-type flares, a signal mirror, a repair kit, a sponge, and four or five packs of soggy tissues.

Harvey observed: 'If we needed papier-mâché for anything, we would have had plenty.'

In addition, St Clair had three more pen-type flares that he'd been carrying with him since his days in Vietnam. The raft also contained two paddles, a sea anchor, a life ring, a pump and a two-part EPIRB, with the battery pack separate from the transmitter. The wires between the two had pulled out, making the EPIRB inoperable.

'I opened two cans of water and let everybody drink a fair amount,' said St Clair. 'We'd all swallowed a lot of salt water, and the kidney and liver damage that can result from that is no fun.'

While Munroe and Gittelman rested, Harvey and St Clair spent much of Wednesday hanging out of the opening in the canopy with the paddles, trying to keep the opening to leeward of the breaking seas, which even after the wind subsided remained large and dangerous. Occasionally, Harvey would remove his seaboots and bail with them. 'The raft kept filling, but at least we were doing something.'

On Wednesday the raft's two inflatable ring sections began to separate from each other. Using line from the sea anchor, the men lashed them together again.

That evening they drank two more cans of water; and St Clair, noticing signs of hypothermia, encouraged the men to huddle against each other for warmth.

'We were experiencing cold and little pains,' he said. 'Every time we'd get the water fairly warm from our bodies and start to doze off, a wave would come in and make it cold again.'

Thursday, before daylight, the hallucinations began. St Clair saw what he thought were the lights of Jamaica. He was picking out street lights and cars driving along the shore. 'There it is, guys, we've got it made; it's right there – look.' The others looked and saw nothing there. Harvey heard a dog bark and people talking. Munroe saw comic books.

Later, St Clair spent much of the day talking to a bird that had landed on the top of the canopy. 'The bird was real,' said Gittelman. 'But it couldn't talk.' That afternoon they drank their last can of water and, because Munroe's condition seemed to be worsening, they gave most of it to him.

St Clair recalls:

'At point I took one long look at Michael and told myself he would be dead by that time tomorrow. He was starting to get

81

incoherent. His eyes were sunken in. I've seen men like that before; just one step away. And that would be it. He was going to be the first. Finbar had been throwing up a lot of blood, too, so I figured just from blood loss alone he would go next. I had some broken ribs; that made me the next weakest, so then I'd go. And Bob would probably go just from the psychological shock of watching us three die.'

Harvey, however, had no intention of seeing the script played out that way. He'd slept most of the day so that he could stay awake through the night, when he figured they'd have the best chance of signalling any ships they spotted. That's how he came to be staring through the canopy opening at about 2200 when a light appeared on the horizon. He watched it for a while; then, in a low voice, almost without emotion, he announced: 'There is a ship.'

Instantly, the other three were at the opening. As soon as they all agreed that what they saw was a ship and not a low-lying star, St Clair fired four red flares, one right after the other. Then he lit a hand-held flare. Harvey, who knew Morse code, began to signal with the flashlight. Among other things, he signaled 'S.O.S.' and 'Out of water'.

On the bridge of the Norwegian tanker *Jastella*, the second mate spotted a red pinpoint of light to the north. At first he thought it might be a lighthouse on Cuba, but his chart showed that light to be white and forty miles away. He figured that it must be a fishing boat. Then he saw a blinking white light; somebody was trying to signal him. He picked out the word 'water'. He tried the radio and did a radar sweep. Nothing. It had to be, he reasoned, a raft.

Two days later, the crew of the *Island Princess* were in hospital in the Cayman Islands – the *Jastella*'s destination – and after a week's stay, they were home again in Key West.

Afterwards, Gittelman said:

'It has played on our minds, sure; but we are sailors, and it won't keep us from going back to sea. What we'll do is go back with a few lessons learned. We learned about life-rafts, about survival, and we learned about what it takes to sink a boat – but most of all we learned where not to be when. We learned to stay the hell out of the Caribbean during hurricane season.'

—————— ,, ——————

From: *SAIL*, February 1981

82

12: Over in the Atlantic

Yacht: *Boatfile* (Val Class 31ft trimaran)
Skipper: Nick Hallam
Crew: Nye Williams
Bound from Newport, Rhode Island, to the Isle of Man
Time and date of loss: 2300, May 8th, 1981
Position: approx. 200 miles WSW of Mizen Head, Ireland

After sailing her to Newport in the 1980 OSTAR, Rob James left *Boatfile* in the U.S. until he had sold her to a new owner in the U.K. who engaged Nick Hallam to sail her back. Twenty-one days out from Newport, *Boatfile* was lying ahull, riding out a Force 8 Atlantic gale in much the same way as she had done before:

——————— " ———————

'We had been lying ahull reasonably comfortably for 24 hours, the B.B.C. Shipping Forecast at 0625 had talked of an improvement soon and the wind remained steady at Force 8 with regular seas of perhaps 20 ft. Our drogue and warps were ready in the cockpit in case they should be needed, but the boat was lying quietly with the daggerboard fully retracted and the helm lashed down, drifting off to leeward leaving a conspicuous path of flat water upwind. Any wave crests that broke over the windward ama hull seemed to have little energy, while the boat's reduced lateral resistance, coupled with the high buoyancy of the amas, allowed her to rise easily and keep out of trouble. We had ridden out previous gales in this fashion and didn't think this one would be any different. I was also not keen to run before the weather until it was strictly necessary, as that course would take us towards the centre of the low, rather than allowing the system to pass away from our area. It was Friday, 8 May, and we were about 200 miles WSW of Mizen Head, keeping watch from below and waiting for the 1355 forecast.

   We never heard it. At about 1300 we were picked up by something very

big, and in a rush of broken water *Boatfile* was rolled rapidly over to starboard and settled into an irrevocably inverted position. The thing that had happened only to others had happened to us; we had been capsized.

The tiny, inverted cabin was a surging mess of loose gear, washing back and forth with every wave. The constant change of air pressure hurt our eardrums, but fortunately there was a surprising amount of light through the submerged windows, so we were able to get at our survival suits quickly and put them on, then secure our EPIRB (Emergency Position Indicating Radio Beacon) unit and switch that on. Looking at its tiny indicator lamp, I prayed that its signal was radiating out through the upturned hull.

We then jettisoned all superfluous gear and rescued anything remotely useful, planning to stay with the boat on the assumption that, like other capsized trimarans, she would stay afloat. To that end, we began laboriously to cut a hatch in the hull above our heads, to give us an escape to the open air and a safe lookout point from which to attract attention. It was a frustrating task: our collection of drills was wonderfully blunt and the GRP/Kevlar hull proved wonderfully tough, but we had to keep thinking and working. It was no use stopping to worry about the obviously worsening weather outside, nor to think of the 200 miles still separating us from south-west Ireland; of course that's just what we did, but working helped . . .

When the boat's stern was plunged into the trough of a wave, twice within 20 minutes, both times trapping us underwater in the cabin, we began reluctantly to suspect that the trimaran was starting to sink. We had difficulty accepting this; still trying to convince ourselves that we could carry on cutting holes from outside, we gathered tools, flares, "panic bag" and the precious EPIRB and dived out via the main hatch to the world outside.

Conditions were appalling. There was no question of working, just hanging on desperately while steep, breaking seas repeatedly swept over us. The daggerboard had dropped out of its case and was lunging madly about, hitting the hulls; the impact of every sea was terrible, and Nye later reported seeing longitudinal cracks opening in the ama hulls. With no integral foam or other form of buoyancy, the little boat was clearly not going to remain tenable for long, even if she stayed awash, so we agreed to take to the liferaft. In the struggle to release it, I must have failed to cut one last lashing, because it had great difficulty in escaping from its valise, and when finally it did, it had lost so much CO_2 via the relief valve that it was perilously soft.

At this point, two things happened: Nye saw the Nimrod, and *Boatfile* sank, tilting inexorably over and threatening to drag me down by my harness. I escaped and also cut the liferaft free. Our last sight of the trimaran was of the stern of the port ama pointing up at 45 degrees like a bright yellow finger, and the blurred, ghostly outline of the rest of the boat underwater. Within a few minutes, *Boatfile* had gone.

While Nye clung on outside, I scrambled in and tried to inflate the raft fully, but somehow was unable to make a proper connection between bellows and valve. Finally, in full view of the Nimrod, our raft was hit by yet another breaking sea and torn.

The Nimrod came in straight and level from dead downwind and dropped a pair of big rafts joined by a long line. This we grabbed, but were unable to pull ourselves to the rafts because of the surge of the seas (by now between 35 and 40 ft, with the wind at 60 knots, according to the Nimrod crew). The aircraft made another run; this time we made it to a raft, but it had a major leak in both chambers and after an hour of grim pumping to try and keep at least one chamber and the roof inflated, it too was overwhelmed and torn apart by a succession of breaking seas.

We spent a dismal time, perhaps an hour, clinging to the bright orange remains of the raft, our Nimrod having disappeared. We felt utterly alone and very anxious. Had they lost contact? Had they waited until we seemed to be safe before leaving the scene to refuel? Our prayers were duly answered as the great white machine reappeared (a second aircraft, we later learned) and in an astonishing display of precision flying dropped two more rafts with such accuracy that the connecting line fell within arm's reach. We righted the nearest raft and clambered aboard, by now exhausted, as night fell.

A big Shell tanker had come on the scene and tried to come close enough to pick us up but her motion was too violent for a safe approach, so her captain moved away to keep station with us, while the Nimrod kept up a pattern of wide circles over us and the ship, marking us from time to time with blinding white floating flares.

Two more hours passed. We were both very tired, but tried to keep ourselves occupied by bailing and sponging out the ten-man raft and by keeping watch from the doorway. Finally, a new set of lights appeared downwind, quickly resolving itself into a big Sea King helicopter. Flooding us with an array of mobile spotlights worthy of a scene from *Star Wars*, it manoeuvred overhead and lowered the winchman who scored a direct hit on the canopy, bounced into the doorway, said "Hi!", and was immediately jerked into the air again as the raft sank 30 ft into a trough. After a few more such violent jerks and heavy splashdowns (accompanied, I suspect, by some non-regulation verbal comments on the part of Bob Griffiths, the man on the wire), airman and raft successfully made contact, and in a very short time we were all safely aboard the Sea King, bound for Cork Airport for refuelling, exhausted, bemused, but alive!'

———————— ,, ————————

From: *Yachting Monthly*, December 1981

PART II: FAULTY NAVIGATION

13: *Song* – the Final Episode

Yacht: *Song* (26ft hard-chine, twin-keel sloop)
Skipper: George Harrod-Eagles
Crew: None
Bound from England to Australia
Time and date of loss: early hours of January 19th, 1982
Position: on Roncador Reef, E coast of Puerto Rico

George Harrod-Eagles set out, single-handed, from Lowestoft in Suffolk in the late summer of 1981, to sail the 26ft hard-chine sloop *Song* back to his native Australia.

Song could be described as a smaller version of the Maurice Griffiths designed 31ft Golden Hind class. Her auxiliary engine was an 8 H.P. two-stroke Stuart Turner.

After calling into several ports on both sides of the English Channel, Harrod-Eagles reached Madeira during the last week of September and left Santa Cruz, Tenerife on November 3rd, 1981, bound for the Bahamas.

Song reached Barbados in forty-two days and Christmas was spent in Carlisle Bay. Then there followed a week in Fort de France, Martinique, before leaving for Fajardo on the east coast of Puerto Rico on January 14th, 1982.

———————— " ————————

'We laid course hard on the wind for St Croix, our first landfall, some three hundred odd miles to the north west. No need to describe that long tedious passage; suffice it to say, with no possibility of a sight, beacons not working, and the extremely poor conditions, there was little sleep for me. We were making a fair amount of leeway, being closehauled, which, when corrections were applied, meant we were unable to point up enough to make St Croix, and that landfall had to be abandoned in favour of Punta Tuna, our second option, preferable now that strong northerly winds

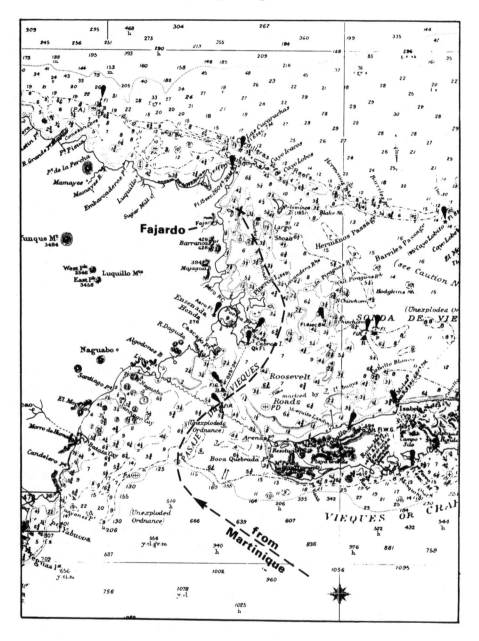

would put us on a lee shore, were we to attempt the passage to windward of the Island of Vieques.

As we were unable to obtain a sight, it was fortunate that the beacon at Punta Tuna was operational, and gave us a bearing, which we could run down until we were able to pick up the light. In the early hours of the third morning, this light came into view and was positively identified. We had made our landfall on the extreme south east corner of Puerto Rico.

This portion of the Puerto Rican coast lies in a roughly north east–south west direction, the distance from Punta Tuna to Fajardo, our destination, being thirty-eight miles. The wind, as we neared the coast, was lighter than before, and about NNE. A big swell generated by several days of northerly winds made more tedious the long tacks necessary to traverse this coast, with the wind in the north quarter. The navigation was complicated by the Island of Vieques, with a long unmarked spit protruding from its south western extremity, far out into the passage between it and the Puerto Rican coast; and by the dearth of navigational aids in these waters, abounding with natural hazards.

We crept through the passage de Vieques, our progress further slowed by the wind (affected by the presence of land on each side) becoming both light and uncertain in direction. There came a time of decision, keeping in mind the golden rule of reef-strewn waters, *"do not sail at night"*. I weighed the odds of reaching our destination before the fall of darkness. The choice lay between finding a suitable anchorage – hazardous, in view of the uncertain weather, no information as to the holding quality of the bottom and the horrible consequences if we dragged – turning around and running back until there was enough searoom to stand off – the safest course, but one, it seemed, that would make pointless all the hours spent getting this far. Or else to continue sailing towards our destination.

It was early afternoon and warm in the sun, now shining through great blue rifts in the cloud cover: a scene to grace the cover of a glossy brochure advertising the delights of the Caribbean and its islands. But we were about to enter an area with few navigational aids, with islands and unmarked reefs on either side, the mile or two between them a very small distance, particularly once darkness fell. A decision had to be made, and, calculating all the factors, I chose to go on – a fateful and perhaps imprudent decision in view of the contrary winds and the slowness of our progress up to then, but one prompted by the consensus of opinion, and a desire to end this tiresome passage.

To assist our progress the engine was started and run at half throttle. We motor sailed past Roosevelt Roads, the U.S. Naval Base, and as we cleared Punta Puerca and the Isla Cabeza de Perro, the wind, no longer diverted by the land, and unaffected by the small islands and reefs in its path, reverted to NNE about force 3. The swell was still with us, and I estimated the tide which was making was exerting about a knot against us, a factor which, with no information about the tides and currents hereabouts, had not entered into my calculations. Nevertheless, Fajardo and the Isleta Marina were visible, and slowly becoming clearer, as we continued to tack into the wind, heading for Isla de Ramos and the last buoy before Las Croabas, which lies on the north side of the Bahia de Fajardo and some five miles distant from Isla de Rumas. As we passed this rocky island with the most difficult miles of this passage still to be traversed, the sun was already low over the mountains of Puerto Rico, the shadows growing longer, the outline of Isleta Marina's two islands becoming difficult to distinguish from the darkened hills behind them, and within us there was a growing realisation that we were unlikely to make the anchorage before the fall of darkness. I took a bearing of the buoy lying behind us, close to Isla de Ramos, and one on the buoy ahead near Las Croabas. These were the only lit buoys in the area that would be visible to us, and if we could adhere to these bearings we had taken, we ought to be well clear of reefs, particularly the long reef guarding Isleta Marina, named El Roncador, The Snorer.

The difficulty of keeping in view one light among a confusion of unrelated lights and the bright glow from the shore is well known. Not surprisingly, as night with tropical swiftness descended upon us, the light astern became impossible to discern, leaving us with no reference except the buoy ahead, the light from which we could see reasonably well. To continue tacking in the stygian darkness that now surrounded us was plainly foolish. We therefore lowered all our sails, and continued under our engine, keeping the light from the buoy ahead. The shore lights of Punta Gorda were directly ahead, and those of Isleta Marina to port, partially obscured, but coming more into view as we plodded on into the blackness – for, with the stars obscured by the overcast, our only light was from the distant shore.

We were stowing sails and watching for white water; the echo-sounder was on, and registering thirty feet of water, and the lights from the complex on Isleta Marina were in plain view now way off to port. The depth shown on the echo-sounder plunged to fifteen feet then up to twenty feet, the chart indicated a number of relatively shallow spots, and I thought to have a look at it, to see if I could relate our position to the depths indicated, when the depth shown on the echo-sounder plummeted to five feet and immediately the boat struck, crunching and bumping half a dozen times before coming to a stop. There was a horrible, cold, heart-sinking moment of realisation, before I reacted and put her hard astern, hoping that she would come off: a forlorn hope, for the set which had by its invisible and unknown presence put us up on the reef, was, aided and abetted by the strong swell, acting on our bows, pushing them round, pivoting the boat on the stern, which (being the deepest part) was stuck hard, forcing the bilge plates against and between great jagged coral heads, which were crunching and grinding in a horrifying way against the hull.

The swell, now that we were aground, was lifting the boat up and bumping it further on to the reef. Clearly we had to get an anchor out and try to pull ourselves off. The inflatable dinghy was unlashed and inflated, and the anchor got ready, but the tide was falling and what was a swell now became breakers. Great rolling walls of water were roaring down upon us, lifting the boat and smashing her down, with shuddering impact, onto the cruel coral, amid great clouds of spray and solid water which broke over the boat continually. Obviously the boat could not take much of this pounding, and I think it was then I knew that *Song* was doomed.

I do not think I can describe the sickening despair I felt at that time, the self-recrimination, followed by intense feelings of being terribly alone and forsaken. It is an awful thing, the knowledge that all you have striven for, over so many months, is being destroyed while you are impotent to prevent it. The continued pounding of the hull and the bilge plates against huge coral heads was not long in taking effect. Within what seemed no time at all, but must have been an hour or more, during which, wet through and continually pummelled by the breaking waves, we struggled to get all in readiness so that we could kedge the boat off, the boat heeled sharply to port and water appeared with a rush inside her. She settled on her side, and as the port bilge plate had broken, it was now just a matter of time.

What difference it would have made I am not sure, but only the shortage of time and the lack of equipment prevented me from cutting off the bilge plates before I left England. Not to offset the effects of striking a reef (I had not envisaged that problem) but because, having read accounts of attacks by killer whales on sailing boats, I thought them an invitation to disaster, should a whale decide to attack head on.

In the uncertain situation that prevailed, a distinct possibility existed of danger to our limbs if not our lives. It was time to call for help, and the U.S. Coastguard was contacted on the VHF radio (not without some difficulty), details of our situation and position given, and an assurance received that assistance would be forthcoming. Whilst we waited, we gathered together what each considered most essential, wading waist deep inside the boat in the dimming light of the overhead fluorescent light to transfer books and equipment, threatened by the invading sea, to the crowded but still dry starboard-side lockers and shelves. We were thrown violently off balance as each wave, striking with thunderous impact, lifted the boat and having passed let it fall back again. The tide, ebbing fast now, even in the still intense darkness, revealed the previously unruffled surface of the sea, a foaming expanse of white water informing us, too late, of the implacable El Roncador.

Several hours elapsed as we waited for the Coastguard. Inside the cabin the light had winked out some time earlier and we were in total darkness. Incessantly soaked with spray, we remained in the cockpit, with some difficulty because of the acute angle of heel, wet, cold and bedraggled in spite of the relative warmth of the water. The wind had dropped with the outgoing tide, and was now gentle from offshore, conveying the cinnamon scent of the land on its back. We sat in silence, each with our own thoughts locked within our minds.

At last there appeared a fast-moving light searching the area of the reef, but away to the north west. Concluding it to belong to the Coastguard, we flashed a Mayday with the torch I always kept in the cockpit. This soon brought a response, and the light described a wide circle to the north, flicking from side to side, gradually approaching until it was revealed to be a large inflatable, powered by two large outboard motors, and crewed by four men in the uniform of the United States Coastguard. They hailed us, while still a considerable distance away, to enquire whether we were indeed the originators of the radio Mayday. They would not come closer than about twenty yards from us, requesting that we use our dinghy to traverse the, now smaller, but nevertheless formidable, waves that were still breaking onto the reef.

Taking with us only our valuables, and a sailbag containing dry clothing, we launched the dinghy on the port side, and clambered aboard. I cast off and rowed around the stern to face the waves, taking great pains to keep head on to them, for a broach would have tumbled us out into the jagged coral, with terrible injuries, at the least, as the result. There was now little depth of water covering the reef, giving us great cause for concern, should the fragile bottom of the dinghy be caught and rent upon the coral, with the result similar to that of broaching.

The dinghy bottomed each time the water receded, but was lifted up once more with each new breaker as it roared in, high upon the crest, enveloped in spray and solid water. I rowed as hard as I knew how, so as to maintain momentum and keep head on to the waves. Perhaps ten minutes passed between leaving *Song* and reaching the quieter waters clear of the reef, but they seemed endless minutes, calling heavily on my physical and mental reserves. Once aboard the Coastguard boat, the dinghy was made fast astern, jumping and rearing in the wake, as at high speed we made for the shore. I felt exhausted and quite drained, only the recollection of *Song*, as we left her, lonely and forlorn, lying on her side like a sea bird with a broken wing, still imprinted on my mind.

A mere half hour later we were nosing into Puerto Chico, put ashore and transported to the Coastguard station at Cabo San Juan, where hot showers, coffee, and dry clothing made new men of us. After going through the usual formalities, we discussed our position with the Coastguard men, who were of the opinion that, with the improving weather, the swell should diminish enough to allow us to approach the boat from the inside of the reef, so as to salvage what we could. But they advised us to make the attempt at first light, for there were scavengers who knew the reef intimately and would soon take advantage of our misfortune.

We accepted the good sense of this advise, and relied further on the good nature of these kindhearted men; some phone calls and a ride back to Puerto Chico brought from his bed Carlos, who runs the diving shop there, and an agreement that he would run us out to the reef in the morning. A visit to the Water Police who are stationed at Puerto Chico, and an explanation of our circumstances and our fears, produced complete indifference to our plight. It was past midnight when we returned to the Coastguard station, spending the remainder of the night in fitful sleep on makeshift beds.

The morning dawned bright and clear, with a light wind from the NE. A cup of coffee, and we gratefully accepted a lift to Puerto Chico, where we found Carlos and his charming wife June waiting for our arrival. They made us most welcome, with sympathy for our loss and offers of whatever help they could give us. Leaving our meagre possessions with June, we boarded the 18-foot aluminium open boat used by Carlos in his business of supplying equipment to, and taking out to suitable areas, people who wished to snorkel and dive. He informed us that El Roncador was not a place to which he would take any of his clients. On average five boats were wrecked there each year. This number included several small coasting vessels. It was a dangerous and poorly charted place.

With our dinghy in tow we made the half-hour run out to the reef, gleaning much information from Carlos, and recounting in detail our tale of woe. Our approach was on the lee side, where although we would have to cross the full width of the reef, the waves would have expended most of their energy. We dropped anchor in a few feet of water onto white sand, and prepared to row the dinghy across to where *Song* lay on her side, still shuddering as each wave lifted her; but now the sun was shining and the seas moderate, no longer breaking over the boat. Progress across the reef was slow, with a need to pick a safe passage between coral heads just below the surface, and it was not until we were quite close that it became evident that something was wrong. Where was the boom with the main sail stowed upon it? Where were the Genoa and working jib we had left firmly lashed to the pulpit? With a sinking feeling within, we scrambled on board, to discover the full extent of this second catastrophe to overtake us.

The boat had been stripped of everything easily removed from on deck and from below. Sails, anchor, rope were gone, lockers rifled, empty spaces only remained where once had been the VHF radio, tape recorder, short-wave radio, camera case with all the lenses and film, clothing and equipment. In their search for valuables they had swept books from shelves and emptied the contents of containers, all of which had been still quite dry, into the swirling waters, invading the boat, turning them into sodden pulp or shattered pieces. Saddest of all was the loss of my sextant and my log book, with its record of the memories of my grand venture. I think then I reached the depths of bitter despair, looking into the chaos and destruction wrought upon my boat. I pitted myself against the sea and lost, but it would have been better had the boat sunk in deep water and everything been lost, than to have my boat thus defiled by such human dregs.'

——————— ,, ———————

From: *Lowestoft Cruising Club Journal*, 1982

14: Last Time Over

Yacht: *Northern Light* (45ft Colin Archer type gaff-cutter)
Skipper: Lt. Cdr. James Griffin R.N.
Crew: Ann Griffin
Bound from Horta, Azores to Gibraltar, Spain
Time and date of loss: 0315, September 10th, 1982
Position: on Spanish coast, 6 miles S of Cadiz

Lt. Cdr. James Griffin and his wife Ann had lived aboard *Northern Light* for 22 of the boat's 52 years. After four years pottering around the Bahamas and the coast of Florida, the Griffins had decided to sail back to Europe. In this personal account Ann Griffin tells what happened after they left the Azores:

———————— " ————————

'We were almost at the end of our fourth Atlantic crossing, only 100 miles to our destination – Gilbraltar. I looked around at our beautiful ship – we had never had a house or a car – our transport was bicycles and they were lashed to the guardrails. We had survived Force 9, gusting 10, on August 28th to 31st, during which time we were hove-to and had been carried 60 miles to the south by leeway. No hope now of seeing Cape St Vincent and creeping round the corner to anchor and recover. During the blow a new steel strap holding the crosstrees to the mainmast had snapped seven out of its eight stainless-steel bolts and was hanging down swinging back and forth threatening to fall on our heads at any moment. It had sawed through the topsail and jib halliards, and was now threatening the main. We had fitted rigging screws inside the shroud lanyards and all of them had broken their fittings, making it impossible to climb the ratlines and secure the wretched thing, nicknamed Damocles. We were sailing at one knot under mainsail and staysail; we had lost the mizzen gaff jaws in the blow, and the mizzen and the jib were our main driving sails. Jimmy had spent the day repairing

97

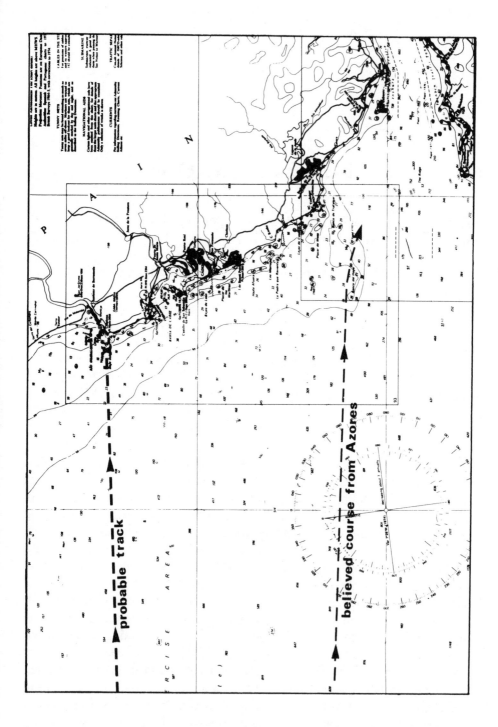

seams on the mainsail – the terylene had stood up to seven years in the tropics, but the stitching hadn't. Everywhere I looked on deck we needed repairs, but there was nothing wrong with the hull, thank heavens.

Northern Light is a 45 foot Colin Archer type Gaff Ketch, with 15½ ft beam and 8½ ft draft, built of 2½ inch Burma teak, copper sheathed, 52 years old, but good for our lifetime. One of our four daughters, Heather, was itching to push us out and buy her off us, but after living in her for 22 years no way would I give her up.

The wind was dying, but there was still a heavy swell. It had been north east or east all the way across from the Azores. Only enough fuel was left to get us in the last four miles to enter harbour. No sign of shipping, but there should have been; another frustrating night ahead.

We had had a hasty crossing to Bermuda from Florida, then a glorious 19 days for the 1850 miles to the Azores, light favourable winds, fantastic sunrises and sunsets, and starry and moonlit nights we would never forget.

Jimmy and I had taken her across the Atlantic in 1974 having left behind all four daughters, now married, but as we were now 62 thought it prudent to invest in a new automatic pilot. It left us very low on cash, and one day out from Bermuda it packed in. We were watch and watch about for the rest of the trip. We don't carry a radio or liferaft, or any aids to navigation apart from a sextant, but had lots of flares and a nine foot ply and glassfibre dinghy.

It had been so hazy that sights had been unreliable for the last two days, but the log was accurate and we were allowing for half a knot current carrying us into the Straits – the charts and the Pilot Book said it was so.

Just after sunset we saw a ship, and during the night twenty-one went past us heading due east . . . we must be near. The ninth dawned heavily overcast – no sights today. At last the wind went southeast . . . we should go northeast. At midday we were suddenly over green water with a fishing boat on it a mile away. A check with the chart revealed where we should have been, on the Banco de Trafalgar, but no sight of land eight miles away. The wind pulled round and went west at last – and we were able to sail direct towards Gibraltar. At 1930 we saw a lighthouse flashing twice every six seconds and went wild with delight . . . we had done it, after 20 days at sea. We celebrated in tea!! We'd be in Gibraltar before dawn, God willing. We got to the lighthouse, but where the heck was Tarifa light? We looked at the lights on the shore – far too many of them, unless Tarifa town had changed a lot in nine years. Feeling very uneasy we put on the engine and hauled off. Shortly after we struck rock and stuck. The rudder broke off with the first impact, and jammed the propeller. For the next three hours we banged every five seconds. For the first two hours she held, during which time we sent up 20 flares, and signalled with the Aldis lamp to every car that stopped to have a look. Then the water crept over the floorboards and started to beat the pump. I sat on deck in a state of frozen shock, trying to stop three terrified cats from jumping over the side, watching and waiting with the signalling lamp to shine on our sails when help arrived. Nobody came.

Jimmy collected ship's papers and passports; we launched the dinghy, and then he said, "I'm sorry, darling; it's time to go; if we wait she might fall on the dinghy." I couldn't believe it; we had been on coral reefs in the Caribbean and always got off, but they were soft by comparison. We put the cats in a sack, and rowed clear, then let them out.

Jimmy rowed two miles inshore, then two miles along through breakers trying to find a beach. Half full, we saw a lit one . . . how I got through the surf I'll never know . . . I slipped on rock, but held on; we got the dinghy ashore and tried to capture three soaking wet and petrified cats.

We had landed on a top-security naval beach. We had left the engine and bilge pump running, cabin and deck lights on. The navy hadn't any English, we hadn't much Spanish, but found we were in Cadiz. We found out later there had been Force 6 and 7 easterlies in the Straits of Gibraltar which had stopped the south-going current. The bank had been the entrance of the Guadalquivir River and the lighthouse had been the Santa Caterina, flashing twice every seven seconds. The Spanish navy was very kind, gave us cognac and coffee at six in the morning . . . water was running all over the floor from our soaking wet clothes. They offered showers and breakfast, but we were anxious to contact Lloyds and help.

Jimmy himself is a marine surveyor for Lloyds, and for the last four years has been working as such for the Bahamas Government. We got to town (two cats in a box, the other one on my lap), and spent three hours trying to get things organised, but as there wasn't a British Consul in Cadiz, went on to Algeciras. After a little difficulty we found a pension that would take cats; sent cables to the girls, and collapsed into bed, cuddling cats.

We were lucky . . . we had each other, and the clothes we stood up in, but oh! the heartache of leaving behind 40 years' diaries and photographs – to say nothing of all the letters the children and grandchildren had written us. The tears came in the middle of the night when the shock wore off. Next morning, down to the ferry to go to Gibraltar – but they wouldn't take the cats. Over the next day *Northern Light* came off the reef and drove herself onto an army firing range: a salvage team went down . . . they could get her off without any difficulty when we could get the army to stop firing.

We were only insured for total loss, but we would have used our life's savings to get her back. It took five days to get permission, by which time vandals had been aboard, stripped her and taken the bronze strips off our 32 deck lights. The water inside pushed them out and she was held down.

The weather deteriorated on September 19th – my birthday – and the answer came that salvage was impossible. At this time both Jimmy and I broke down, but fortunately our eldest daughter, Geraldine, had come over with her fourth child, and that helped. Next day Jimmy went over to see *Northern Light* for himself, and said his own farewell.

Now the tears have stopped; it's only material things we have lost – we must find another boat, and get the cats back . . . they are in a kennel in Spain. We are in Gibraltar with our daughter. We'll never get another boat as beautiful, but nothing will ever take away the memories and we were lucky to own her for 22 years.'

―――――― ,, ――――――

Extracted from an account by Ann Griffin

15: A Gaffer's Grave

Yacht: *Quiver* (21½ft gaff cutter)
Skipper: Michael D. Millar
Crew: Richard Penn
Bound from St Peter Port, Guernsey to Lannion Bay, Brittany
Time and date of loss: 0300, June 4th, 1971
Position: NE side of Les Triagoz Rocks

Michael Millar, a past President of the Old Gaffers Association, accompanied by his grandson as crew, left Chichester harbour on Saturday May 29th, 1971, with the intention of attending an Old Gaffers Rally in Braye Harbour, Alderney, later that weekend. Millar had owned *Quiver* for 16 years, and Richard Penn had sailed with him for almost as long.

Quiver was thought to have been built in Cowes in 1895 – the exact year was not known – and was probably converted from an open boat around 1920. Late in her life she was fitted with a small inboard petrol engine.

Because of contrary winds, they did not cross to France directly, but called first at Yarmouth (Isle of Wight), Poole, and Lulworth Cove, where they spent the Sunday night.

After setting out on Monday morning to sail to some Devon port, the wind became favourable for crossing the Channel and they decided to set course for Alderney. They arrived in Braye Harbour early on the Tuesday morning (too late for the Old Gaffers), and moved on to Guernsey after hearing a forecast that it would soon blow from the north east.

Two frustrating days were spent in St Peter Port, which they left on the Friday morning.

————————— " —————————

'We decided to head for Lannion Bay in the eastern end of Morlaix Bay; it appeared to be easy of access by day or night (we should probably arrive in the dark, and those French leading lights are terrific), was reputed to be good holding in firm sand, and should provide a cosy anchorage on a weather shore. Furthermore, it was downhill all the way. We did not then realise how steep that hill was to be.

The direct route from St Martin's Point (SE corner of Guernsey) took us between Les Sept Iles and Les Triagoz, two of the reefs lying off the Brittany coast, then between Les Triagoz and Ile Grande, the latter being on the 'corner' of Morlaix Bay, there being a safe gap of over three miles between the two. However, this course (so far as I can remember it was 240° Mag) was dead downwind, and as the wind was a bit fresh for spinnaker work for a crew of two, it would have meant a very tiring day at the tiller. So we decided to make a dog-leg of it, and steer due west until the DR put us north of Les Sept Iles, then due south until we found them. This worked very well, enabling us to keep the headsails drawing all the time, especially when the wind fell light during the afternoon, at which time we shook out the reefs with which we had started, and changed up from no. 2 to no. 1 jib.

During the afternoon we saw a French fishing boat executing some alarming manoeuvres, and stood by to take evasive action in view of the stories one has heard of yachts being attacked by such vessels; however, it seemed that she was only locating and picking up her pots on the Banc des Langoustiers, and we were able to exchange cheery greetings as we passed them, kedged by their gear.

Soon after dark, we picked up the Les Sept Iles light where expected, and, crossing this with a radio bearing on Les Roches Douvres, got a satisfactory fix which showed that we were back on our rhumb line.

Being quite happy with the fix, we altered back to the original course of 240° M, and in due time picked up the light on Les Triagoz where expected, fine on the starboard bow. We were now sailing on a dead run, boom to port and staysail goose-winged to starboard. The log was giving us 5 knots, the fixes indicated that we were making good 3½, which confirmed the rather meagre information gleaned from the charts and tidal stream atlas that there was a 1½ knot head tide. This tide was supposed to run till about 0400, dropping to about one knot in the last hour.

Until about 0130 the sky was clear though the visibility was still apparently poor, and a brilliant moon, three quarters full, moved steadily round until it was right in our track. If only it had stayed there . . . but it was not to be. Some heavy cloud came up from the south, across the wind, and blotted everything out, leaving us with nothing but the two lighthouses.

By 0200 we had drawn abreast of Les Sept Iles, and I had a feeling that we were being set somewhat to the SE towards the outlying dangers at the western end of that reef. I therefore altered course more westerly, until the

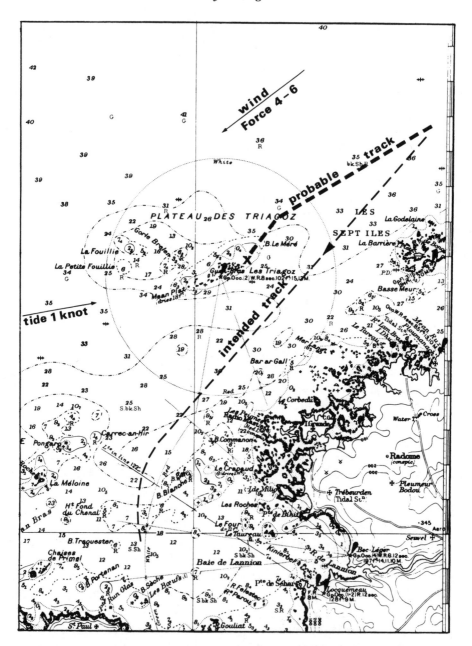

Les Triagoz light was just open to port, for about half an hour, and until I was satisfied that we were well clear of Les Sept Iles. I then altered back about double the amount until Les Triagoz was well open in the starboard rigging; a quick check on the chart confirmed that at 3½ knots made good (and nothing had changed to alter this), we would clear the eastern tip of the Les Triagoz reef by about 1¼ miles, a comfortable margin. At about 0300, I was just contemplating resuming the compass course, when *Quiver*, with a resounding crash, stopped dead.

There is, of course, no excuse for wrecking one's ship on a well-charted reef, especially when one can see two lighthouses and has a commanding wind. There are, perhaps, reasons. I will suggest three. The first is that during that last hour we had done the full 5 miles over the ground; in other words we had lost the 1½ knots head tide which we had been experiencing, and which we should have had for another hour at least. One can only assume that it was masked by the reef into whose shadow we had sailed; there may even have been a counter-eddy: at any rate we were undoubtedly 1½ miles further on than I thought we were. The second reason may have been that I made my detour by eye on the lighthouse, rather than on compass courses – not very seamanlike. The third reason was undoubtedly because it was 3 o'clock in the morning. We both felt wide awake, and were thoroughly enjoying the ride. I was (thank God) at the helm myself, while Richard was below planning the next move. But at that hour one is not at one's brightest, we may have been taking careless bearings, plotting carelessly, or simply doing our sums wrong; we shall never know, as the deck log and chart went down with everything else . . .

After the initial impact, which probably broke the stem and certainly opened up the hood ends, *Quiver* shook herself free of the half-tide rock she had struck, luffed a bit, and went charging off again into the dark. She took a great tombstone square on the bowsprit end, and again stopped dead; in the dim light from the cabin one had the feeling of being in a flooded graveyard, with great slabs of granite sticking up all round, and the water boiling on unseen tombs beneath. She swung round, hinging on the bowsprit, until the port bilges found some of these on which she then pounded for several minutes. We let go all sheets to try to take some of the weight out of it, but the swell kept her pounding until she finally slid clear in a northerly direction. To keep her quiet (and reduce the frightful din of flogging sails), we furled the jib and backed the staysail leaving the main sheet free; thus hove to, she fore reached at about a knot in water which within a few yards gave a depth of 35 fathoms. We had hit the top of a 200 foot cliff!

A quick look below revealed a hopeless situation; Richard was already on the pump, but the water in the cabin was rising at an alarming speed. Water was gushing in both sides of the stem forward, under the port bunk, and again under the cockpit. It would not have been easy to try to deal with one puncture in force five on a pitch black night in a fair old seaway; four or more holes were out of the question – we had to abandon.

While Richard set about releasing the dinghy (9 ft Nautisport, fully inflated, upside down on the coachroof), I started in on the flares. My main armament was some seven or eight of the "Roman Candle" type; they burn a steady red flare in your hand, while throwing up a succession of red balls to a very satisfactory height. They all went off beautifully, and the display must have lasted at least four minutes, possibly longer; the only snag was that there was no audience. The mainland coast was a good three miles off, but the visibility was much less than that; I felt sure that the lighthouse should be keeping a watch, but at 0300. . . ?

We started loading up the dinghy: oars, rowlocks, pump, bailer; food? a big plastic gash-bag, shove in cakes, biscuits, tarts, tie a knot in it; water? all in the tank, tiny galley pump, no container to hand! At that moment, six long-life milk cartons conveniently floated out of their locker, in they went; what next? I grabbed my wallet and travellers cheques; personal kit – one large travel bag each; next? my second bag, with all the ship's and personal papers – in it went (it wasn't until two hours later that I realised that it was the wrong second bag; all I saved was a lot of useless hardware). By this time the water was over the cabin bunks, slowing down a bit as it had more room to spread out, and the relative buoyancy increased, but still rising visibly. We grabbed a few more bits and pieces, but then decided we had better get out in case she took a wave into the cockpit and plunged suddenly. We had been something over ten minutes, probably about quarter of an hour, from the first impact. After we let go, *Quiver* went on fore reaching in a northerly direction, while we started drifting rapidly WSW. The direct cabin light disappeared quite quickly over our limited horizon, but the glow from it on the sails could be seen for another five minutes or so as she sailed sluggishly into the darkness. Then she just disappeared.

I won't go into all the sordid details of the next ten hours. It was a hell of a long time. Every quarter of an hour or so a wave would sweep right over us, to make sure that we were kept as cold and wet as possible. We bailed it all out again, though there was not really much point. We never saw a suspicion of land or vessel the whole time. Cramp was rather trying.

I found that I had in my pocket my plastic "Offshore" hand bearing compass. It was comforting to confirm, by sighting up wind, that we were being blown WSW, and that therefore France lay somewhere to leeward. I tried rowing, but found that I could not do anything very effective except in short bursts which were very tiring. I felt however that I had to try to do something useful, so kept gently paddling across the wind in a generally southerly direction, thereby reducing the possibility of missing France altogether. We decided that we really did not know what the tide might be doing to us. Even if we had managed to grab any charts or pilot books which were floating around in the cabin, they would have dissolved before we could have made any use of them.

Sometime about midday, Richard declared that he had been watching for a timed quarter of an hour the same two slag heaps directly to leeward. Unlike all the other land we had been imagining, they were still there. They could only be Ile de Batz. Soon they joined up and became a proper island, with the cliffs above Roscoff appearing opposite. Then a buoy went past, obviously the landfall for the Roscoff channel. Things were looking up . . . or were they? As the actual coast became visible, it was increasingly apparent that it was very knobbly; the lighthouse in the channel had spray bursting 20 to 30 feet up it; what would happen when we got in amongst that lot? I decided to try to row across our track sufficiently to guide the dinghy into the Roscoff channel, in the hope that we might be able to pop into the harbour as we went past, or at least find a lee behind it.

Just as I started the lighthouse dodging operation, I saw the bows of a vessel pointing at me from windward. Digging in my bag, I found a large yellow towel which we hastily lashed to an oar, and which Richard waved vigorously aloft, while I resumed rowing, trying to dodge being flogged in the face by the wet towel. The langoustier, for such it was, altered course away from us to keep to his channel, and we quite decided that he had not seen us. Then figures appeared on deck; the ship stopped, turned, and slowly took up station to windward of us; a rope was thrown, we were hauled alongside. The rolling of the ship made getting aboard relatively easy; you step on the rubbing strake as it rolls down, then you are catapulted over the bulwarks as she goes back. They gaffed our gear with an outsize boathook, then hauled up the dinghy as well.

After that life became somewhat more civilised. The crew took us down to the aft cabin, stripped us off, and delving into their own bags, found enough spare clothing to kit us out warm and dry. They brewed coffee and laced it with rum; they found some hard tack and butter, chocolate and fags; they did it all with great good humour; one can ask no more of any man.

We were not, as we thought, bound for Roscoff, but for Mogueriec, some five miles further west. *Le Rayon de Soleil* (she was the only sunshine we saw that day) was heading for home and Sunday dinner, and the tide being right, was taking the short cut inside Ile de Batz; otherwise . . .

On arrival at Mogueriec, we met our host for the first time; he had been at the helm hitherto. M. Jean Baptiste Le Bihan is a great powerful jolly man, patron-pêcheur, a man of substance, and with a great heart. Initial difficulties over language soon became easier, as he has some English acquired from frequently marketing his catches in Cornish ports.

Our first visitor was the douanier who took one look and decided he was not interested in us. Then came a gentleman who introduced himself as of the French navy. He was subsequently described in the local newspapers as 'syndic des gens de mer à Roscoff' and 'L'administrateur de l'inscription maritime de Morlaix'. We never did discover which hat this M. Balcon was wearing that day, but he made the civilised suggestion that it would be more comfortable if he were to interview us with a glass in our hands, so we adjourned to the local cafe. Having satisfied him that *Quiver* was not a danger to shipping (he must have been Receiver of Wrecks as well), he undertook after making his report to his own authorities to notify the British Embassy in Paris; they in turn reported to the Foreign Office, who telephoned Richard's parents with the true story of what had happened, thus forestalling the inevitable inaccurate press reports.

Meanwhile, Mme Le Bihan had gathered up all our wet garments, plus our saturated baggage, shoved them into the boot of her car, and taken all home. There she rounded up some neighbours, and they spent the whole of Saturday afternoon and evening feeding it all through the washing machine, hosing out our bags, spreading out all our other bits and pieces to dry. Sunday she spent drying and ironing, so that by Sunday afternoon we had the whole lot back, ready to pack.

Now came the embarrassing bit. We had no passports, therefore my travellers cheques were useless. We were rapidly eating our way through the few francs I had fore-armed myself with at the local hotel. I could not get any more money till I had a passport; I could only get a passport in Paris; how to get the fare? I offered Baptiste (as our host is known to his friends, amongst whom I now count myself lucky to be numbered) some English money, knowing that he frequently visits British ports, but he would have none of it; we might well need that before we got home. He would buy our rail tickets; and he did just that at 6 o'clock on the Monday morning, after driving us 20 miles into Morlaix to save a taxi fare.

After sorting ourselves out in Paris, we duly obtained temporary passports; then, liberty at last, some money! An evening in Montmartre was indicated, and enjoyed.

We caught the night ferry back from Dunkerque to Dover, where, just to rub things in, the ship went aground while turning to back into her berth. We were rather glad to get home.'

———————— ,, ————————

From: the *Old Gaffers Association Newsletter*

16: Goodbye to *Smew*

Yacht: *Smew* (30ft cutter)
Skipper: Edward Nott-Bower
Crew: Angela Nott-Bower
Bound from Tresco, Scilly Isles to Waterford, Ireland
Time and date of loss: 0220, May 29th, 1951
Position: approx. 1 mile E of Mine Head

Smew was designed for a Col. Smee by a Mr Trew and built by Aldous of Brightlingsea in 1893. She was of lap-strake construction and originally had a centre-board, although this was removed in 1899. Immediately after World War II, *Smew* was owned by Edward Allcard, from whom Edward Nott-Bower bought her, on the spur of the moment, when looking for somewhere to park his caravan at Richmond on Thames.

After Allcard had given the new owner some brief instruction and accompanied him as far as Dover, Nott-Bower and his wife Angela spent the next five years making some very successful cruises to Brittany and round Spain, which voyages are amusingly described in the book *Ten Ton Travel*.

In the spring of 1951, *Smew* was on passage from the Scillies to the south coast of Ireland when, due to extreme tiredness, her skipper lost track of their true position and she was wrecked.

—————— " ——————

'On Saturday morning, 26th May, 1951, we sailed out past Cromwell's Castle and between the rocky headlands of Tresco and Bryher into the Atlantic. Outside there was a truly enormous swell. It did not trouble us in the least, for the motion it gave the boat was comparable to going slowly up and down in a well-operated lift every ten or fifteen seconds. We should have slept but for the fickleness of the breeze which kept us busy setting and resetting our light-weather canvas to its vagaries. I ruled on the clean

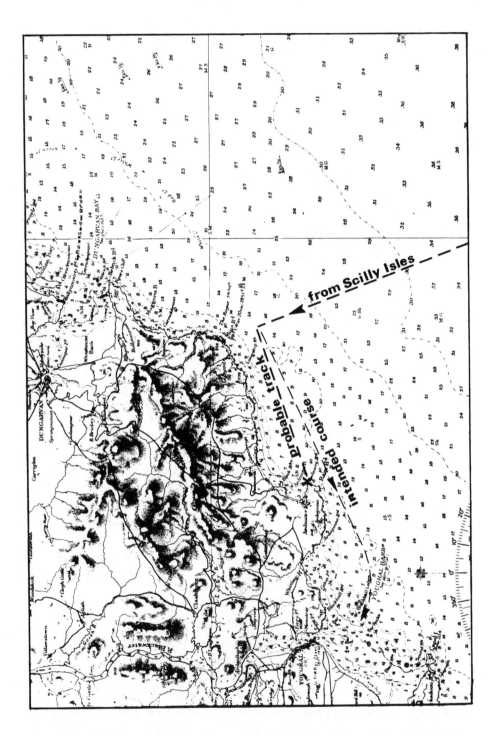

new chart a neat line from Tresco to Dunmore, a small harbour near the entrance to Waterford, and laid off the course – north by east. Very slowly the green islands faded astern, but soon after one o'clock, when I took an observation for latitude, I noticed with some annoyance that the lighthouse on Round Island was still plainly visible. This dead accurate but entirely useless observation was the only one I was able to get during a passage in which our position was nearly always in some doubt.

6 p.m. The weather forecast says a depression is moving north from France bringing strong to gale force winds in its train; direction as yet uncertain. We discuss this and decide it is grossly unfair. We have had no spell of really good weather since April, and of this we had only taken advantage to complete *Smew*'s fitting-out. Angela asks when we may expect to arrive, and after some thought I reply:

"Perhaps on Monday in the middle of the night."

"As usual. Have you got a decent chart of the place?"

"Yes. Bang up to date, with an inset of the Waterford entrance. No trouble at all."

9 p.m. A steady breeze from the NNW. This is good, for it enables *Smew* to sail herself on the course close-hauled with the helm lashed, and we are thus able to have a pleasant supper together, followed by a game of Angela's favourite patience to which, in the happy conditions prevailing, I am permitted to contribute pieces of advice. Afterwards we divide the night watches into two-hour periods. But somehow the desire for sleep is entirely absent. I find it impossible to dismiss from my mind all thoughts of the boat's progress and of the implications of the weather forecast. If the wind is north-westerly surely the depression must be somewhere to the NE of us. If it comes towards us presumably the wind will veer more north. Or will it? I have to get up and draw a diagram on the table. Is the wind increasing? I shout to Angela and she comes down, leaving *Smew* to plunge on by herself. Yes, she says, it has piped up a bit; it might be as well to take in the topsail. Up above conditions are still quite comfortable though the sky is overcast. The ship is rising and falling rhythmically over a sea as yet hardly disturbed by the breeze. There are no white horses and no spray; just a decent bow-wave and a perceptible wake streaming out aft. I take in the topsail and stow it under the dinghy. Then I note the course: NNE. The wind *is* veering more northerly and it is beastly cold.

Sun. 27th May. A fine drizzle began in the early hours of the morning, and the wind steadily increased and headed us till we were pointing roughly towards Milford Haven. The ship's motion from a gentle pitching became a violent bucketing. When the periodic "three big ones" came along she buried her bowsprit in each wave, then paused, heeling sharply, to gather way again in the succeeding lull. Water began to percolate in through the forehatch and the cabin-top coaming. In the cabin water began to appear on the lower part of the floor, and swished across at the more violent rolls.

6 a.m. We take a reef.

9 a.m. We take two more reefs.

It is difficult to trace the exact stages by which one is transmuted from a reasonably energetic and companionable person at sea to a silent, dyspeptic, slow-moving being whose mind and muscles are clogged with a heavy lassitude, and whose every thought and movement demand a conscious effort of will. I was approaching this unenviable state by 11 a.m., when it was blowing really hard, not far short of gale force. The barometer had fallen three-tenths during the night and was still going down. We took in the jib and hove-to. Angela made hot soup, washed up the mugs, and started another game of patience. Heroic, I thought. The fact that every now and then long snakes of cards slid over each other did not seem to worry her in the least. To me it seemed an intolerable addition to the discomforts attendant upon a storm at sea. I went up and cast a jaundiced eye on the scenery, comparing it unfavourably with Tresco. It was raining in buckets and the sea was a grey desolation of tumbling crests and mountainous waves.

8.30 p.m. I decide to give up the idea of going to Ireland and press on for Milford Haven. The wind seems somewhat less violent. We let draw the staysail. *Smew* protests violently at being woken up and retaliates by bucking viciously and drenching us with semi-green seas. However, the thought of a harbour even 60 miles away serves to raise our spirits, and we keep her at it.

10 p.m. I trim, light and fix the lamps.

A simple enough operation, you would think, but as I recollect it, it went something like this:

I take one lamp from the locker at the after end of the cockpit and, after awaiting a lull, climb down into the cabin with it, placing it hurriedly on the leeward side of the floor where there is a puddle of water. The next lurch seats me violently on the lee bunk, pale and panting. I open the lamp and withdraw the burner assembly which is covered with a mixture of paraffin and soot. I wonder if it is prudent to put it on the clean chart on the table. I decide that it is not, and put the chart on the bunk beside me. It falls off into the puddle. I get up, balancing precariously, retrieve the chart, and wait for the next roll which flings me across on to the weather bunk. I am now in a position to put the chart in its rack above the table. Crossing over again, I begin to clean the burner with a dirty rag and trim the wick; then I clean out the inside of the lamp. Finally I put the burner in and light the lamp. My grabs to preserve my balance as I get up to carry the lamp on deck result in dirty finger-marks on the cream paint. A small matter, but one which drives one more nail in the coffin of my malaise. Perhaps after all the maroon leather and varnish would have been better. Having placed the lamp on the cabin-top on the weather side I climb out of the cockpit and work myself and the lamp slowly forward to the shrouds, loudly protesting to Angela that I have no intention of falling overboard. At length I stand erect and slide the lamp into its socket. The process is then repeated with the other lamps.

Mon. 28th May, 2 a.m. I am in the lee bunk thinking almost enviously of Sir Cloudesley Shovel. The slamming of the boom and quarter blocks is added to the general turmoil. Angela shouts down that the wind has suddenly gone altogether. I join her in the cockpit, and together we get our great intractable boom, which sticks out 5 ft beyond the transom, tamed and secured in the gallows. Now what? The barometer has hit the bottom and shows a tendency to rise. It looks as if we are in the middle of the depression and that we may get a change of wind.

And so it was. We had only a quarter of an hour to endure of that most agonising of all motions, the rolling of a small sailing ship windless in a confused sea; then miraculously we were away before the wind carrying full mainsail and feeling the big forward urge of the waves instead of the vicious crash of their resistance. Our course was once more for Ireland, distant 90 miles.

3 a.m. We take a reef.

3.30 a.m. We take two more reefs.

At 4 a.m. we took in the mainsail altogether. I went below to the fo'c'sle and got out the trysail, but when I got up on deck again I decided not to set it. We were travelling at great speed and *Smew* was tipping her stern cleverly to the crests of the big overtaking waves and roaring down their steep sides in a smother of foam. Our small jib and staysail were almost bursting with the force of the following wind. Angela demonstrated with a pleased smile that the tiller was quite free and demanded no attention from her. I watched the course on the compass. It was steady at NNW. The first signs of light were showing to the eastward; the wind cut through our damp clothes. We went down to the cabin where conditions were less depressing than before. The motion was again like a lift, this time operated by a novice in a hurry. I re-checked our position from our estimated courses and came to the conclusion that NNW should be just about right for Dunmore.

8 a.m. The wind has backed and moderated somewhat. I have set the trysail and am experimenting with a tiller lashing to ascertain what course we can now hold without attention. It is NW.

It was here that a lack of resolution induced by strain and sleeplessness first made itself felt. A north-westerly course, according to my reckoning, would take us to the westward of Dunmore, towards a part of the coast of which I had no charts other than the very small-scale passage chart. But, I argued to myself, my dead reckoning is so susceptible of error that for all I know NW may be a better course; at least it will ensure that we do not miss the south-east corner of Ireland altogether and carry on into the Irish Sea. Anyway it was cold and wet in the cockpit, and I felt an overpowering desire for rest and inaction.

The sky remained overcast all day with occasional rain, and pray as I would for a glimpse of sun for an observation it refused to show. We rolled on and on, the thought ever uppermost in our minds – could we reach harbour that day, or must we spend yet another night of toil and anxiety? From tea-time onwards we were up on deck every five minutes scanning the northern horizon for signs of land. Four hours later in a dimming light we were rewarded with a vague smudge on the starboard bow, then another dead ahead. Feverishly we examined the chart and tried to draw deductions, but it was no use: there were too many places it might have been. Time seemed endless as the smudges faded in the gathering dark.

10 p.m. A light shows wide on the starboard bow. Its flashes are so intermittent owing to the rise and fall of the waves that it is impossible to identify it.

10.15 p.m. Another light shows on the port bow.

Here now was the crux. If the latter showed a flash every three seconds it would be the Hook Head light off the Waterford entrance, and the following wind would carry us right into the estuary where Dunmore was easy to find and enter with a good chart. But as we stood straining our eyes to detect a regular periodicity in the flashes our hopes gradually fell. More and more the light to starboard showed the three second flash. The other was Mine Head far to the west.

I should repeat that *Smew* was not clever to windward. Under full mainsail in smooth water she concealed this disability very creditably, but reefed down in a big sea, although she made a brave show of pointing well up and bashing the waves with laudable tenacity and much foam and noise, her actual progress over the land was quite surprisingly at odds with the direction indicated by the compass. Give her a trysail and a real beast of a sea, and she would say in effect: "Well, *really* . . . !" and turn away to leeward with a wry chuckle. We could, I suppose, have set a reefed mainsail and embarked upon a heroic beat to the Waterford entrance. Had we had only one night out we should no doubt have done this. But this was our third night without sleep, and the idea of turning to windward at all, with the violent motion it would have entailed, was quite contrary to my inclinations, and I believe even to Angela's; while the business of stowing the trysail and unleashing the boom to a Force 6 wind was one which I felt incapable of facing. We rolled on towards Mine Head.

Tues. 29th May, 2 a.m. We are approaching the Mine Head light. I estimate it as a mile ahead. I alter course to WS'J', a safe course to clear the coast beyond. I do not want to get too far out, otherwise we may have a beat into Youghal Harbour at dawn. I have been trying to read the *Irish Coast Pilot*, but it danced before my eyes and I could not make much sense of it. I thought perhaps we might try and get into Dungarvan Harbour, just east of Mine Head, but the place seemed beset with the most complicated dangers. Better to keep on till daylight. Angela is asleep below. I am feeling like nothing on earth or on the sea. *Smew* seems to hold the course steadily with a slight adjustment of the tiller lashing. I go below and turn to Youghal in the *Pilot*.

2.20 a.m. I am on my way up to the cockpit when there is a crash and a shudder.

"Blast!" is my first thought, "we have gybed."

Angela is out of her bunk and following me.

"What on earth is that?" she asks.

"Gybed, I suppose," I reply.

At that moment there is another crash. As I look up into the dark sky I see a darker mass towering up on the starboard side. It looks exactly like the mainsail boomed out. As I try in a muddled way to work out how the mainsail has hoisted itself and gybed from port to starboard there is a third and final crash. Now we are suddenly motionless with the waves breaking round us.

"Good Lord, we're aground," says Angela, "that thing's a cliff!"

I can remember that my first reaction was one of immense physical relief at the lack of motion, which in an instant made me feel capable of energetic action. I sprang forward to where the dinghy was lashed on the foredeck, cast off the lashings, upended the dinghy, and slid it into the water where it banged against the rocks. Then I got the end of a warp and began to bend it to the anchor. Angela came up from below carrying a handbag and two loaves of bread.

"What on earth are you trying to do?" she asked, "she's holed below and making water fast. Come on."

"I'm going to get a kedge out to haul her off," I replied.

"Don't be a fool," she said, "you'll just get drowned."

I looked round at the sea. The force of the waves was considerably broken by an off-shore reef; nevertheless it looked distinctly unpleasant for dinghy work, and there was a good deal of noise and spray. I left the dinghy and made my way back to the cabin. Rather miraculously the boat remained on an even keel, wedged into the rocks. As each wave came along she rose fore and aft and fell again with a thump. In comparison with half-an-hour ago the scene was peaceful. But the water on the floor was deep; it was above the level of the drawers below the port bunk. I opened the nearest one quickly and fished out my camera and binoculars; both were under water. Then I took a hand torch and went up on deck again. Angela was ashore and calling to me.

"Come on. It's a bit slippery but quite easy."

At the end of the bowsprit was a big black rock against which the waves were breaking. I worked myself along the bowsprit shroud, sat on the bowsprit end, and waited for a wave to pass. Then I dropped off and scrambled up on to the rock. I looked at my watch. Two-thirty.

I am still uncertain of the immediate cause of the accident – a shift of wind, a slip of the tiller lashing, or possibly a mistake in setting the course. All that I am certain of is that, had I been in anything approaching a reasonable frame of mind, I should have been very much further out. As it was, *Smew* was lost, despite all efforts at salvage. She broke up a week later. Nothing remains of her but memories; her faults forgotten, the grand times she gave us always fresh.'

———————— ,, ————————

From: *The Yachtsman*, Summer 1952

17: *Kelpie*'s Last Cruise

Yacht: *Kelpie* (26 tons gaff cutter)
Skipper: Conor O'Brien
Crew: None
Bound from Oban, Scotland to Limerick, Ireland
Time and date of loss: early hours of September 1st, 1921
Position: on rocks off Portpatrick, Galloway, Scotland

When Conor O'Brien bought *Kelpie* in 1910, she was already twenty-three years old. At first he sailed her with William Brady as skipper, but in 1914 the Irish Volunteers 'accepted the service' of *Kelpie* 'as being the most improbable outfit for a gun-running expedition'.

By 1921, O'Brien felt that he knew his ship well enough to be able to manage a passage from Kingstown (Dun Laoghaire) to the Shannon without any outside help. The plan was to go north about and the voyage started in a southerly wind, but this changed to a westerly by the time O'Brien needed to round the north coast of Ireland and, instead of attempting this, he altered course for Oban, where he spent some time on climbing excursions with the crew of the yacht *Molly*.

Eventually, having had a new stove fitted, *Kelpie* left Oban, bound for Limerick at the end of August.

———————— " ————————

'Alas! that I did not use that easterly breeze for another purpose. As long as it lasted the stove-fitters of Oban kept holiday, and when the work was done the wind had settled into the south-west, a foul wind for my destination. I wanted a fair wind for a start, to get me clear of the land before night and allow me to turn in with a good conscience; anyway, I did not want a head wind in any narrow channel, for the ship was not rigged for handiness in making short tacks. So naturally I had to begin with a beat down the extremely narrow Sound of Kerrera in very baffling airs and too

117

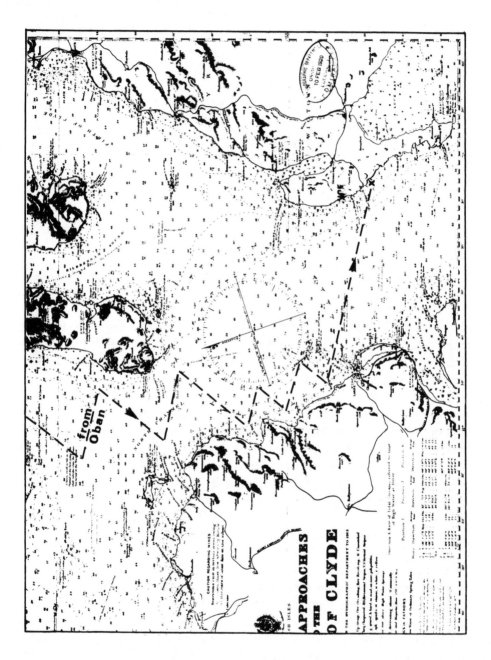

early to get any help from the tide. At nightfall I was still only between Colonsay and the Torranan Rocks, of which, as Alan Breck said, it sticks in my mind that there are 10 miles. I did get an hour's sleep after passing them, and, being set far to leeward out of my course by a heavy swell, nearly hit Dubh Artach. I resigned myself to keeping clear of dangers, and probably made more leeway than headway during this unprofitable night.

At daybreak the prospect was no more cheerful. I could do nothing whatever to the westward, for the swell from that quarter stopped me dead, but on the other tack I should sooner or later get into smooth water, and might with luck fetch Lough Swilly; so I stood away southwards. And gradually southwards became south-eastwards, and as all my information – a three-days-old weather chart out of *The Times* – pointed to a continuation of southerly winds on the west coast, I reckoned I would rather have my southerly wind in smooth water, made a virtue of a necessity, and wrote down in my log-book that I was bound for Dublin, always on the way towards Limerick, but south about.

This time the North Channel was at its calmest, but the wind was at its highest, and for my second night I took things easy. It was rather a wonderful night, clear overhead, though the fact that one could only see stars of the first three magnitudes and that the horizon was hazy showed that there was something in between me and the sky. There was, and a most surprising thing; quite heavy rain. I believe this phenomenon of a "serena" is not uncommon in some countries, but it was the first and only time that I ever met with it. Towards dawn the rain stopped without any sign of cloud having appeared, and in the morning a scorching sun dried out my sails. And I didn't like the look of those sails at all, especially that of the mainsail, which ought to have been all right, for it was a new sail that had only just enough wear to knock the stiffness out of it. Nor did I like the set of the topsail, and I argued that if the mainsail had been the right shape the topsail would have fitted over it all right. So I became cross and impatient, and pulled and hauled on sheet and halliards, and produced very little improvement at a vast expense of energy. And since when once my appetite is whetted by fiddling about with ropes the vice grows on me, I discovered a lot of small defects in the rigging and set them right; and really when we came to beat down the coast of Antrim from Fair Head we weren't looking so bad aloft; and if I had had the sense to anchor in Bangor for the night I should not have been afraid of comparisons between Dublin and Belfast yachting. But unfortunately, like Jimmy Hicks, I became too ambitious – which is sailors' slang for working too hard – excess of work is a vice just like any other excess. I went into the galley to gloat over my new stove, for the nights were getting chilly and I wanted to get her good and hot before sunset, and one of those shifting lockers to which I have already alluded caught my eye as being quite intolerably crooked; so I must needs secure and straighten that. Last of all there was dinner to be cooked, and I felt I wanted a good dinner; and I had it. And that was the end of a pretty strenuous day, and I felt inclined afterwards to blame it all on the cut of the mainsail; though I don't think it is quite fair to blame anything, for I enjoyed the day's work thoroughly – only I lost my ship because of it.

After dinner I was undeniably tired, but I saw the navigation lights burning brightly, and the alarm clock set to warn me a safe time before we neared the land, in case I might fall asleep, and then I sat down with a pipe in the saloon and wrote my journal up to date. As I reviewed the events I thought that, even with the anxieties of the gale in Scavaig, this was the pleasantest cruise that I had yet undertaken. But I was beginning to wish it were over; the collapse of the potato-locker had worried me, and the bulkhead had never come so badly adrift before. I began to doubt whether I should ever bring the ship as far as Limerick; the prudent person would of course break her up at Arklow, build a new hull at an insignificant price, and put into it her valuable fittings. But this I could not bear to do, so strong was my feeling for her. Then I reflected that the prudent man does not go sailing alone, at least not in narrow and crowded waters, and that such a practice is not even morally justifiable; and I wrote down in my journal, in order that others might learn from my precept, if not from my example, that close-hauled on the starboard tack, as I was then, I might hit seven different kinds of ships and be to blame for the collision; an overtaken vessel, a vessel to leeward holding a better wind, a vessel not under control, a vessel laying telegraph cables, a fisherman with his gear out, a vessel at anchor, and a light-vessel; and then I must have dropped asleep, for I was next aware that I had hit an eighth thing, which was the coast of Galloway. That damned alarm had failed.

I knew at once that it was all over; I had killed my poor little ship. She, who worked for me unaided night and day, found me asleep upon my watch, and for all her virtues the reward was her destruction. To any seaman the death of a ship is a tragedy only second to the death of a shipmate; and *Kelpie* was not only my ship but my shipmate as well.

I launched my little boat and drifted up the coast in the dark, seeking for a landing, and as the yacht's light faded out in the distance I wished that good ships might go to heaven, so that my *Kelpie* might carry a message to the men who designed and built her of my thanks for the pleasant years I had spent in her company, and of my contrition for her murder. She, poor thing, in her death had spared me the protracted agony of uncertainty. Her end came so quickly that I hardly realized my loss till I stepped ashore on the quays of Portpatrick in the grey light of dawn, to find myself homeless, earth-bound, and dependent on others for my movement.'

———————— " ————————

From: Conor O'Brien *From Three Yachts* (1928), Edward Arnold

18: The Loss of *Sea Breeze*

Yacht: *Sea Breeze* (49ft Bristol Channel pilot-cutter)
Skipper: H.W. Tilman
Crew: Brian Potter
      Mike Clare
      Brian McCleagan
      Dougal Forsyth
Bound from Lymington, Hampshire to W coast of Greenland
Time and place of loss: 2100, August 21st, 1972
Position: in entrance to Sermilik Fjord, Greenland

Within a month of returning from Norway after the loss of *Mischief* (see pages 241–247), Bill Tilman was offered another Bristol Channel pilot-cutter – the *Sea Breeze*. Despite the fact that John Tew, the surveyor, advised against buying her, Tilman could not resist the temptation, although he knew 'that much renovation and rejuvenation' would be required, since she was only one year younger than Tilman himself, who was 70 at the time.

The first voyage in *Sea Breeze*, in 1969, did not go well, and within 25 miles of Scoresby Sound, Tilman's crew 'mutinied'. He had to return, sadly reflecting that 'Once before I had had the melancholy experience of sailing homewards with a disillusioned crew.'

In 1970, *Sea Breeze* was short of a complete crew and to augment it, Tilman advertised in *The Times*: 'Hands wanted for long voyage in small boat. No pay, no prospects, not much pleasure.' The objective that year was the south-west coast of Greenland, where 'there are plenty of mountains of the order of 5000 to 7000 feet!'

In 1971, with another crew including 'Two guitar players and their instruments, a bugle and a mouth organ,' *Sea Breeze* attempted to reach Greenland again, but was stopped by ice 70 miles off the coast.

In 1972, Tilman's plan was to take *Sea Breeze* to the west coast of

Greenland, to Baffin Bay and Ellesmere Island. Having left Lymington on May 1st, they met 'dirty' weather in the Atlantic and while some 500 miles east of Greenland's Cape Farewell, suffered a broken boom which made it necessary to 'set a tops'l abaft the mast as a sort of trys'l' and alter course for Reykjavik in Iceland, 300 miles to the north. They arrived there on July 2nd, and a new boom was made by 'laminating together eight lengths of one-inch planking.'

While in Reykjavik, the crew was rearranged to include a student from California and they left on July 10th, intending to call first at Jan Mayen Island; but:

———————— " ————————

'Within a couple of hours the unfortunate Californian had retired to his bunk retching and groaning where he lay for the next five days in a sort of coma, a bandage over his eyes, neither eating nor drinking, nor even moving. We thought he was dead. So we put into Isafjord to land him, and no sooner were we alongside but he was up and about, looking remarkably sprightly considering his five days' ordeal. Brian promptly telephoned his friend and secured the son whom he did not know but guessed would be in his early twenties with considerable sailing experience. Two days later, on returning to the boat after a walk in the hills, Brian and I learnt that Dougal Forsyth had already arrived and that he was a schoolboy of sixteen. This rather staggered me but there was nothing to be done, and young Dougal, sturdy for his age, proved to have the makings of a useful hand.

We sailed from Isafjord on 18 July and reached Jan Mayen (No. Lat. 71° Long. 8.28°W) on the 25th. Some 70 miles north-west of Horn we sighted our first ice, a field of heavy pack-ice close aboard to the west. There was no ice anywhere near Jan Mayen this year. The steep cliff that marks the south-west Cape was sighted from 40 miles away, the ship happily pointing straight at it. We anchored first in the small bay off the Norwegian base, the bay of evil memory where *Mischief* took such a battering from the ice in '68. One of the small party awaiting Mike and me as we rowed ashore greeted me with, "Mr. Tilman, I presume." He had been on the island in '68 and seeing our yellow hull had put two and two together and concluded it was that man again.'

———————— " ————————

After a couple of days they were under way again and were off Scoresby Sound by August 3rd, not meeting any ice until within ten miles of the coast.

———————— " ————————

'We hung about for several days while all the ice disappeared except that inside the Sound where, from Cape Tobin south to Cape Brewster, it remained chock-a-block. Along the coast, too, north from Cape Tobin there remained a belt of shore-fast ice so that we were unable to anchor anywhere, and it was the more frustrating because at one time we were within three miles of the settlement and could see the wireless masts. On 8 August when we tried the engine it started reluctantly, made a queer noise, and finally refused to start at all. A friend who knows the engine has diagnosed the trouble as a broken valve spring and thinks that the engine could have been run on one cylinder had we had on board anyone able to cope. So we gave up Scoresby Sound and went south to Angmagssalik where by the time we arrived, which was not until 21 August, there should not be much ice. The entrance is long and narrow but would be possible to sail through were there no ice; we needed water and stores for the voyage home and having come so far the crew deserved something more than a view of Greenland. It would have been prudent to go home.

The absence of ice off the Sound led me to think that the coast to the south would be ice free, and we started off with the pleasant thought of keeping this magnificently mountainous coastline close aboard all the way. However, south of Cape Brewster we began meeting ice, and the further south we went and the further away from the coast – for the coast falls away to the south-west – the thicker the ice became. When a field of close pack-ice showed to the *east* it became clear that this was no place for a boat with no engine. So we sailed north again, rounded the pack to the east, and gained open water. It was a slow passage and we had another unpleasant encounter with ice in thick fog only some 70 miles north-west of Iceland, probably the remains of the field we had seen on the outward passage. Unusual, too, were the number of bergs we kept sighting from a point 30 miles west of Iceland right across Denmark Strait to Greenland.

On the night of 19 August when some 30 miles east of Cape Dan we met a north-easterly gale, the hardest blow of the voyage, which went on for 24 hours. Hove-to and reefed down with only some 8 ft of luff on the mast we lost a lot of ground to the south-west, and on the 21st, the gale having spent itself, a bank of fog over the land made it difficult to identify.

I intended spending the night at sea but when an opening appeared in the floes, decided to sail through in order to anchor in Sermilik fjord which lay temptingly wide and open to the south-west. Having reached the open water with nothing but a few bergs about we thought our troubles were over until the wind became fluky and finally died when we were still a mile or so from the shore. Towing with the dinghy did little to help – a couple of long sweeps would have been more use.

After the gale the glass has risen smartly and was high and steady so that the fierce blast of wind that came in about 9 p.m. when it was getting dark, the herald of a dirty night, was quite unexpected. The first blast laid her over until the lee deck was half under water. The boat shot ahead and was soon within a quarter-mile of the dimly seen shore. She had plenty of way on, and the rate we were going and the fear that we might hit something induced me to get the sails off in a hurry – prematurely, as it happened, for we got no bottom with the lead. By then a lot more ice had come down the fjord, too much to sail among with safety in the wind then blowing. So for the next three or four hours we drifted slowly away from the shore, the crew hard at work fending off floes. We had not even enough respite to get the dinghy on board. When a rock islet loomed out of the darkness to leeward we set the stays'l in an effort to clear it, and might have done had not a floe got under the lee bow and stopped her. Her heel caught and she swung round to be pinned by wind and wave broadside on against the rock, the cranse iron at the bowsprit end striking sparks off the rock face. Dropping the stays'l all hands shoved desperately and vainly with boathooks. She could not be got off and was taking a terrible hammering. Fearing she would break up or fill and slip off into deep water I told the crew to abandon her. A little later she did slip off so that at first light only a few feet of mast showed above the water.

Mike got ashore first with a rope which he anchored to hold Dougal while he jumped. We should have secured the rope on board to serve as a handrail. Without waiting for the rope to be thrown back Brian followed, slipped on the rock and was washed back almost under the boat until the next wave took him forward to be grabbed by Mike, wet from head to foot. The only loose rope handy was the lead line so young Brian got ashore on this while held by me. This left me with the weight end and thinking that 7 lb of lead round my waist might be a hindrance if it came to swimming I had to go below for a knife to cut it off. After being first thrown violently to the deck with a crash that made me think the deck above was caving in I found a knife and presently joined the others, wet only from the waist. I'm ashamed to confess that my faculties were so numbed by the sudden disaster that while all this was happening it never even occurred to me to collect such valuable and portable things as diary, log book, met. log, films, camera, money, sextant. The crew were no better. Sleeping bags were all that most of us got ashore. A sack of food had been thrown ashore but a wave washed it away.

The wind continued throughout the night and in the morning rain set in, to continue throughout the day. At daylight we moved to the top of the rock. Mike had brought a very light bivouac tent into which we put Brian and Dougal who were wettest and coldest. The rest of us, having looked into every nook and cranny and found nothing – our rock was rich only in pools of water – spent the day pacing up and down, speculating on the chances of a boat passing, and if one did on whether we would be seen, and on the number of days a man could last without food. There was a small settlement a few miles up the fjord and no doubt communication between this and Angmagssalik, but how frequently or infrequently was the question.

But our luck was in. Late that afternoon we saw a small local boat bound up the fjord. She was passing a good mile away and on account of the drizzle visibility was poor. All five of us stood on top of the rock waving sleeping bags and even shouting, a perfectly futile exercise since her three-man crew were warmly ensconced in the wheelhouse. For several agonizing minutes she held steadily on until at length to our heartfelt relief she began to turn towards us. The Greenlander crew acted smartly. Two jumped into their roomy dinghy, brought it close to the rock stern-on and, in spite of the swell still running, took us off in turn without mishap.

The lesson of this sad story for me – at present no one else seems likely to profit by it – is not to mess about in Greenland fjords without an engine, especially when they are full of ice. Nevertheless I think we were the victims of an unlucky chain of circumstances – first the failing wind that prevented us from anchoring, followed by a wind of such strength that we could not safely sail among ice, but for which we would have come to no harm.'

———————— ,, ————————

From: *Roving Commissions 13* (1973), published by
The Royal Cruising Club

PART III: FAILURE OF GEAR OR RIGGING

19: Four Pumps – and Still She Sank

Yacht: *Mariah* (86ft staysail schooner)
Skipper: Ed Clark
Crew: Bruce Paulsen
      Chip Williams
      Beth Brodie
      Jimmy Joner
      Jay Linsay
      Elisabeth Storm
Bound 'south from City Island', New York State, U.S.A.
Time and date of loss: abandoned 0130, October 26th, 1980
Position: approx. 200 miles SE of Cape May, New Jersey

Mariah, an Alden designed staysail schooner, was built in 1931, and her owner, Ed Clark, wanted her down south for the winter of 1980–81. They left City Island, N.Y. at 0100 on the morning of Thursday October 23rd, having 'flushed out the bilges, using every pump on board – to see that each was functioning properly.' Bruce Paulsen relates the subsequent events:

———————— " ————————

'The night was cold, but crystal clear. The huge clock at the Watchtower Building read 44 degrees at 0600; a beautiful day, with crisp Canadian air and northwest breezes. Both Bendix and NOAA predicted good weather for the Northeast, with a slight trough developing over the middle Atlantic region which could produce some storm activity, but nothing serious. We were not worried since we would be well east of any trouble.

At 0900 we left Ambrose Tower to starboard and were joined by a family of sparrows. The wind was northwest at 15 knots as we broad-reached under full sail. Beth set our course at 140° magnetic, which would take us out across the Gulf Stream. We had a beautiful day of sailing, but by evening clouds began to roll in, and the wind picked up. It was time to shorten sail, so Jimmy and I furled the flying jib, while Ed and Chip double-reefed the main. This left us a bit under-powered but made for a manageable, balanced rig. After a chicken dinner and a brief sip of Jay's renowned homemade wine, we broke into watches.

Jay and I were on deck as the day came to an end. The clouds continued to build as we looked to the west. "There'll be no sunset tonight," I told Jay. By 1900 the wind began to veer and increase. At 2000 we dropped the main staysail. The wind, now 25 to 30 knots, swung around to the northeast. We had trouble holding course at 140° and headed down to 160° magnetic. At 0400, we spotted a school of porpoises and had to confess they lifted our spirits on a cold, grey night.

The wind increased as daylight approached, and continued to shift to the right; by 0600 it was straight out of the east at about 35 knots. The sunrise was a brilliant red; the sparrows had disappeared.

Friday was cold and unpleasant, as the wind kicked up to 40 knots, and veered south of east. *Mariah* was working hard and began to leak, which was hardly unusual for a boat of her age. By afternoon our small seven-gallon-per-minute electric pump had trouble keeping up.

Mariah had four bilge pumps aboard; besides the electric pump there was a Whale Gusher on the deck. Its capacity, however, was only about a quarter of a gallon per stroke. Then, there were our big guns: a 50-plus gallon-per-minute Jabsco that ran off the Lehman diesel, and a 75-plus gallon-per-minute firehose/bilge pump that ran off its own one-cylinder diesel mounted in the lazarette. Either could handle any kind of problem. Both had functioned properly ashore. I had said with pride to visitors, "If we have anything aboard *Mariah*, it's bilge pumps."

By 1900 Friday we were leaking badly enough to engage the Jabsco. Ed turned over the diesel, and flipped the pump. It worked for a minute or two, but then grew hot and stopped pumping altogether. He took the pump apart and discovered the impeller had been completely destroyed. We inspected the intake for pieces of debris, but the fine screen was still intact. Confused but undaunted, we scraped out all the remnants of the old neoprene impeller, making sure to leave the cylinder perfectly clean. Ed then installed a spare impeller and reassembled the unit. By the time the pump was back together, however, the water in the bilge was over the level of the belt that drives the pump, causing it to slip around its pulley whenever the pump was engaged. Before we could operate the pump, the water level had to be reduced. We then began the grueling process of bucket-passing which was to last for the next 30 hours.

Beth, Jay and I bailed for about half an hour before the water level was low enough to try the pump again. Ed cleaned the belt with degreaser and once again cranked over the diesel. As before, it functioned for a minute or so before growing hot and stopping completely. Jimmy began pumping the deck pump, but its small capacity made it relatively useless. The rest of us kept bailing with the buckets.

Still not overly worried, we had yet to engage the automatic-priming, one-cylinder diesel, our USCG-approved monster pump. However, once turned on, it would not prime, perhaps because of the 10-foot waves. Jay, who knew pumps, assisted Ed, but after repeated attempts, it still would not hold a prime. By 2400 the decision was made to head for New Jersey and safety. We could still keep up with the incoming water, but we had no pumps. We were 300 or more miles from Bermuda with the wind southeast at 40 knots and increasing. Beating and bailing for three or four days did not seem particularly inviting. Cape May, however, was about 200 miles to the northwest. We could perhaps pick up some gas-driven pumps there and then continue. At 0100, Saturday, we jibbed and began to run with the seas at 290° magnetic. We kept bailing.

The wind increased to 50 knots, and squalls were frequent through the night. Seas grew to 20 feet or better, leaving both Jimmy and Elisabeth incapacitated by seasickness. Bailing was constant and unbearable, thanks to a break in the main fuel line leaking diesel into the bilge. There was no time for rest, and daybreak brought no relief.

By 0600 the water was a foot over the floorboards. Something had sprung, and it was getting difficult to keep up. At this point, the first of a long series of MAYDAYs was sent, and the tanker *Navios Crusader* relayed our message to the Cape May coastguard. At 0830 the coastguard informed us that an aircraft was on the way to drop a 140-gallons-per-minute bilge pump. The news gave the whole crew an emotional lift – the cavalry was coming over the hill. At 1030, Beth, manning the radio, told us that an aircraft was near.

We expected a helicopter, but a huge C-130 transport appeared instead. Slightly taken aback, we hoped they were good at high-speed air drops. Our only sail was the double-reefed main staysail, which gave just enough steerage to manoeuvre in the mounting seas. I tried to keep *Mariah* heading 300°; the plane would make its final approach on the reciprocal course. After several practice runs, the pilot approached with amazing speed; we watched anxiously for the drop, but nothing happened. Then Ed spotted a bright orange parachute about 200 yards behind us, to weather. Recovery was impossible, since we could not head upwind. The C-130 headed back to Elizabeth City, N.C., for more pumps and would not return for four hours. For the first time, we realized we were in danger of losing the schooner and possibly our lives.

Shortly, the coastguard informed us they had despatched the 210-ft cutter *Alert* to our position. The 30-ft seas, however, were keeping her under 10 knots, and she was over 100 miles – 10 hours – away.

At noon, two of the main staysail seams blew out, and within minutes, the sail was in ribbons. Now running under bare poles, we were pushed by waves as big as houses. Steering was difficult and tiring as the waves continued to mount, yet it provided the only relief from bailing.

At 1430, the C-130 reappeared. This time the orange drum containing the pump was dropped about 300 yards ahead of *Mariah*. I steered toward the drum, visible only every two or three waves, and finally it appeared on the crest of the wave ahead of us. Ed gaffed the parachute which immediately began to tear. The drum submerged as the pressure on it increased, and finally broke away. Strike two.

Another pump was dropped well ahead of us, and once again I pointed *Mariah* toward it. The trail line was difficult to spot in the foamy sea, and once we saw and gaffed it, it was too late. There was no loop in the end of the line; it slipped off into the sea. Strike three.

At 1600 the C-130 departed, telling us an H-3 helicopter was on the way with more pumps, and that another C-130 would circle us until he arrived. *Alert* was getting closer, and the merchant vessel *Dorsetshire* was standing by. By now, however, we had bailed for about 20 hours, and the diesel fumes had formed a thick haze over the knee-deep water in the bilge. Diesel coated everything in the cabin, and the floorboards on the leeward side were floating. Exhaustion was setting in. We were losing ground quickly.

The radio chattered again; it was the coastguard telling us that the helicopter had been delayed and would not arrive until 2200, four hours away, and we received a message from *Alert* that due to our rapid forward progress, even under bare poles, she would rendezvous with us around the same time. Perhaps our long-awaited pump would finally make it. Meanwhile, we kept working. Ed stopped to rest for a while, knowing that one of us would need to be fresh when the pumps arrived. With Beth on the radio and Jimmy doubled over with pain, that left three of us to bail and steer. Seasickness could not hold us back; Jay vomited into the buckets as he dumped them overboard.

At 2145 the helicopter arrived. The winds were up over hurricane force with waves well over 40 feet. I brought the boat up as close to the wind as possible, about abeam to the seas. The water in the saloon was chest high, and the heavy maple floorboards began to slam around, tearing apart the interior. The lee rail was down, with only three feet of freeboard on the cabin port and side. In the pitch dark, the helicopter had trouble manoeuvring around our 86-ft mainmast, and after half an hour backed off and radioed that instead of lowering a pump, he would begin evacuation procedures. We still wanted a pump more than anything else, but were obviously in no position to disagree.

We were told to inflate our Avon raft, which Chip had readied, to place two people at a time into it, and trail it aft. Elisabeth, not a sailor, was overcome with fright, so the captain decided to put her and Jimmy into the liferaft first. Ed streamed the raft out behind *Mariah*. The helicopter's huge floodlights illuminated the monstrous waves as the basket bounced across the water and the liferaft. Jimmy strained to grab the basket, but half an hour passed before he got a good grip and helped Elisabeth into it. Overall, it took nearly 40 minutes for both to reach the helicopter.

As Ed hauled the raft back into the boat, a gust of wind flipped it over, partially filling it with water. He brought the raft upright and alongside, however, and Jay and Beth prepared to jump in. Before they could do so, a huge wave broke over the boat, knocking both of them over the lifelines. Ed hung onto Beth and hauled her aboard, and, Jay, thanks to his safety harness, was brought back aboard. Once the wave had passed, we saw that the top ring of the liferaft had deflated. Beth, back on the radio, told the pilot of the fate of our liferaft. We were then told that the operation had to be abandoned, but that the cutter *Alert* was standing by to complete the evacuation.

Our batteries were long since dead, and the wave had drowned the generator that had been running a single light bulb that was our sole means of being identified. As *Alert* steamed straight for us in the darkness, Ed searched the wreckage below for *Mariah*'s flaregun. He found it and fired when the cutter was about 150 yards away.

Below, I grabbed my wallet and car keys. The cabin was a mess. No one had bailed since the helicopter arrived, and all the floorboards were floating; they had destroyed most of the interior. Diesel fumes filled the air; I got out as quickly as I could.

Meanwhile, *Alert* launched a 19-foot, hard-keel Avon inflatable with two frogmen aboard. They brought it quickly alongside *Mariah*, and we all jumped on as quickly as possible – Jay head first. *Mariah* had only three feet of freeboard on the windward side, and the leeward rail was awash. We hoped she could make it through the night. By 0030 we were safe and sound aboard *Alert*.

The captain of *Alert*, Commander Armand Chapeau, informed us that we were to lay by the schooner through the night, and perhaps, if she was still afloat at daylight, a pump could be taken aboard and we could take her in tow. But around 0130 *Alert* received orders to hurry to another distress call to the southeast. *Reliance*, another 210-foot cutter, would proceed to *Mariah*'s last known position to search and perhaps take her in tow. But 24 hours of searching proved futile. *Mariah* surely went down during the night.

The schooner was lost; but we still didn't know how lucky we were.

Later we learned that the storm of the weekend of October 25th claimed many boats and many lives; it was vicious, unpredicted, and caused extensive damage and losses all along the northeast seaboard. *Mariah* was not her only victim; another was the 33-ft *Demon of Hamble* with her owner, Angus Primrose, the noted English ocean racer and designer of *Gypsy Moth* in which Sir Francis Chichester had sailed alone around the world.

Every time a storm of such intensity strikes, all of us on the water learn many lessons, most of them the hard way. Questions are raised about sailors and their equipment. Why is it, then, that a main chapter in almost every sailing disaster story is pump failure?'

———————— ,, ————————

From: *Yachting*, August 1981

20: The End of an OSTAR

Yacht: *Livery Dole* (35ft trimaran)
Skipper: Peter Phillips
Crew: None
Bound from Plymouth, England to Newport, Rhode Island, U.S.A.;
in the 1980 Observer Singlehanded Trans-Atlantic Race
Time and date of loss: 0600, June 28th, 1980
Position: 42° 20′ N 54° 10′ W (approx. 700 miles E of Newport)

Livery Dole was one of the 88 starters in the 1980 OSTAR race, in which trimarans gained the first five places. But Peter Phillips, a police sergeant from Plymouth, was not so fortunate. *Livery Dole* was sponsored by a charity in aid of needy children, and she had been 21 days at sea:

———————— " ————————

'I have just over 700 miles to go to the finish. By 05.00 the wind is up to about 35 knots and I have three reefs in the main and the number 2 jib. *Livery Dole* is not at her best. She is doing 6–7 knots but slamming and dipping the lee float well under the water. The weather float is another problem. The seas are so big that every now and again a wave hits the up float with alarming force.

Not much later I have the fourth reef in the main and the storm jib, and I have got the speed down to 4–5 knots. I shall try and hold at that but as *L.D.* is such a lightweight trimaran I may have to run off under storm jib or heave to for a spell. The seas are the biggest problem. I reckon they are 12 to 15 ft with heavy breaking crests. It's about 06.00 and I look up on deck. Not much different. I then hear a roar behind me and I look back to windward. There is a big wave, much bigger than the others, coming towards me with a vicious, already breaking top. It hits the windward float and throws it in the air. The tri is virtually standing on its starboard float with the mast along the surface of the water. I am convinced we are going

135

right over and will capsize. The wave picks up the main hull and then moves upright but the down float goes on up and the windward float gets slammed back down on to the water to windward with an almighty crash. I hear a crack and to my utter surprise the whole front section of the windward (port) float has just snapped off and is gone. The waves crashes on through and we are nearly capsized again.

We are still afloat, but for how long? She is sailing on the good float but slamming so badly I ought to heave to, but I cannot because the other float will fill and capsize us. The windward float and front crossbeam are taking a terrible bashing. The seas crash into the open end and put undue pressure on the crossbeam. The broken edge is right at the crossbeam and the bolts are beginning to tear out. If the remainder go the float will come off and fracture at the rear beam by pressure alone. There is little doubt: I am in trouble.

I start to get things organized in case I have to leave the tri, but almost immediately there is a crack and part of the front crossbeam is broken off by another wave. I go on deck and cut the liferaft straps and pull it out ready to go if need be. The problem is that I cannot launch the raft at this speed, about six knots again, but I cannot reduce too much for fear of a capsize to windward by wave action. I tune my radio into 2182, the distress frequency, ready for use. The front end of the port float is breaking away from the beam. I broadcast a "MAYDAY" and give my position several times. Fortunately my navigation is up to date and I reckon my position to be 42° 20′ North and 54° 10′ West. I get a part confirmation from St Lawrence coastguard that they have got my message but they want the name of the yacht and the nature of the trouble. I give it to them and repeat the position.

Suddenly the lee (down) float is pushed up by wave action. The open end of the windward float digs into the water and we stall. We begin to capsize to windward. I grab the emergency beacon from my bunk and jump up through the hatch. We are gradually going over to windward.

I throw the liferaft over the side and operate the "panic" button on the Argos Satellite transmitter. The tri is almost over. I climb up and jump over the side into the water near the liferaft, hanging on to the emergency beacon. The mast hits the water, momentarily stops, and then carries on going. Then it's upside down – completely inverted. The whole process has taken only seconds.

I grab the liferaft painter and pull it several times. It inflates right way up. I put the beacon inside and get in myself, leaving the liferaft painter still attached to *Livery Dole* which is still floating, albeit low in the water. The damaged float has already torn itself off and is attached just by the bracing wires. I try several times to get into the tri through the safety hatch to get more food and water but the big seas break and wash me off. It is obvious that with these seas I am not going to succeed. I make my way back to the liferaft and get into it. I set the emergency beacon going and put it in the water on its line. The pulsating light is operating well and that makes me feel a whole heap better. If a search does get under way soon and my position is correct it will help them locate me. I close the canopy on the liferaft to conserve body heat as hypothermia and exposure are the real killers in situations like these.

I decide that I will stay in the liferaft attached to the tri for as long as is possible. If people are searching it will give them a bigger target to look for. She looks in a terrible state and I feel very sorry about what has happened and for all the people that have been involved in the project from beginning to end. I was doing well and it should have never ended like this.

I decide to wait until the weather moderates and then try to gain access yet again. I get most of the water out of the liferaft and curl up on the floor for a bit of wet and uncomfortable sleep. I wake up after maybe a couple of hours; I don't really know as I didn't even have time to pick up my watch from the chart table.

I look out and there is a problem. The starboard float has completely snapped off with most of the crossbeams and the main hull has gone deeper in the water by the escape hatch. The seas are no better but I am going to have another go to get in before I cannot reach it at all.

I pull myself in and climb back on the bits of crossbeam – there isn't much of them left – but try as I may I cannot get to the hatch, I just get washed off every time by the seas. I eventually get back into the liferaft somewhat exhausted by the effort.

About an hour later I hear an aircraft. I look outside and see a Search and Rescue plane flying straight for me. What luck, and so soon. He flies over the top and straight on. I watch for him to turn but he goes out of sight and I am puzzled. I wait for him to return but no such luck. He should be if he is homed on to the beam from the emergency beacon. The beacon is lying around the back of the liferaft so I pull it into sight. The flashing light is *NOT* working. No wonder the plane went on. I pull the beacon in, check the battery connections and everything. It looks okay but is not working. Just my bloody luck – my Mayday was received, the plane is there but he has no beacon to home in on. Visibility is not good and I doubt that he will see me from the air.

I take stock again. Without the beacon they will have difficulty in finding me and it will take a lot longer. I am going to have to last without the food and clothing, but I will stay attached to the tri for as long as is possible, to aid identification. *L.D.* is now lower in the water.

Later the visibility improves – I have no idea of the time but it is still light. The tri is very much lower in the water and the main hull is trying to roll over. I cannot risk staying attached any longer so I cast off and gradually drift away from it with the wind. I have never seen such a sorry looking mess, and yet to me it was a beautiful-looking craft. I gradually lose sight of it in the swell and I am pleased when I can no longer see it.

The weather has eased, as is always the way. The swell is still large and I cannot see much chance of being spotted, particularly from the surface, but I hope and get ready to spend a cold wet night in the raft. Funny thing, I haven't noticed the lack of food and water yet. I shut up the raft and try to sleep to conserve energy. I hear aircraft and look outside. There are two Search and Resuce planes flying in circles not far from me. They are about 50 feet off the water and obviously conducting a visual search. I am elated. Their circles are coming closer to me all the time. As they reach me they pass over several times and show no signs of having spotted me. I can't let the chance go. I get three red flares ready and wait until one of the aircraft is flying straight at me. I light all three flares at once and stand up and wave at them. Nothing and then YES – something is dropped from the plane. It hits the water and goes off; a smoke marker. He has got me. I suddenly feel on top of the world. The plane approaches again, very low this time. I wave and can see the pilot wave back. It is a Canadian plane and I notice that the other is American. More smoke markers around me and I begin to feel secure and relieved. Even if I don't get picked up for a couple of days it doesn't matter. I can wait.

The American plane begins a long run in and makes a drop. As the items hit the water two dinghies inflate about 600 feet apart and joined by a floating line. I am going downwind towards the centre of the rope. A great drop by the pilot. Packs are floating attached to the dinghies. They are obviously survival packs and I presume it means that there are no ships immediately to hand and I am in for a wait.

I decide to help things along and paddle my way towards the rope. I eventually reach it and pull myself along and secure my dinghy to one at the end of the line. I pull in the survival pack containing space blankets, water and sweets and begin to get myself sorted out for a stay. The plane still circles around replacing the smoke markers, and it is comforting to have him there.

Later I look up and see a ship approaching. This is great. I am not even going to have to spend a night in the dinghy. I can hardly believe my luck. As it comes closer I see that it is a container ship well loaded. It slows up and then comes forward until the bow protruder picks up the rope between the two dinghies only feet away from me. Lovely positioning. This brings my dinghy alongside the starboard side of the ship. It isn't rough but in the liferaft I am moving up and down quite a bit. The scramble nets are in position near the stern and ropes along the side. I learnt later from the Captain that the ship's boats were crewed ready for use if needed. I catch hold of one of the ropes and begin to pull myself along the ship's side. The gangway is being lowered ahead of me and that looks like a very civilised way of going aboard. Someone is at the bottom of the gangway ready to help. I approach slowly because of the up and down movement. There are lots of people to help. The liferaft comes up, one step and I am on the gangway. The man at the bottom catches hold and pushes me past him, and in seconds I am on deck and it's all over.'

—————— ,, ——————

From: *Royal Naval Sailing Association Journal*, Autumn 1980

21: **Disaster in the Mouth of the Elbe**

Yacht: *Pentina II* (33ft Bermudian cutter)
Skipper: Robin Gardiner-Hall
Crew: None
Bound from the Island of Borkum to Cuxhaven
Time and date of loss: 0600, July 4th, 1979
Position: half a mile S of Scharnhorn Beacon

Robin Gardiner-Hall was sailing single-handed from Hellevoetsluis to the Baltic. His yacht, *Pentina II*, was a 33ft Kings Amethyst with Bermudian cutter rig. She was slightly under-powered by a reliable single-cylinder diesel engine capable of giving her 4½ knots – but only in calm conditions. Having left Hellevoetsluis on June 27th, they were in Borkum, by way of Amsterdam (Sixhaven), Harlingen and Dokkum, by July 2nd.

Local advice persuaded Gardiner-Hall to go direct from Borkum to Cuxhaven, although he now thinks he should have gone to Helgoland and not left there until conditions were really suitable.

After leaving Borkum on 3rd July, they followed the coastal buoyage up to the Accumer Ee, whence a course was set for the Elbe No. 1 light-vessel, which was seen at dusk. Soon after midnight on 4th July, they were in the well-buoyed channel of the Elbe and the wind was fair, force 4–5 from the NW. Big ship traffic was busy, and to keep clear of it a course was maintained close to the line of starboard-hand buoys. As the channel turned more southerly, *Pentina II* came on a dead run and her skipper decided to hand the main and then proceed slowly under jib alone, since he preferred to reach Cuxhaven after dawn:

———————— " ————————

'I therefore rounded up to port to hand the main. However, the main was stuck – presumably because a screw had worked loose in the track, although I shall never know for sure. I could only lower the main about

140

141

two-thirds of the way, and we were effectively hove-to on the starboard tack and slowly fore-reaching southwards. Realising this I gybed, made some offing from the side of the channel and rounded up to try again. I did not go as far as I should have done, because a nearby merchant ship was approaching. This time I made an error of judgement and struggled unsuccessfully with the stuck main too long. The result was that we drifted too far out of the channel and suddenly heeled over to an extreme angle, running well and truly aground on the edge of the Scharhörn Riff. Our position was about 53° 59′ N 08° 23′ E; this can be clearly seen on German chart no. 44, which shows just how steep the bank is very close to the buoyed channel. The area is marked *zahlreiche Wrackreste* and I regret that I have made the wrecks even more numerous.

I immediately laid out my 35lb C.Q.R. anchor and twenty fathoms of chain and handed the jib. I was still unable to lower the main completely, but lashed it to produce minimum windage. I confess that I was not very worried: there were still five hours of tide to rise, the anchor was holding and I thought that I could wait for the tide to lift her off and then recover the anchor under engine. About an hour later the tide had risen enough to keep *Pentina II* afloat most of the time, but she was bumping and a heavy surge had built up over the bank. The engine was running full ahead and the chain was snatching violently. Suddenly I heard a loud bang and found that the chain had sheared the port samson post off at deck level. With some difficulty I resecured the chain to the starboard samson post, having veered more chain to give a better catenary. Half an hour later we were again in heavy surf and pounding badly when the second samson post sheared in the same way as the first. The chain ran out and was lost; it parted the bitter-end lashing in the chain locker and the whipping end cut the lower starboard lifeline.

The situation was now serious: we were losing ground on to the bank, the engine was not really helping much – although I kept it running all the time – and the pounding was very bad indeed. As always on such occasions the wind was increasing, or at least seemed to be (I doubt that it was ever really more than Force 6), and we were, of course, on a lee shore. Clearly the time had come to sink one's pride and let off distress flares.

Despite the heavy traffic in the estuary it was about an hour before I made contact with a ship; by that time I was down to mini-flares and flashing with a torch. I cannot really say that mini-flares are better than rockets and hand-held flares, but they produced results. My flashed S.O.S. was finally acknowledged. Many ships had passed, and I think the problem was that in a busy channel like this they are far too busy looking for their marks and at other ships – to say nothing of the radar – to notice what is happening abeam, well out of the channel.

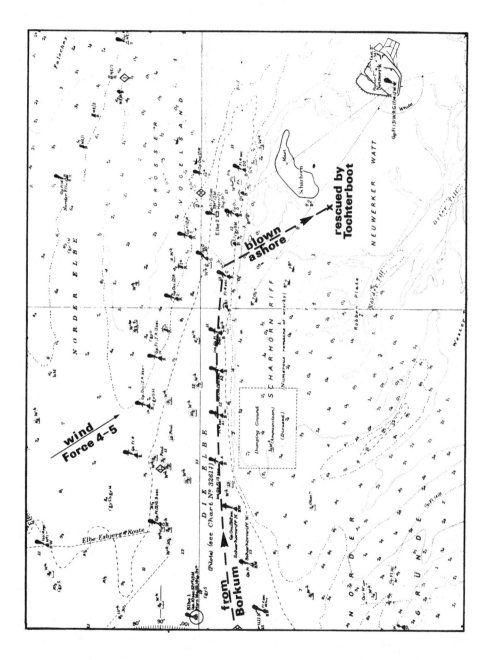

I now knew that rescue would be only a matter of time, but the incessant pounding made things very difficult. Fortunately I had two very thick kapok cockpit cushions, and most of the time managed to keep one of these underneath me; I think that this probably saved me from serious injury. I did, however, suffer two cracked ribs, and sitting down was uncomfortable for some weeks afterwards; in addition, below the waist, my body was more black and blue than white. I was also soaked through but not really cold – there was always plenty to do. At one point I went below to make up an emergency bag containing ship's papers, passport, wallet, chequebook and so forth, but I was worried about doing this as several stainless steel bottle-screws had parted, the mast – which was stepped on deck – was rocking through quite an angle, and I was afraid that it might fall on the dog house and trap me below. The cabin was a sad sight with oily bilge water everywhere.

As dawn broke it was possible to see how far we had been carried down on to the shelf. We were now about half a mile south of Scharhörn Beacon (approximately 53° 58′ N 08° 24′ E) but at high water still about a mile from the Island of Scharhörn. At about 0600 there was the welcome sight of an approaching lifeboat, but it could not get within half a mile; they launched their *Tochterboot*, a shallow draft skimmer carried on the afterdeck, which appears to have a powerful engine and carries a crew of two. Shallow water prevented it from sailing round on to my lee side. Handled with great skill, it made one or two trial runs with a bows-on approach, during which I handed over my emergency bag. They shouted to me to climb out over the lifelines – not an easy task as we were heeled over and still pounding. The *Tochterboot* has a steel post forward, against which the crew member braces himself with both arms free and outstretched. On the next run I was able to jump for it and was caught in his arms. While the boat backed off, he opened a forehatch and I was bundled below; it was rather claustrophobic with no head-room, but at least there was a bunk to lie on.'

———————— ,, ————————

From the lifeboat captain Robin Gardiner-Hall learned that flares should always be let off in pairs, at an interval of about ten seconds. Otherwise someone sees what might or might not be a distress signal, watches for a bit, and if he does not see another flare tends to assume that it was only his imagination.

The temporary lifeboat doctor, Reinhard Kohfahl, took care of the shipwrecked skipper and the members of the Cuxhaven Yacht Club helped him to find a replacement yacht – the *Lorbas*, in which he continued his cruise on July 20th.

From: *Roving Commissions* (Centenary Edition, 1979), published by the
Royal Cruising Club

22: The death of *Banba*

Yacht: *Banba IV* (38ft gaff-rigged cutter)
Skipper: Malcolm Robson
Crew: Merrill Robson
        Tex, Hank and John
Bound from Cape May, U.S.A., to Sark, Channel Islands
Time and date of loss: approx. 1700, July 6th, 1969
Position: approx. 1200 miles E of New York

This laconic account by Malcolm Robson, and the one that follows by his wife Merrill, tell how they lost first *Banba IV* and then the *Maid of Malham*.

Banba IV was a 20 ton cutter designed by Fred Shepherd and built by the Whitstable Shipping Company in 1911. Malcolm Robson and his wife Merrill had left Annapolis, Maryland, towards the end of June, after giving *Banba* a very thorough refit, including 'New rigging, all running gear replaced, sheets turned end-for-end, new bowsprit rigging, new parts for the vane steering, scrubbed and painted and sails strengthened. Fuelled up to the eyebrows, watered and victualled for five men for eight weeks, for the non-stop voyage to Guernsey, about 3500 miles.'

——————— " ———————

'At midday our new crew arrived, three husky American yachting types between 17 and 24, and an hour later off we went, through the Chesapeake and Delaware canal to Cape May, our jumping-off point.

Armed with a five-day forecast of Atlantic weather from the U.S. navy, it was unfair of the gods to send us east winds for three days. What could we do except battle on, southward? Runs of 20, 70, 50 miles a day weren't going to take us home at record speed! The next day it blew. Not the ocean winds we had had on the southern route westward, but good old North Sea wet-

145

'n-windy force 7+ and ten-foot swells into the bargain. Then it stopped. Yes, dead calm and poor old *Banba* stumbled down holes in the ocean, crashed into solid walls and skidded into mountains. And all with sails lowered and the engine using precious fuel just to keep her head to the seas. When eventually the winds came they were force 1, but from the north. On for an hour, force 8 from the west, then another day of dead calm. This continued for five days and we gloomily watched our fuel dwindling until in the end we stopped the motor and drifted.

It was about here that we knew that the bread was mouldy, so every loaf was unwrapped and dried in the fitful sun. Not serious though, as we had plenty of nosh aboard and water for 75 days. About here, too, the port forebrace parted with chafe and the yard fell on deck. Again not serious as later that day we put her on a reach and were able to send a man up the mast for repairs.

So far, so good; and the crew were in good heart. By July 5th we had nearly 900 miles on the log and only a quarter of the fuel used. "Pity about the fuel," I thought, as after the 23rd sail change the squaresail tore from yardarm to yardarm! Heigh, ho, we have plenty of spare canvas aboard, though stitching would be impossible until the weather moderated a bit. It was reefed, too!

It was that evening that we first noticed that something not altogether right was happening to the mast. We could hardly set up the starboard runner lever, the backstay was too tight. Too tight? Now I know *Banba* would much prefer a docile cruise around Brittany than these antics in mid-Atlantic, but I thought of her wrought iron framing straps, the 4 in by 5 in frames, the oak planking and more. Besides, she wasn't making any water, except through the decks above our bunks, so I puffed away the cloud no bigger than a man's hand. But when, the following day, the mast must have been a foot out and it took two men to flip the runner lever over, I thought again (strumming a top *E* from the backstay) and decided that either the mast step had moved or the tongue at the foot had broken off. *Banba*'s mast, of solid pine, is 52 ft long, and weighs half a ton and is held up with massive ⅝ in shrouds, forestay and topmast shrouds, but the thought of this stick waving about in a force 9 breeze was a cloud a bit bigger than a man's hand.

So we hove to under tiny staysail immediately and considered the situation. Newfoundland? 450 miles and against the prevailing winds, and on the starboard tack, dangerous for us. Azores? Some 1100 miles away and very far south of the sailing ship recommended track, and against the prevailing wind for the last part. Bermuda? 700 miles upwind. Total fuel about 90 hours in calm, say 270 miles at half speed. Total Trinidad rum about three cases: say your prayers, lads, and away with prohibition!

The Death of *Banba*

We had seen several ships along this Atlantic highway, though by now we were a little to the south of the main steamship tracks, and I had a small secret thought that . . . well. But what a decision! To carry on. IF the wind didn't exceed, say, force 7? We read the U.S. pilot chart for this July and it showed us 1.5 gales above force 8. IF the swell-after-gale wasn't as bad as we had already had? IF we could hoist sail properly . . . so many ifs. Or to abandon *Banba*. With the round trip almost complete? With our home for a year to go to the bottom? 600 charts, instruments, clothes, tools, nautical books, everything? What about this funking lark, too?

All day I turned over the problem, sitting mostly in the cockpit being rained upon, until about teatime I spied a large freighter a mile away to windward in the grey murk. The problem solved itself. I called the crew aft, read them chapter 23 of Hornblower, put on life-jackets and sent up a red flare. "Passports and money only," I said, starting the engine. For nobody would have a second chance once near the freighter, it would be "Jump" and then would come the crashing of rigging, splintering of planks, etc.

With the exception that my trousers fell down at the critical moment, all went well: the ship made a lee and I brought *Banba* alongside the scrambling nets. The yacht alternately smashed into the vertical walls or rose and fell crazily ten feet or so. But we all made the deck and willing hands rolled us over her rails! I staggered to my feet and counted the heads, five, and looked back to see *Banba* rolling her decks under 50 yards away. Her engine was still running in astern gear and within a few minutes she was lost in the driving rain.'

———————— ,, ————————

From: *Ocean Cruising Club Journal*, 1970

23: What Went Wrong?

Yacht: *Maid of Malham* (48ft Bermudian sloop)
Skipper: Malcolm Robson
Crew: Merrill Robson
Bound from Galapagos Islands to Marquesas Islands
Time and date of loss: 1973
Position: 7° 48' S, 110° 57' W (About halfway between Panama and Tahiti)

Maid of Malham was designed by Laurent Giles as an ocean racer for John Illingworth and was built by King and Sons at Burnham on Crouch in 1936. She was very different from *Banba IV*, but her fate was the same.

———————— " ————————

'Let me give you the facts. Some half-way between Panama and Tahiti *Maid of Malham*'s rudder came adrift at the foot, and, though we could steer, the Pacific came in through the trunk, with only Merrill and me to pump it back again every hour or two. We bore away under a small jib only in the rumbustious SE Trades for two days, and discussed survival with more than just academic interest. Our landfall in the Marquesas was 20 days away; the Galapagos Islands were 1,000 miles back, upwind, upswell, upcurrent; the Pacific Routings showed shipping to be as good as non-existing. Thinking about the inflatable life-raft made morale, if possible, lower. At this point – over to Merrill.'

'I was baking bread. Malcolm was working out his morning sight. Finished, he went on deck, gave a roar: "a ship". I thought he was joking, there never was a ship. Then I looked at his face, near tears of relief. Hurrying below. "The flares." "I've been dreaming about this, the million to one chance." Bang. Bang. Two red Verey lights soar up. "Are they slowing down?" "Can't tell." "What nationality?" "Port something . . .

London." "Yes, they're turning. Thank God." "Down with the jib, ready with the sheet?" The engine starts but oh dear . . . "Don't forget the wheel's disconnected." "It's the tiller – you work the controls."

"Get some stuff together, there may not be much time. Where's that sail bag?" "In the booze locker stopping the rattle." Now then. Passports, ship's papers, money in that box. Into the bag with it. Oh, there's that photo. Tear it off the bulkhead – the lovely ones of the children. Now the small clothes locker. Thank goodness I had put shore things in a plastic bag for dryness. "Malcolm, put some shoes on. Have you got your specs?" "I'll bring life-jackets." In the flag locker. Put mine on then help Malcolm with his. Nearly alongside. Lovely big ship, grey and red. Rails lined with people. They've thrown down a warp. Round the anchor winch and make fast. What's that fellow with the walkie-talkie saying?

Near enough now. Malcolm bawling: "We're making water. Can you take us two on board?" Talk. Shout. Crash against ship. "What's your weight?" "15 tons." "We have crane to lift 25 tons." "Malcolm, he says they might lift us on board." "Our draught is 8 feet and the mast 65 feet. It's going to be a job, but we'll help." Down snakes a pilot ladder. "Can you let down a line for this bag?" Catch it now. No panic, it's over. Tie it firmly, proper hitch. Over the side, no matter if it trails in the water. "Up the ladder, Merrill." Slow now. Wait until the *Maid* is at her highest point. Then up, no hesitating. Nearly there. My leg hurts, must have scraped it. The top. Willing hands, jump down on solid ground. Steel. Malcolm next. "Come this way to the Captain." Walk. People. Grim faces. Cameras. "Welcome on board, on board, on board." "Lord, how we feel for you." "Are you all right?" Four long flights to the bridge. Out of breath. Shake hands. Malcolm talking . . . four, five officers. Captain and Chief Engineer having second thoughts of lifting operation. Crew might get bashed about. Must take out mast first. Operation scrubbed. Malcolm going down ladder for more salvage. Sack on heaving line. Water sloshing in cabin. There he is in cockpit, jolly good, sextant, chronometer. Wonder if he has remembered second sextant we bought from Canal pilot? What's he holding? Hand bearing compass. Come up. Don't wait too long, they're casting off the *Maid*. Long warp trailing astern, that's bad, could get in ship's propeller. Our *Maid* won't leave, she hugs the ship. That crosstree is going to spike a porthole in a minute. Lord, how it's scraping. What a noise, scattering paint. Now both spreaders broken, poor *Maid*, what an awful end. Doesn't she look long and slim from so high up, never seen her from here before. There's the jibstay gone, still she won't leave the ship. Seems to be sucked in close, though the ship is going slowly ahead. Right under the stern, can't bear to look at her.

"No, we don't carry a transmitter, what's the point? The range is so small when you are on the oceans." "Our guardian angels certainly were hovering when this ship chose to be in the same spot of water at the same time." I can't see our boat any more; oh yes I can. There she is rocking about, getting smaller. She's low in the water. Poor, lovely, *Maid of Malham*.'

―――――――― „ ――――――――

From: *The Cruising Association Bulletin*, June 1973

24: The Tri that Broke Up

Yacht: *Triventure* (29ft Islander trimaran)
Skipper: John Nicholls
Crew: Malcolm Beilby
Bound from Aldabra Is., Indian Ocean to Lourenço Marques, Mozambique
Time and date of loss: 0900, November 11th, 1979
Position: Mozambique Channel, Indian Ocean

Under different titles in several magazines, John Nicholls has described the loss of his 50 ft ketch *Heart of Edna* on a New Guinea reef in 1979, but it was his friend and crew member, Malcolm Beilby, who, ten years earlier, had told the story of Nicholls' previous loss of the trimaran *Triventure*.

Nicholls built *Triventure* in a backyard in Sydney in the early sixties, and for a year after launching her he sailed around Sydney harbour and the nearby coasts. In 1968 he planned to sail the trimaran back to his native England.

The first leg, 'with three friends on board, was a leisurely voyage up the resort-studded Queensland coast and across the Coral Sea to Port Moresby', where Nicholls met Beilby, who agreed to join *Triventure* as crew as far as Durban.

From Port Moresby the voyage continued via Timor, the Christmas and Cocos Islands, the Seychelles, Aldabra Island and then south into the Mozambique Channel, where their troubles really started:

———————— " ————————

'The opening act of *Triventure*'s tragedy began on John's 29th birthday, Friday, 31 October. We'd hand-steered through a quiet night and in the morning a southerly breeze began to pick up. We set Angus up and went below to sleep.

151

Just before midday *Triventure*'s motion and the wind noise awoke us to freshening conditions with black clouds and rain ahead.

By 1400 hrs the wind working against the current had whipped up a nasty, steep sea and were were slogging into it under reefed main and working jib.

At 2000 John had just relieved me on watch when we heard a loud, sharp crack. A torch search failed to reveal anything wrong in the main hull or the wing decks, and we tried to convince ourselves that it must have been caused by some small floating object that had been thrown against the hull. But ominous creakings became apparent and persistent and John took a torch into the port float to investigate.

Watching from the cockpit it seemed an eternity before he emerged and when he did his words dropped the bottom from my stomach.

"Get the sails off her!" he shouted. "The float's coming off!"

Together we had the canvas down in seconds and *Triventure* lay beam on to the seas and rode them like a raft while John, with characteristic calm, prepared a cup of tea.

The plywood main spar in the forward edge of the wing deck, he explained, had broken inside the float where it butted against one of the major bulkheads. The bulkhead also was broken, and water resistance against the fin was flexing the float outwards away from the main hull. With the sails off the stress would be minimised and he proposed G-clamping the broken frames to hold them overnight until repairs could be made in daylight.

We fished four clamps from the tool box and John took them into the float, while I packed a haversack with tinned fruit and prepared some water bottles in case we had to take to the raft.

John was amused by my dire interpretation of the situation and assured me that leaving the boat was the last thing in his mind. Then he climbed into his bunk and went to sleep. Lucky him. I lay awake for hours listening to the creaking of the fractured plywood.

In the morning the wind had dropped a little, but the sea was still steep. Sea sickness repeatedly forced John from the cramped confines of the float, but he bolted strutting either side of the broken spar and bulkhead and we set about getting *Triventure* under way again. The outer shrouds, from the float gunwales to the masthead, were disconcertingly slack, a sign that the mainspar was no longer straight, but there was nothing we could do but take them up and hope for the best.

Under sail the severity of the damage was more obvious. With the port float to windward we could see the gunwale rising and falling as the float flexed in and out on the edge of the wing deck.

The first night after the break was spent hove to under reefed main, but the next day, Sunday, the weather eased and on Monday we were becalmed again. We awoke after an afternoon sleep to find half a dozen large dorado and twice that number of sharks circling the boat. The dorado refused to take a hook and John spent a futile half hour hanging over the side trying to shoot one with his speargun. When an evening breeze got the boat moving again the sharks lost interest, but the dorado stayed with us and through the night they cut phosphorescent streams through the dark water as they paced *Triventure* towards the African coast.

We decided to abandon plans of making Lourenço Marques and to head instead for Inhambane, a Portuguese port several hundred miles north and correspondingly closer to us. Inhambane is situated 8 miles up a wide tidal estuary, which we reached late on Tuesday afternoon and anchored about 6 miles from the town. Not knowing what to expect, we sat on deck that night and speculated on the significance of the distant lights, and John, an unseamanly teetotaller, dreamt of Coca-Cola. In the morning we battled up to the town against a very strong tide and anchored about midday off a long wharf.

Remembering our difficulties in Portuguese Timor, we were surprised by the affability of the Inhambane harbour authorities who quickly cleared us to go ashore. The harbour master himself drove us to a timber yard and advised us where to get supplies.

Inhambane was quite a surprise. We expected a dusty, one-horse, one-street town and found instead an extensive, substantial town with lawns, trees and sidewalk cafes along the main thoroughfare. My chief recollection, however, is of alarmingly high prices. In the five days we were there we spent more than $US60 on a minimum of timber, glue and a modest amount of supplies.

Through the days John laboured in the oven-like confines of the damaged float, reinforcing the broken bulkhead and mainspar and securing the inside planking of the float hull back to the stringers and frames from which it had pulled away.

I attended to minor jobs about the boat and got the stores and water aboard. In the evenings we'd go ashore and join the citizens at the cafes or stroll along the front. In this fashion the days slipped quickly by and though we did not realise it, the good weather was passing with them.

On Monday morning, 10 November, we went ashore early to clear our papers and get a weather report before sailing but the harbour master, who had agreed to translate the previous night's forecast for us, was not in his office. His deputy handled the paper work but when the harbour master had not returned more than an hour later we decided to snatch what was left of the ebb tide and take a chance on the weather. As it was the tide turned before we were halfway down the estuary and as *Triventure* battled against it, it became sickeningly apparent that the float was still flexing badly.

We reached the open sea in the late afternoon and John entered the float but could see nothing working there. Evidently the main spar break had been the primary trouble but fixing it had done nothing for the weakness that had developed inside the wing deck itself between the float and the main hull. John accepted the fact with fatalistic resignation and decided to press on for Durban 400 miles south. But his plans, shaken by the first troubles, had now come crashing down around him. Ahead had been another year of cruising and the hope that successful completion of his voyage might help him win sponsorship for an attempt in the singlehanded transatlantic race. In Inhambane he thought his repairs had removed the threat to his boat and future but now he was faced with the certainty that *Triventure* could not be taken past Durban.

Meals at sea are usually looked forward to as highlights of the day but tea that night was a bleak affair.

Overnight our luck finally ran out. The wind picked up steadily from the south and the reaction on the current quickly resulted in a steep sea. By dawn we were hove to in a 40-knot gale and it was worsening.

At 0700 hrs the rending sound of tearing wood told us the end had come. We scrambled from our bunks and into the cockpit to see the port float, fortunately to windward, swinging up and down through almost 60 degrees as though on a huge hinge along the edge of the wing deck.

John put up the jib, and I eased her away in an attempt to run west for the coast which we knew could not be far away; but it was immediately apparent as we gathered forward speed that the float was tearing off even more quickly.

In no time the arching stanchions crushed and flung the fibre glass dinghy overboard from its chocks on the wing deck, and as we put *Triventure* back on to the wind the float came away completely. While I held the boat into the wind John cut the guardrail wires between the cockpit pushpit and the float stanchions. But he could make no impression on the port outer shroud, the only thing now keeping the float beside us. Tethered by that, the float plunged wildly up and down, smashing into the remains of the wing deck, and we feared it would push a stanchion through the main hull.

Luckily the chain plate pulled out first, and the float swirled away astern as I put the helm over to head for the coast again. Now all the strain was on the port inner shrouds, and as John ran forward to attend to the jib they gave way. The mast and sails came down on him and he disappeared beneath them.

One moment *Triventure* had been gathering speed and the next she was lifeless and wallowing with her spars and canvas half overboard.

For an instant I thought my companion was overboard too. I think I stood frozen until he freed himself from under the mainsail. Most other things of that morning I can remember with crystal clarity but actually seeing him emerge from the tangle on deck I cannot. Certainly he was on his feet before I had moved from the cockpit.

Amazingly, he was unhurt. The mast had actually hit his back, throwing him to the deck, but the starboard stanchions and guardrails had checked its fall and prevented it from pinning and crushing him.

Now things were right out of our hands. Together we attempted to drag the mast back on board, calculating that its weight lashed down on the starboard float top would hold the float down and prevent the boat from flipping over to port on the backs of the waves. But in the pitching seas the mast's weight was too much for us. We could not get it fully on board, and instead lashed it as best as possible diagonally over the cabin top with the end hanging over the starboard side.

Below, the cabin was a shambles and every violent lurch made it worse. The wind was already easing and few of the waves were now breaking, but every so often a white top would slam into the port beam and push *Triventure* violently to starboard. Then she would lurch alarmingly to port as the crest passed beneath.

John was thinking as clearly as ever though when he suggested breakfast and, on the understanding that he wouldn't be too demanding, I put the kettle on and buttered some bread. I was passing him his second slice when he looked around the crushed weathershield and spotted *Slavisa Vajner* looming past not 400 yards away.

Breakfast was forgotten as we waved from the cockpit but it seemed the tanker had not seen us as she steamed majestically past. The first flare was blown into the water, the second was a dud and John was preparing the third when we saw the ship turning slowly to starboard. Back she came, this time so far upwind that only her superstructure was visible. As she went by two smaller ships came into sight and away to the west the coast was visible.

John considered taking a gamble on being washed ashore, but we decided against it when we found the radio, with its aerial down, could not contact the tanker which was obviously making rescue preparations. The 70,000 ton ship was manoeuvring to be directly upwind of us when she lost forward motion. The 40 minutes that preceded our pickup was necessary to switch the single big diesel engine from the crude oil used at sea to the fuel oil used in manoeuvring.

A couple of hundred yards away two rope ladders dropped down her towering side, and as we bumped alongside down came throwing lines and a hawser. John made it fast, then followed me up the ladder clutching his typewriter and precious *Times Atlas* under one arm. Then, barefooted on the slowly rolling steel deck, we found ourselves skating helplessly to either side as we attempted to follow a crewman to the bridge where Captain Uros Lombardic was waiting. In good English he offered to hoist *Triventure* on to his deck but explained 15 minutes would be needed before auxiliary steam could be raised to power the winches. John, considering the risk to crewmen, decided against it. Instead he asked for time to go back aboard and get off what he could. Capt. Lombardic agreed, and we returned to the rail where John donned a safety harness and went down the ladder.

I took pictures from the rail, then followed him down. He was at work in the cabin when I reached the deck and noticed the float bow cracking under the pounding against the steel plates alongside.

"Hurry it up! She's breaking up!" I yelled in alarm, and panicked us both. We grabbed the bare essentials, bagged and sent them up on the heaving lines, and cast *Triventure* off.

Then, as the tanker slowly gathered way, we paced *Triventure* along its deck and she fell astern looking like a crippled seabird exhausted and helpless on the water.

"I can always build another," said John as we stood at the rail watching and filming until his yacht was lost to sight among the swells.'

———————— " ————————

From: *Yachting Monthly*, July 1970

PART IV: FAILURE OF
GROUND TACKLE OR MOORING LINES

25: A Gallant Dutchman

Yacht: *Maaslust* (45ft yawl-rigged boeier)
Skipper: John P. Wells
Crew: Margaret Wells
      Frank Philips
      Freda Philips
Children on board: Peter Wells (22 months)
                  Nichola Philips (12 years)
Bound from Deauville, Normandy to Langstone Harbour, Hampshire
Time and date of loss: abandoned 1300, July 29th, 1956
Position: off Selsey Bill

This account of the loss of *Maaslust*, one of the Dunkirk 'Little Ships', is by Margaret Wells, whose 22-month-old son Peter was on board at the time.

Maaslust, a boeier, was built of steel in Holland in 1923. Having left her mooring in Langstone Harbour on July 20th, 1956, she made an uneventful night passage to Cherbourg. Visits to St Vaast, Isigny and Ouistreham followed, and by the end of the week she was in Deauville:

———————— " ————————

'It is very difficult for me to write of preceding events when my mind's eye can see nothing but the picture of a gallant Dutchman, *Maaslust*, abandoned to fight a losing battle against fantastic seas; but this is to be an account of the happiness she gave us during her last weeks and a requiem for her brave spirit.

Neither John nor I had been very keen on the idea of Deauville and Trouville, knowing that all "the best people" go there and feeling that it would not be our "cup of tea" at all. However, we were favourably impressed and unhappily allowed ourselves to be talked out of our plan to make Fécamp on Saturday and to return to Shoreham on Sunday. Had we not succumbed to the fleshpots, how different would be the ending of this story! However, it must be admitted that we thoroughly enjoyed ourselves, meeting by chance old friends from Le Havre and being hospitably entertained by them and by the Monks. We visited the casino, where we gained entrance to the Inner Room without even our passports! We basked and bathed to the music of the negro orchestra at the swimming pool, we shopped in the market and bought presents in the sloping streets. On the first evening I had surpassed myself by producing a dish of *moules* which were voted nearly as good as those in Cherbourg.

Having been lured to remain in Deauville, neither John nor I was anxious to move, and so we did not entirely regret the falling barometer, suspecting that our departure would be delayed by weather conditions. However, by Friday the glass had steadied, the thundery atmosphere had passed and we decided that subject to a satisfactory weather report, we would set sail for England on Saturday afternoon. On Friday evening John radioed Niton, requesting a report from Dunstable for 11.00 hrs next day, together with a long-range forecast for the Channel area. The message came through at 09.00 hrs: southerly wind, force 1-2 veering westerly, and increasing to 4-6 on Sunday evening. This obviously gave us no excuse to tarry, and Saturday morning was spent on a provisioning orgy in the market.

We had arranged to refuel at 14.00 hrs, and were more than annoyed to find the fuelling wharf abandoned and no one at all interested in telling us where to find the mechanic in charge. It was here that a factor arose that was for us to have fateful consequences. The skipper believed in having ample reserves of fuel at all times, and this rule will never again be relaxed. But time was passing and, having waited for the attendant for over an hour, there was no immediate prospect of receiving our expected replenishment. We had on board fuel for four to six hours' running in case the wind failed. So, impatient to be on our way, we cast off from the wharf and made sail. But had it not been for intransigence at the fuel depot we should, no doubt, have brought the ship safely to port at the end of our journey.

We eventually left Deauville–Trouville at 15.00 hrs on July 28th, immediately meeting a lumpy sea. The weather was fine and the wind free, but the sea, meeting *Maaslust*'s plum bows, knocked her way off. John had to be talked out of a farewell visit to Le Havre. We blamed our late visit to the casino the previous night for our unwonted lack of enthusiasm for the homeward journey, and turned our eyes resolutely from the coast of France – more's the pity.

Being a great believer in the nourishment of the inner man, I made a gargantuan stew on the way out and Freda was the only one who did not partake to capacity. She, perhaps wisely, preferred Dramamine. I took the

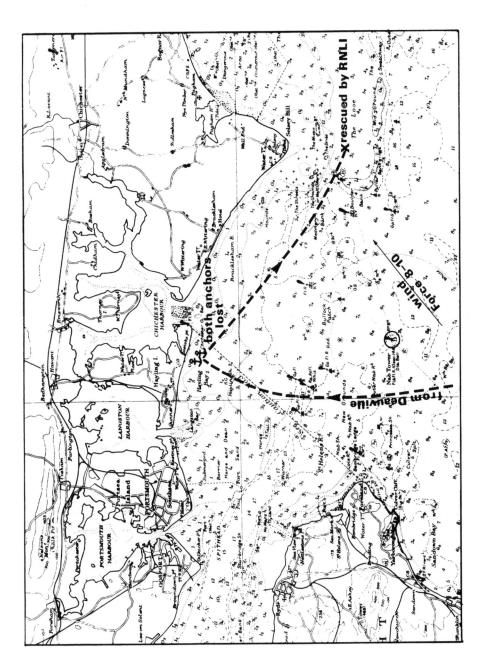

first watch from 21.00 to 23.00 hrs and did not enjoy it. It rained, and the seas made the old girl extremely heavy on the wheel – one moment's lapse of concentration and she would do her best to gybe. The breeze was not excessive, however, and there was nothing to indicate that we should turn back. We had a little trouble with the diesel's water pump, and the man off watch had to keep an eye on the gauge in case the filter clogged again – we motor-sailed to help her through the waves. At 01.00 hrs on Sunday, July 29th, we took the staysail off her because it was doing no good and at 04.00 hrs the first reef was taken in. From then on conditions deteriorated rapidly. The increasing SW gale brought squall after squall and the seas rose higher. We had long abandoned the idea of making Shoreham, since the entrance is a nasty one in any weather, so we headed for the lee of Bembridge Ledge. It was soon necessary to take in the second reef, and she still made seven knots, with seas 12–14 ft high to surmount. We watched the two 12-ft dinghies with anxiety as comber after comber crashed down upon them, but their gripings held them firmly against the davits. Twice seas filled the mainsail and *Maaslust* lay right over, but up she came again like the gallant fighter she was. The scene below decks was indescribable – the stove jumped its gimballs, the cutlery broke out of its locker, crashing to the ground with devastating noise; the saloon table lifted itself bodily, abandoned its weights and came to rest, none too gently, upon my recumbent form; the combined radio and television set took charge; in fact everything that was not screwed or bolted down became a potential menace. Small Peter slept peacefully enough until the vessel first lay over, when he became a little frightened and, once awake, very seasick. He needed a prolonged cuddle to calm him but eventually resigned himself to the double-cabin berth with Freda and Nicky, where the three of them shared their misery with mute stoicism. Poor Freda, who feels sick at the suggestion of a ripple on the water, was heroic, for when the whole mattress rose up and landed half on the floor she wedged herself against the bulkhead to hold the children in. It was indeed hellish down there, but, even so, those below had little idea of the seriousness of the situation with which we were faced.

After settling Peter and stowing and wedging all that I could in the saloon, and having parted company with the stew, I went up into the wheel-house to survey the scene. One has read of the icy hand which grips one's vitals in moments of dread, but although I have had several hazardous occasions at sea I had never felt it before. The sight of the waves, 30 ft from base to crest, green-grey and streaked with spume and sand, was for the first moment truly petrifying. Later there was no room for fear, although one accepted the fact that survival was unlikely. I remember a feeling of thankfulness that the three of us would be going together, regret that Peter

162

had seen so little of life, sorrow for our parents, and regret about our dogs and our lovely home, but no fear of the end. Perhaps our sensibilities were numbed by the physical battle in which we were involved, for, discussing it later, we found that we had all reacted the same way.

By 09.00 hrs it was evident that our hopes of finding a lee under the Isle of Wight were groundless; in fact we were now in a far worse situation, for the seas were steeper and closer together. Before we reached the forts the tide turned to the eastward against us and, despite all that Frank could do at the wheel, we had soon driven past the Nab towards the lee shore of Hayling. It was impossible to keep the vessel head to the seas, for they came so rapidly that she could only take every third one, the others breaking over her with 6 ft of solid water upon the decks. She could not free herself of the weight of the first before the second was upon her, and the side decks were perpetually awash, but still she rose. The backlash of the wheel was so great that Frank refractured an old wrist injury (we knew nothing of this until later) and it was physically impossible to stand on deck against either the wind or the sea. I doubt that the three of us would have survived had it not been for the high bulwarks and stout handrail, for in such weather lifelines were quite ineffective. Near the Nab the parrels of the double-reefed mainsail began to go, and a rent started in the leach, so we decided to take it off her. To do so I had to let go the lee signal halyards against which the gaff had fouled, and they blew out of my hand to stream away like wire at 60 degrees from the mast. Shortly after this the mizzen blew out – the heavy canvas tearing down a cloth like calico. We now depended for our lives upon the gallant Porbeagle with its limited fuel supply.

When we were a few hundred yards off Hayling shore we let go both our anchors, one a 2-cwt C.Q.R., the other a 2-cwt fisherman. As the fisherman bit in, the chain vibrated so violently that the whole forepart of the ship trembled and in a few minutes the claw stopper jerked off and the whole chain went over the side, leaving the C.Q.R. to take the strain alone, until its chain also parted under water with a crack like a whiplash. At this moment I yelled to John to hold on as an enormous comber came crashing down on us on the foredeck; I was to leeward and clung to the binnacle bolted through to the deckbeams below. It came away in my hand as the sea hit us; and it, the kedges on deck and John came down upon me. We can only ascribe it to a miracle that I ended up under the dinghy, which must have risen to receive me, surrounded by clutter but unhurt with the dinghy's keel pressing the back of my thigh. But with its weight supported by the combing I was extricated from this uncomfortable situation before the next ton of water descended.

By now Frank had won sufficient offing to pass the Chichester Bar buoy and there was a rapid consultation as to the advisability of trying to make the harbour. Seas mountains high were breaking upon the Winner Bank and we realised that one touch and the children at least would be doomed – our chances of getting through were to say the least remote, even at full throttle. So we decided not to risk it. John and I turned our attention to the engine bilge, which had taken a lot of water through the wheel-house doors and a loose skin fitting. The bilge pump was not man enough for the job and priming it was virtually impossible with the motion of the ship, so we set to with a bucket and basin, bailing alternately. The engine was partially submerged by now, the water slimy with diesel oil and green paint from a tin which had burst asunder, and as it surged from side to side great spurts flew up into our eyes from the belt pulley driving the dynamo. We cannot speak too highly of that beloved machine, newly installed and greatly prized as it was. We certainly owe our lives to it and would like to thank Parsons of Southampton for the craftsmanship which enabled it to chug faithfully on even after we had abandoned ship. We hope that another Porbeagle will grace the new *Maaslust* when we have her.

By the time we had bailed out the engine bilge and repaired the skin fitting, Frank had got us past the Mixon Rocks. At odd moments we had been sending up rockets and handflares with little hope of attracting attention – visibility was less than 100 yards because of the height of the seas, the tops of which were broken into a welter of flying spume – and we sent one up for luck to a vessel to seaward of us. At this moment the after end of the rudder parted, the vast iron girthe snapping off like tin. We realised that there was little now to do but to keep the water out and hope as the beach at Selsey drew nearer. I went below to look at the main bilge, which needed attention but was not alarmingly flooded. As it was of steel, we had always kept it bone dry and had omitted to test the pump, which not unnaturally refused to function now. Accordingly I spent an unhappy time bailing into the galley sink and being sick! Freda and the kids looked as if they were past caring, until an enormous jolt shook them to life. My immediate reaction was that we had hit a buoy (of all things, in those waters!) and I prepared to bail harder in case we had sprung a leak. I could hardly accept the fact that it was actually the lifeboat.

My only recollection of the next few minutes is of the sight of Peter, suspended in nothing but his pyjama top over the seething water, as John handed him across to our rescuers. My bare feet were slippery with paint and oil so that I came a cropper on the lifeboat deck, knocking myself out momentarily on a cowl, and the next thing was the incredible sight, which I shall never, never forget, of our beloved vessel battling there alone. I could not believe that we had actually left her, and even now, in spite of everything, I wish we hadn't. It was desertion of a faithful friend, and, though human life is infinitely valuable, we shall always feel remorse, knowing as we do now that the wonderful old lady did not give herself over to the whim of the seas, but fought on for many hours after we left her.

Who knows to how many anxious hearts she brought relief and joy, at the darkest period of the last war, bearing home husband, son or loved one. One of the "little ships," she bore the proud battle-honour, "Dunkirk, 1940."'

———————— ,, ————————

The rescued crew of *Bloodhound* were already aboard the Selsey lifeboat, so that by the time a third rescue had been made and the crew from the yacht *Coima* had been taken on board, the small hold was crammed with seasick bodies for the four long hours it took to reach and enter Portsmouth Harbour.

That same night, John and Margaret Wells went to Shoreham to contact their insurance broker, feeling sure that *Maaslust* would already be ashore and might be salvaged, even though her engine had been left running to keep her head to the seas when they had abandoned.

On the Monday, hoping against hope, they scoured the coast between Selsey and Newhaven and found nothing, but at Littlehampton they learned that the Dutchman had been seen lying off at 10.00 hrs on the Sunday and had looked as though she was waiting for the tide, to come in!

She was seen again, 'clawing out to sea'. Lloyd's List gave her as being afloat on Monday morning – but after that – silence.

From: *The Little Ship Club Journal*, 1956.

26: *Girl Stella*'s Going

Yacht: *Girl Stella* (40ft gaff-rigged ketch)
Skipper: Frank Mulville
Crew: Richard Morris (mate)
      Celia Mulville
      Patrick Mulville
      Andrew Mulville
Bound from Bermuda to England
Time and date of loss: early hours of April 24th, 1969
Position: Porto Piqueran, 1 mile N of Santa Cruz, Flores

On August 1st, 1968, *Girl Stella* left Heybridge Basin in Essex, on a voyage to Cuba. On board were Frank Mulville, his wife Celia, their two sons Andrew and Patrick and a friend, Dick Morris. The 24-ton *Girl Stella* was an ex-Cornish lugger, built in 1896, but completely rebuilt and fitted with a diesel engine by the Drake brothers at Tollesbury.

On the way to Cuba, *Girl Stella* stopped for a while in Spain, the Canaries and the West Indies, before spending Christmas in Kingston, Jamaica. They arrived in Santiago de Cuba on December 28th, and spent several weeks cruising along the south coast and around the western end of the island, including twenty-four hours aground on a reef in the approaches to Santa Lucia. For the last month of the ten-week stay, *Girl Stella* lay in the harbour of Habana, finally leaving Cuba on March 15th, 1969.

After calling at the Bahamas and Bermuda, the Atlantic crossing commenced on April 9th.

———————— " ————————

'Being to the southward of our course had put the Azores almost in line between us and home. "Of course we'll go in," Patrick said, "it will be nice to get a run ashore in a brand new island." I was doubtful. "Wouldn't it be better to go straight on home?" Celia and Adrian agreed. "Let's go home,"

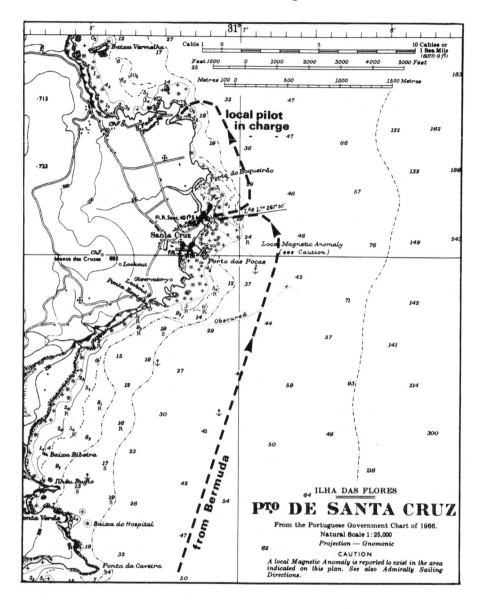

Adrian said, "we'll be late for school – and anyway I want to see the dog." Dick, if anything, seemed to be in favour of seeing the Azores. "I must say I'd like to see the whaling boats," he said. The argument kept us amused for days. "Look here, Daddy," Patrick said, "you can't go right past these lovely islands and not go in."

In the end I compromised. If we just went in to Flores, the most northerly of the islands, and stayed for a short time, two days at the outside, it wouldn't waste much time or take us far out of our way. We studied the Pilot book. Flores had a harbour of sorts, although it didn't say much about it. It was a whaling island – the last place in the world, I believe, where whales are still hunted with pulling boats using hand harpoons. If the whaling boats used the island there was no reason why we should not, and the port of Santa Cruz was on the lee side and should be well sheltered. "After all," Patrick said, "Sir Richard Grenville lay in Flores of the Azores, why shouldn't we?" "All right – we'll go into Flores. But two days only," I decided. "We'll fill up with water," Celia said, "and get some fresh vegetables."

It was a bad decision. I knew it was a bad decision because a little voice inside me told me so – a decision dictated not by considerations of careful seamanship and what the Pilot book would call "A proper regard for the safety of the vessel", but by nothing more tangible than a passing fancy – a set of frail desires. It was trusting to luck instead of careful planning. Once embarked on, it led inexorably on to other decisions, taken one by one and in themselves innocent enough, which built themselves up to produce a misfortune which, to our small world, was a disaster.

The wind worked its way round to the south-west as we got closer to Flores and the glass went down slightly – nothing to worry about, but if it was going to blow a gale from the south-west it would be just as well to be safety tucked away in the lee of a high island. There is no radio beacon on Flores and, unlike any other of our major landfalls of the voyage, I would have to rely completely on my sextant. Flores is not a big island, perhaps half as long as the Isle of Wight, and there was no other island within a hundred and thirty miles of it except Corvo – a very small island immediately to the north-east. I supplemented my sun observations with star sights in the morning and confidently pronounced an E.T.A. "You'll see it at half past two this afternoon, lying on the port bow, and there's ten shillings for the first boy to sight land." It was Tuesday, April 22nd and we had covered 1,700 miles in thirteen days – an average speed of over five knots. At two o'clock Adrian sighted the island pushing its bulk out of low cloud fine on the port bow.

It took a long time to come up with the southern cape of Flores and it was evening by the time we rounded it and came along the east side of the island towards Santa Cruz – close under great cliffs and mountains that dropped sheer into the Atlantic. White houses high up on the mountainside blinked their lights at us – we could see the gulls wheeling in tight spirals against the sheer rock face, and ahead of us the small town of Santa Cruz could just be seen before the sun went behind the mountain and everything was suddenly submerged in darkness. "What a pity. I thought we'd just get in before dark," I said to Celia. "We'll have to hang off till morning – how disappointing," she said.

We took the sails down off Santa Cruz and just as we were making a neat stow of the mains'l, two bright red leading lights suddenly showed up, one behind the other, showing the way into the harbour. "Well, what do you think of that?" I said to Dick. "Do you think they switched on the lights specially for us?" "Perhaps they did. Anyway it must be quite O.K. to go in at night otherwise the leading lights wouldn't be there." I went below where Celia was. "They've switched on two beautiful leading lights," I said. "I think we'll go in rather than flog about here all night." "I think we ought to wait till we can see where we're going," she said. I consulted Dick again and we overruled her. "Is everything squared up? – get the ropes and fenders up and we'll go in," I said. I knew, deep inside myself, that it was a silly thing to do. The little voice told me so again. "You're a bloody idiot Mulville," it said. "Oh shut your blather – I'm tired – I want a night's sleep."

When everything was ready to go alongside – the mooring ropes ready, fenders out, side lights lit, boat hooks handy, anchor cleared away ready to let go if needed, I put the engine slow ahead and went straight for the leading lights and straight for the black cliff which was all we could see behind them. Soon we could hear the surf pounding against the rocks. "I don't like it, Frank," Celia said, "I'm going below." "It's not too late to turn back," the voice said. "Don't be such a bloody fool."

"Can you see anything, Dick?" I shouted to the fore deck. "Yes – there's a gap right ahead – starboard a little." "Starboard she is." "Steady as you go." "Steady." Suddenly we were between the rocks – close on either side. There was no turning now. A swell took us and swept us forward. "Hard to starboard," Dick shouted. I spun the wheel, my mouth dry as the bottom of a bird cage. "There it is – right ahead – put her astern," Dick shouted.

There was a small stone quay right beside us – a dozen men on it, all shouting at us in Portuguese. The swell was terrific. *G.S.* was rearing up and down alarmingly. Dick threw a rope, it was made fast and *G.S.* was pulled in towards the quay. "We can't lie here," I shouted to Dick, "we'll have to get out again." Just then *G.S.* grounded on a hard stone bottom. She only touched once, not hard, and I put the engine astern and brought her a few feet along the quay – but it was enough to be unpleasant. "Anyone speak English?" I shouted. A big man came forward. "I pilot," he shouted. "This harbour no good for you – tide go down – no enough water." He and two of his friends jumped on board. "Full astern," he said. I put the engine astern and opened the throttle. The pilot took the wheel from me. "Neutral – slow ahead," he said. We seemed to be surrounded by rocks on all sides and the swell was playing round them, leaping into the air, and crashing down with a noise like a steam train pulling out of a station. The pilot manoeuvred us back and forth – turning *G.S.* round with great skill as if he had known her ways all his life. "I don't know how you get in here," he said, "no one come in here at night." "Then what in Christ's name are the leading lights for?" "Fishermen," he said.

It was like the middle of Hampton Court Maze, but somehow the pilot got us out, backing and filling and turning until *G.S.* was clear in the open sea again. The saliva slowly came back to my mouth. "Give me a drink of water," I asked Celia whose white face was looking anxiously out of the hatch. "We take you Porto Piqueran. One mile up coast," the pilot said, "You O.K. there." We motored for a quarter of an hour to the north and then the pilot put *G.S.*'s head straight for the rocks. "Don't let him do it," a voice said. "Shut up for Christ's sake. I can't tell him his job."

There were no leading lights here at all – only the black face of the rock. "No worry," the pilot said, sensing my apprehension, "you O.K. here. Quite safe – no swell – I know way." "Ça va bien," one of the other men said, thinking for some reason that I was French and wishing to air his grasp of that language. "Le Monsier Pilot – il le connait bien ici." The pilot was as good as his reputation. He took us straight towards a tower of rock, looming sullenly in the weak light of the stars, then hard to port for a few yards, then to starboard and to port again until suddenly we were in a small cove – a cleft in the rocks no more than sixty feet across but calm and still. "Let go anchor. Now we tie you up."

The pilot and his helpers climbed into our dinghy and ran out ropes to the rocks. They jumped nimbly ashore and fastened every long rope we had in the ship – three on each side. "Best ropes forward," the pilot said, "bad ropes aft. Wind come from west," he said pointing to the sky where the clouds were racing towards England. "Always strong wind from west here." I thought for a moment while they were working on the ropes. "Pilot," I said, "suppose we have to go out quickly. Would it not be better to turn her round, so she's facing the sea?" "No," he said, "strong wind from west – always face strong wind – best ropes forward." The little person inside me said "Make him turn her round, you weak idiot – this may be a trap." "Stop your bloody nagging."

They tied us up thoroughly, made sure that everything was fast and strong and then they came down to the cabin and we gave them a drink. "By God – you lucky get out Santa Cruz," the pilot laughed. "No ship ever come there at night before. You fine here – you sleep sound." We put them ashore in the dinghy to a stone quay with a flight of steps hewn out of the rock face and they went off home. "See you in the morning. You sleep O.K."

We did sleep sound. *G.S.* lay as quiet as if she were in Bradwell Creek. The glass was dropping again and it was already blowing a gale from the south-west but Porto Piqueran was quite detached from the gale – the only evidence of wind was the racing clouds far up above and an occasional down draught which would sometimes break away from the body of the gale and find its way like some spent outrider round the mountain and down towards Porto Piqueran where it would hurl the last of its dissipated energy at the top of *G.S.*'s mast, stirring the burgee forty feet up, making a faint moaning sound and then dissolving into the night. Dick laughed, "This is a hurricane hole all right – there isn't enough wind in here to lift a tart's skirt." "Don't laugh too soon," the little voice said to me as I went to sleep.'

———————— '' ————————

Next day, Mulville met with some difficulty when customs officials accompanied him into Santa Cruz to the office of the International Police, who wanted to retain all the passports. After much argument Mulville managed successfully to plead with them:

———————— " ————————

'"The wind might change in the night," I said. "We might want to go out at a moment's notice. We must have our passports."'

———————— '' ————————

Before spending a second night in Porto Piqueran, they carefully checked all the warps before they went to bed and found nothing amiss:

———————— " ————————

'The two strongest warps we had were out over the bow, each made fast to a rock. On the starboard side there was a rope from aft to a ring bolt let into the rock by the steps and another to a stone bollard at the corner of the quay. On the port side the longest rope led from aft to a big rock on the south side of the cove and yet another from amidships. It was something of a work of art. "If you got out your crochet needles you could make us a Balaclava out of this lot," I had remarked to Celia. In addition to her ropes the anchor was down, although I doubted whether it was doing any good as the bottom was hard and it had not been let go far enough out to be effective. Dick had been round in the day checking that the ropes were not chafing against the rocks and had served a couple of them with rope-yarns. "I reckon she'll do," I said to Dick and we went to bed.

A boat is always there – you never stop worrying about her whether you are aboard or ashore – she is always a presence in the mind and you're conscious of her at all times. She may be laid up in some safe berth for the winter or hauled out of the water in a yard, but wherever you may be – at home in your virtuous bed or roistering in some gay spot, a chorus girl on each knee and the air thick with flying champagne corks, a part of your consciousness is always reserved. When the wind moans round the eaves of the house it has a special significance, and you check off in your mind, one by one, the possible sources of danger. Men lie awake worrying about their bank balances, their waist-lines, their wives, their mistresses actual or potential; but sailors worry about boats.

A boat is something more than an ingenious arrangement of wood and copper and iron – it has a soul, a personality, eccentricities of behaviour that are endearing. It becomes part of a person, colouring his whole life with a romance that is unknown to those who do not understand a way of life connected with boats. The older a boat becomes, the stronger the power. It gains in stature with each new experience – people look at boats with wonder and say "She's been to the South Seas," or "She's just back from the North Cape" and the boat takes on a reputation in excess of that of its owner. *Girl Stella* had become a very real part of our lives – we each of us loved her with a deep respect.

I slept badly, frequently waking and listening. At two a.m. it began to rain, softly at first and then more heavily so that I could hear the drips coursing off the furled mains'l and drumming on the cabin top. At four a.m. I heard a slight bump and wondered what it was – then I heard it again and I knew what it was. It was the dinghy bumping against the stern. I froze in a cold sweat. If the dinghy was bumping against the stern, the wind must have changed. I got up, put oilskins on over my pyjamas and went on deck. It was cold – the temperature had dropped three or four degrees – it was pelting with rain and a light breeze was blowing from east by north – straight into the cove of Porto Piqueran.

I undid the dinghy, took the painter round the side deck and fastened it off the bow where it streamed out clear. I went back to the cabin, got dressed and called Dick. I tapped the glass and it gave a small convulsion – downwards. "Dick – the wind's changed. We'll have to get out of here quick. The glass is dropping. We can't stay here in an easterly wind." Dick got up and put his head out of the hatch. The rain was pouring down and it was as black as a cow's inside. I believe he thought I was over-nervous – exaggerating. "We can't do much in this," he said, "if we did manage to get her untied and turned round – we'd never get her out through that channel in this blackness. All we can do is wait till morning and then have another look at it." He went back to bed and was soon snoring peacefully.

The little voice said "Get him up – start work – now." "Shut up – he's right – you can't see your hand in front of you – how the hell can we go to sea in this?" I walked round the deck. There was more swell now, and *G.S.* was beginning to buck up and down – snatching at her ropes so that sometimes the after ones came right out of the water. The forward ropes – the strong nylon warps – were quite slack.

I went down to the cabin, sat at the table and tried to read. I made myself a cup of coffee and sat with the mug warming my hands and the steam wreathing round my face.

Then I went on deck again. The wind was beginning to increase, a heavy swell was now running and small white waves were beginning to overlay it. The rain had increased and was now slanting with the wind and driving into the cove. *Girl Stella* was beginning to pitch and jerk at the two stern ropes with alarming force. Very slowly and reluctantly it was beginning to get light. I went below and shook Dick. "Come on – not a minute to waste – it's beginning to get light." I tapped the glass again and again it dropped.

It seemed an age before Dick was dressed in his oilskins and on deck. "First we'll get the anchor up. It's doing no good there and it will only hamper us. Then we'll let go the head lines – leave them in the water – they'll drift to leeward and we'll come back for them later. Then we'll go astern on the engine and let her swing round on one of the stern lines." We set to work. It was a relief to have ended the dreadful inactivity of the last two hours. As the anchor began to come up, Celia woke and put her head out through the hatch. "What's happening?" "We're going to get out of here – look at the weather – we're turning her round. Better get the boys up." In minutes the boys were up on deck in their oilskins and Celia was dressed.

The anchor came home easily and I started the engine. We cast off the head lines and prepared another line which would take the strain after we had turned, passing it round the bow so that we could fasten it to the stern line to starboard, which would then become the head line to port. Now the wind was howling with real ferocity – increasing every minute. The swell had become dangerous and was slapping against *G.S.*'s blunt stern and sending little columns of spray into the mizzen shrouds. I moved the dinghy painter from the bow to the stern and the boat lay alongside, leaping up and down and banging against the top sides.

We were almost ready when there was a twang like someone plucking a violin string. I looked up and saw that the stern line on which we were relying had received one jerk too many. It had snapped in the middle and the inboard end was flying back towards the boat like a piece of elastic. *G.S.* immediately began to move towards the rocks on her port side. I jumped into the cockpit, slammed the engine into reverse, gave her full throttle, and put the rudder hard to starboard. She began to pick up. "Let go the port stern line," I yelled to Dick. He began to throw the rope off the cleat. "Throw it well clear – she'll come." The engine vibrated and thundered – the spray over the stern drove in our faces – the wind battered our senses but she was coming astern. "Good old girl," I muttered, "we'll get you out."

Then the engine stopped – suddenly and irrevocably – the bare end of the broken line wound a dozen times round the propeller. "Now you're in trouble," the little voice said.

G.S. began to drift inexorably towards the rocks – there was nothing to stop her – no ropes on the starboard side and no engine. "Fenders, over here, quick," I shouted to the boys and Celia. "Fend her off as best you can. I'll go over with another rope," I shouted to Dick. There was one more rope long enough to reach the shore, still in the fo'c'sle locker. The top of the locker was covered with toys and books belonging to the boys and with Patrick's accordion. I threw them off in a pile on the floor and brought the bare end up through the fo'c'sle hatch. "Celia," I shouted, "pay it out to me as I go in the dinghy." As I got over the side into the *Starling* I felt *G.S.* strike the rocks – surprisingly gently, I thought. Perhaps it was a smooth ledge and they would be able to cushion her with fenders until we got another rope out. I rowed desperately towards the shore, the end of the rope wound round the after thwart of the dinghy. The swell was washing violently against the stone steps. I could see the ring-bolt but I couldn't reach it – as soon as the dinghy got in close it would surge up on a swell, strike the slippery surface of the steps and plunge back. I took my trousers and my shirt off, plunged into the sea with the end of the rope, upsetting the dinghy as I jumped out of it, and tried to clamber up the steps. But there was nothing to grasp and three times the weight of the rope pulled me back. With a last effort I managed to roll myself over onto the steps, reach up and keep my balance until I was able to grasp the ring. "All fast," I shouted to Celia. I swam back on board and clambered up over the bobstay. It was bitterly cold.

Dick and I took the rope to the winch and began to heave. The strain came on the rope and her head began to come round clear of the rocks, but she had moved ahead slightly and the rocks under her stern had shifted their position to right aft, under the turn of the bilge, and begun to do real damage. They were too far below the water-line for the fenders to be of any use. Then she stopped coming. The rope was tight but something was preventing her from moving forward. Dick went aft to look. "She's all tied up aft," he reported, "every bloody rope in the place is tied up round the propeller and they're all bar tight." I looked over the stern. It was daylight now and I could see a tangle of ropes bunched up round the propeller. "I'll cut them free."

Dick gave me his razor-sharp knife and I jumped over the side again. I dived and saw that at least two ropes had somehow got themselves into the tangle – I managed to cut one and came up for breath. *G.S.*'s stern was just above me, the swells lifting it and allowing it to settle back on the rock with all the force of her great weight. I could hear the rock cutting into her skin –

the unmistakable cracking sound of timbers shattering under blows of irresistible force. I knew then that she was done for.

I dived and cut the other rope, swam round to the bobstay with difficulty in the heavy swell and dragged myself on board. Dick and I wound furiously on the winch – she moved a little further, and then, as the swells came more on her beam, she lifted and crashed down with an awe-inspiring crunch. She would move no more. As I went aft Celia was working the hand pump and Patrick jumped into the engine room and switched on the electric pump. Adrian came up out of the saloon and I heard him say to Celia in a quiet voice, "Mummy, I don't wish to alarm you but the cabin's full of water." "It's all over," I said to Celia, "everybody get into life-jackets. We'll have to swim for it."

Celia and I went below. The water was knee-deep on the cabin floor and was rising as we watched. She was still bumping, and every time she hit the rock we could hear the heavy frames splitting, the timbers crumbling. I looked at Celia. Her face was grey, her hair hanging in rat tails, and she had an expression of unimpeded sadness. We stood for a moment among the ruin. The ingredients of our lives were swilling backwards and forwards across the cabin floor, soon to be swallowed by the sea. Books given to us by the Cubans, their pages open and eager, as if they would convert the ocean to revolution, Adrian's recorder, clothes, an orange, the cribbage board, the kettle, a pair of chart rulers, rolls of film, my hat, Celia's glasses-case – objects which had somehow jumped out of their context to give mocking offence. The ordered symmetry of our lives was torn apart and scattered – haphazard and suddenly meaningless.

I could see in Celia's face that she had reached the end of a long journey. *Girl Stella* was a precious thing to her – something that was being thrown away in front of her eyes. The years of struggle with the sea were coming to an end – the pinnacles of achievement, the harrowing crises, the light-hearted joys and the endless discomforts had slowly spiralled upwards as we had progressed from adventure to adventure. Now they had reached an explosive zenith and for her there could be no going on. I knew in that moment she would never come sailing with me again. I had at last betrayed her trust – forfeited her confidence in me. Before, we had always come through – snatched victory out of disaster – but now she was facing a fundamental confrontation of truth. I put my hand in hers – pleading for a glance of sympathy.

Celia passed the life-jackets up the hatch to Dick, and then she gathered a plastic bag and put in it the log books – the ship's, the children's and her own – and a few oddments. I found myself unable to think – I was almost insensible with cold. I grabbed my wallet and a book of traveller's cheques, the last of our money, and stuffed them into the bag. I took one last look – the clock and the barometer shining on the bulkhead, the cabin stove, its doors swung open and the water ebbing and flowing through the grate, the lamp swinging unevenly with a stunted motion, and floating lazily across the floor, *G.S.*'s document box, "*Girl Stella* – Penzance" scrolled on the lid.

On deck the boys were calmly putting on their life-jackets. I bent down to help Patrick with the lacings. "This is the end, Daddy," he said quietly, "the end of *Girl Stella* – poor, poor *G.S.*" Now she had settled deep in the water and her motion had suddenly become sickening. She had lost her liveliness and when she rolled to the swell it was with a slow, tired lurch. Her stability, the quick sense of recovery, the responsiveness that she always had, was gone. "Quick. She may turn turtle – we must get off. I'll go first, then boys, then you, Celia and Dick last. Grab the rope and pull yourselves along it. I'll help you up the steps."

I jumped into the sea, found the rope and shouted back, "Come on Pad – jump." Patrick hesitated for a moment and then his body came flying through the air and he bobbed up, gasping with cold beside me – then Adrian, then Celia. We pulled ourselves hand over hand along the rope. Now the swell was much heavier and there were vicious seas breaking in the cove. It was much more difficult to get on to the steps. The ring-bolt was high up out of the water and it was necessary to let go of the rope and swim the last few yards to the steps. My puny strength was of no consequence in the swell – like a piece of floating stick I was swept back and forth across the rock face, the small aperture of the steps flashing past as I was carried first one way and then the other. Then, more by some quirk of the swell than by my own efforts, I was dumped heavily on the bottom step and was able to scramble to my feet. I grabbed Patrick by one arm and heaved him up, then Adrian came surging past and I was able to grasp the back of his life-jacket and pull him on the bottom step. Celia was more difficult. She was all but paralysed by the cold – she was heavy and slippery and there seemed to be nothing of her that I could grip. Then she managed to get her body half on to the step, and with Patrick helping me we pulled and rolled and tugged until she finally got herself clear and struggled to her feet. "Up you go – quick before the sea snatches you back again."

Dick had not come. I looked up and saw that *G.S.* had moved ahead and was now lying athwart a towering rock pillar. I saw that he had been below and had brought up the two sextants and placed them on a narrow ledge of rock which he could reach. *G.S.* was now low in the water and sinking fast. "Dick," I shouted, "come out of it – now." If she sank before he came he would be denied the rope and I doubted whether he would be able to swim through the broken water without its help. He took a last and reluctant look round and then he jumped and we watched him working along the rope, hand over hand, until I was able to grasp his arm and he scrambled up the steps.

We stood in a dejected, shivering group on the little stone quay and watched *G.S.* work out this last moment of her span of life. A thing of grace and beauty – agile, sure-footed, tender in her responses to our demands – at the same time she was a block of solid assurance. We had always felt safe in her – we always knew that she would do whatever was asked of her. She was our home – she gave us a dignity which we would otherwise have been without.

She had come to her end not by any misdeed of hers – not through any wilfulness or delinquency – but by misuse – a sheer disregard of the elements of seamanship. I felt the dead weight of my responsibility settle heavily on my shoulders. It was a score against me that could never be wiped clean – nothing that I could ever do would relieve me of the knowledge that I had destroyed a thing of beauty.'

—————— ,, ——————

From: *In Granma's Wake* (1970), Seafarer Books

27: Bad Luck in Boulogne

Yacht: *Mary Williams*
Skipper: Clementina Gordon
Crew: None
Bound from Etaples (river Canche) to St Valery sur Somme, France
Time and date of loss: approx. 0400, August 7th, 1962
Position: outer harbour, Boulogne

Many people began their cruising careers in Silhouettes, those small hard-chine bilge keel plywood boats designed by Robert Tucker; but not so many of them were women, and surely the Revd Clementina Gordon was the only ordained woman minister amongst them. In 1961, Clementina Gordon had won the Suzanne Trophy for her log of a remarkable cruise in appalling weather from the east coast of England to Zeebrugge in Belgium, and in 1962 she set out to cruise along the Normandy and Brittany coasts, but ran into trouble, as she relates in this simple but graphic account:

———————— " ————————

'I was trying to cruise on the difficult north coast between Boulogne and Cherbourg, exercising great care, as the anchorages are dangerous with vile bars and ripping tides, also drying out 20 ft and more. On Monday, August 6, I left Le Canche river about 3.45 a.m., negotiating the bar with a terrible ebb, and then the SW tide for St Valery sur Somme. At 6.45 a.m. the forecast was a westerly gale coming from Plymouth area, so as I hadn't a hope of making Dieppe, I ran back over a foul tide to Boulogne. (The Somme estuary is murder in on-shore winds.) I came into Boulogne in pouring rain, and brought up just by the inner pier head, clear of traffic, and of course behind the big west breakwater. There I rested clear of the miseries of that inner basin and all ready to slip in when I had sorted myself out. I must have dozed off, thinking myself perfectly secure. When I came to, the wind had flown round, from off shore, to put me on the lee of the

178

inner pier, about Force 7. I thought it a risk to get under way, and placidly waited for a lull or a pluck in from a passing tug. My signals, even red rockets bursting 100 ft, were unnoticed, so I had to hang on with very heavy ground tackle, two anchors and vast new warps and chain.

By midnight, the wind settled in the SW and increased, I guess to Force 8, but another report said much more. I had now the far side of the harbour in my lee, down Cape Griz Nez direction, all rocks and old blockhouses, with heavy surf. She held till just before H.W. 3 a.m., when the west breakwater ceased to function, and a heavy swell came in almost unimpeded. I sent off the remainder of the big rockets (after I learnt that the inner pier head, 80 yds away was manned all night and the life-boat station was 150 yds away!).

I then took the situation seriously and inflated my good rubber dinghy, as it was obvious that if the bitts were not torn out of her something would have to go. The surf and the rocks were so nasty that I had a drink of Madeira to steady my poor nerves, and stop my being sick all the time and therefore inefficient. Just after that there was a bigger heave than usual, and with a roar I found myself trapped under the cockpit with the boat on top of me. (Afterwards, examining the wreckage, I found that the new 2½ bow warp had parted about 15 ft from the bitts, so I presume she was caught underneath by a steep wave and turned bow over stern.) Luckily I held my breath, extracted my leg wedged under the boom, and got out plus dinghy, which my safety belt was attached to. Then a gulp of air, before a monster of a wave crashed me down and down. Eventually I came up, and was rushed ahead for 250 yards or so, nearly torn away from the rubber dinghy. A pause, then crashed down again and pushed violently forward. This was repeated while I weakened physically.

Luckily I missed the rocks sticking out, and after ¼ or ½ mile had slacker water, but a sheer cement wall with an overhang and railings right on top. It was just light, and a Frenchman fishing with a rod was there, so I yelled like an otter hunter, and he slithered down a drainpipe to help. I was too weak to keep hold of the rocks as the dinghy acted like a sea anchor and pulled me back by the safety line. He could not approach to pull me out, as he had a new pair of suede shoes, and leaped back for fear of wetting them – even then I could see how funny it was! Eventually, I had the wits to pull the release of the belt, and was able to hang onto a rock.

I was hauled out. A baker's delivery man had now appeared to join in the fun, and then manhandled me into a pub where Madame had hysterics and tipped filthy French "whisky" down me, such as the fishermen use. As I would insist on subsiding on to the floor in a pool of my own private sea, they sent for the ambulance and tucked me up in a nuns' hospital. There I stayed for a couple of days, as I had only a nightshirt lent by a nun, and it

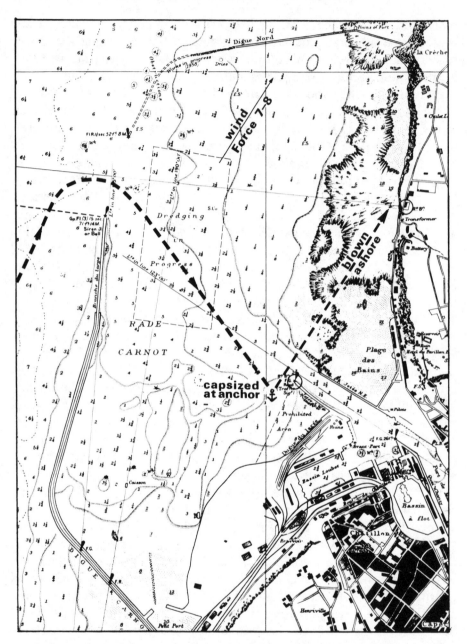

stopped short 1½ ft above my knees; so I was a prisoner of modesty.

The unfortunate boat broke up ¼ mile off shore. The local yacht club picked up the bits at low water and most of my gear was salvaged.

Obviously the whole silly accident was quite unnecessary, I could easily have gone right inside before supper. But it is a sobering lesson on what a dangerous place a harbour is in a gale, and how useful an inflatable dinghy can be (no other dinghy would have had the buoyancy to bring me through that stuff), also on the improbability of one's distress signals being seen. Perhaps one ought to carry a minimum of a dozen rockets and a dozen flares, instead of three of each and some whites, as I had.'

―――――――― ,, ――――――――

From: *The Silhouette Owner*, September 1962

28: *Thelma* Parts her Cable

Yacht: *Thelma* (27ft gaff-rigged cutter)
Skipper: A.W. 'Bob' Roberts
Crew: A.F. 'Bully' Bull
Bound round the world from England, westabout
Time and date of loss: sometime on March 1st, 1935
Position: Chatham Bay, Cocos Island

Long before he won fame as a skipper of Thames spritsail barges, Bob
Roberts and his mate 'Bully' had sailed the little gaff cutter, *Thelma*, from
England to Cocos Island in the Pacific, where she was lost when her anchor
cable parted. Roberts had felt uneasy about their anchorage in Chatham
Bay, but put his doubts behind him when Bully asked why he was worried:

——————————— " ———————————

'It was an open anchorage and no place for rough weather, but being so
calm it did not seem that there could be the slightest danger in lying there
for a few days. It would not take us long to top up our water tanks and get
away for the Galápagos. It was only those queer fancies of mine that made
me dislike the place, and I even went so far as to reveal my thoughts to
Bully as he stirred the porridge in the galley with a sweaty hand.

"I don't like this place much."

"Want to move further out?"

"No, she's as safe here as anywhere with the hook in this patch of sand."

"Well, what don't you like about the place?"

"Dunno. Just a hunch."

In the meantime I altered my ideas about a kedge anchor. We were not so
lavishly equipped as to have two anchor chains, and our custom was to lay
out a kedge on a stout manilla warp. As our two-inch tripping line had
already chafed through on the jagged bottom in only two hours I felt it
would be useless to use a kedge on a warp.

182

After solemn deliberations we decided that if the anchor chain did not hold her it was quite certain a chafing warp would not. Likewise it was impossible for our main anchor to drag. It could not drag from that patch of sand because it was surrounded by mushroom coral. This mushroom coral grows some little way off the bottom and spreads out according to its name. Thus if the anchor dragged, the lower flukes would go under the coral and hold there so fast that it would be unlikely that we should ever get it up again.

So there did not seem to be much danger of *Thelma* dragging her anchor, especially as the weather was dead calm and there was no current to speak of in the bay itself.'

———————— ,, ————————

They spent three days watering ship by ferrying a cask to and fro between *Thelma* and the shore; and then, having met a man named Cooknell, they were persuaded to join in a search for the 'Cocos' treasure. The search was unsuccessful and throughout the five days Roberts remained uneasy and depressed.

The return to Chatham Bay was in a ship's lifeboat.

———————— " ————————

'I was glad to be on my way back. A cloud of depression seemed to be hanging over me all the time at Wafer Bay. While the others scampered in and out of the water and played golf on the beach with a round stone and a crooked branch, I could only sit around and mope. I must have been dull company.

I thought it was sheer tiredness after our efforts in the jungle, but as things turned out it was that vague mental warning to which the human mind is sometimes subjected when something dreadful is going to happen.

At last we got Nuez astern and bore away to cross Chatham Bay; I felt no qualms at not sighting *Thelma*'s stumpy stick straight away. But as we grew closer I stood up in the prow and scanned the bay. *Thelma* was not there!

Wild thoughts ran through my head. Then, far away in a corner of the bay, I caught sight of her. She was but a few yards from the rocks. Even as I watched a huge wave lifted her up and carried her in.

We rowed like fiends, but the tide and current were against us. I stood there and saw her rise again and disappear. When the next breaker came she did not come up. She was down on her beam ends with the surf pounding over her.

There was very little wind but it was impossible to get the lifeboat alongside in the breakers. We anchored a little way off and veered down as near as possible. The sight before us almost broke my heart. There was the gallant little vessel, which I had loved and cared for all these years, which had brought us safely through fair weather and foul for nearly 7,000 miles on this cruise alone, in her death throes on that lonely shore. All our worldly belongings danced and swirled among the rocks. A bunch of dollar notes disappeared in the foam. Pieces of timber floated everywhere.

It was enough to chill the heart of the bravest soul. To complete the mournful scene Jimmy, drenched and scared, meowed pitifully from the masthead.'

———————— ,, ————————

For a while there were thoughts of saving her, but Roberts knew that this would not be possible.

———————— " ————————

'I took one look at the way she lay and knew that the vessel was doomed. She hardly rose an inch to a breaking wave, and there was a sickening grinding and snapping of timbers with each cruel blow. Every wave broke clean over her and forced us to cling on for our lives.

We fought our way down into the tiny cabin. Each wave filled her up and we were imprisoned like rats until it subsided. We choked and gasped as we grabbed such things as were within reach and passed them out on deck. It was impossible to stay below for long at a time, and as I struggled in the cabin I could feel the rocks under my feet. The whole of her starboard side was ripped out. Something was sticking up through the cabin floor. There was nothing to be done except to try to save everything possible.

At low water *Thelma* was almost high and dry and I was able to discover the cause of the wreck. Trailing from her bow were many fathoms of anchor chain but no anchor. One of the links had been sawn clean through as if with a file. It was the work of the mushroom coral. So sharp was the edge of it that in five days it had cut through a heavy link as the vessel swung gently to her hawse. I should never have believed that coral could cut through solid iron so efficiently. Later we found pieces on the beach which would file through any iron or steel we possessed. But the knowledge came too late. The worst was done. Some time after the wreck we found that anchor still firmly embedded in the sand and it took four of us to weigh it from the lifeboat.'

———————— ,, ————————

From: *Rough and Tumble* (1935),
Sampson Low and Marston

PART V: COLLISION

29: Hard Chance in a Nutshell

Yacht: *Dorothea* (32ft Bermudian cutter)
Skipper: Peter Tangvald
Crew: None
Bound from Cayenne, French Guiana to Fort Lauderdale, Florida, U.S.A.
Time and date of loss: 2000, March 12th, 1967
Position: approx. 40 miles S of Barbados

When I told the ocean-wanderer Peter Tangvald that I was preparing this book, he replied, from Las Palmas, that he had himself once thought of compiling a list of 'yacht disasters', with the intention of making a book out of it. However, he had abandoned the idea – 'after having submitted a few of the examples for the approval of the various skippers concerned, who are all very offended by my conclusions, which generally put the blame on them; as they themselves, in every case, considered the fault to lie with everybody else but themselves.'

Nevertheless, Peter did kindly give me permission to use his own account of the sinking of the *Dorothea* in the Atlantic. I have used the title he originally intended for the story.

Dorothea, a Harrison Butler designed cutter, was built in Whitstable in 1935. Peter Tangvald bought her in 1959 and during the next five years sailed in her round the world before writing his book *Sea Gypsy*. After marrying his faithful crew Simone and while in South America, they decided to build a larger boat and decided to sell *Dorothea* in the US, where she could be expected to fetch a higher price.

Tangvald left Cayenne on March 7th with the intention of making a stop on the way at Charlotte Amalie in the Virgin Islands, where he hoped to meet old friends.

———————— " ————————

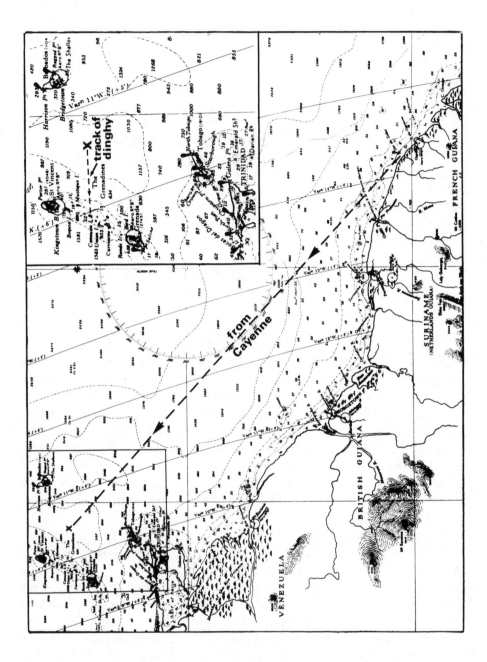

'My wife stayed behind in our newly leased house to watch over the huge pile of lumber and all the machine-tools already purchased for the new ship.

She told me later it had been a beautiful sight to see the ship tack down river towards the sea. Had she seen me when I crossed the bar, however, she would not have said the same thing, as one huge breaker swept the ship from end to end, soaking me to the skin in the process, while I wondered how strange it was that man is able to shoot rockets to the moon, yet be incapable of making oilskin which is truly watertight. Being wet and cold I decided to anchor for the night in the lee of the Iles du Salut about thirty miles from Cayenne.

Next morning, without having gone ashore, I set sail again, this time in much improved weather, well rested and cheerful. The wind was right on the beam and very fresh and gave *Dorothea* her maximum speed. In fact from us leaving these islands till the moment of the accident, she made the greatest average speed of her life, covering an average of 170 miles a day from noon to noon; but I must add that about 40 of these miles were probably due to the strong South Equatorial Current helping us along.

Then on the night of 12 March it happened. The weather had covered up with black clouds and rainsqualls. The night promised to be dark as there was no moon. Although the ship steered herself with her self-steering gear, I sat by the tiller, breathing in the last rays of daylight. The evening meal was on the stove down below and would soon be ready. Then when the new night was complete and I had just decided to go down below for dinner, the ship struck!

She struck so hard that she shuddered. But then she kept on going as before. I knew that I was many miles from the closest land and had about a thousand fathoms of water below me, and thus could not have bounced on a reef. For an instant I thought that I had collided with a native fishing boat, as they often do not bother to use any lights, but dismissed the thought immediately, as I knew that had that been so I would have heard not a little swearing. Indeed, shining my electric torch all around the horizon revealed nothing but water. Thus I can only presume that what I had hit was possibly a large tree-trunk or some wreckage which had been floating just at, or just below the surface of the sea.

Down in the saloon I was horrified to see the water already washing above the floorboards. The collision had sprung a very serious leak in the ship which until then had never leaked more than a bucket of water *a year*. I immediately realized that at the rate the water was coming in, the ship would soon sink unless I was able to localize the damage and make temporary repairs, but this proved an impossibility due to the inside ceiling which hid the planking with its damage. Thus water was leaking in between

189

the outer and inner skin of the boat with no possibility of access for me to the damaged spot. To look for it from the outside would no doubt have been possible in a calm sea and in daylight, and I might then have been able to nail over it a piece of canvas; but as it was, with a rolling ship, in heavy seas and pitch darkness it was an impossibility, and perhaps even suicide as the copper sheeting had no doubt been torn and its sharp edges would soon have cut me to death.

To realize suddenly that one is on a sinking ship, far from land, outside of any shipping lane and with no life-saving equipment on board is most depressing, and perhaps even more so on a pitch dark night, windy and with frequent rain-squalls. But however unhappy I was, I never stopped trying to figure out how to save my own life.

The dinghy was just 7 ft long and of flimsy plywood construction, while the seas were heavy and frequently breaking; but with luck even the smallest boat can survive quite rough conditions. Down in the chartroom with water swirling around my legs I saw that the closest land was Barbados, about forty miles away but dead to windward of me and thus out of the question for me to reach; but to leeward was the long chain of the Grenadine Islands about fifty-five miles away. Presuming that the dinghy would not be swamped before then, these should be easy to reach with a following wind, and the only navigational difficulty and danger would be to avoid letting the wind and current sweep me between two islands and into the Caribbean Sea where we would have no more land to our lee until the American mainland.

Thus with the greatest possible care I launched the dinghy and was greatly relieved when I had been able to do so without damaging it and without letting it be filled with water. To get a dinghy in the water single-handed is not the easiest job in the world even in a calm harbour, but in a heavy sea and a rolling ship it is very awkward indeed. I let her drift off to leeward on a long painter so that she would not get damaged against the side of *Dorothea*, and then went below to assemble all the gear I considered desirable for increasing my chances of making land alive.

First of all I took the two plastic bottles each containing 2½ gallons of fresh water which I always kept as emergency rations should *Dorothea*'s single tank have sprung a leak; then I half-filled a sailbag with food; then another sailbag with some clothes, then the chart and the compass; then an awning, a short gaff and some rope with the idea of a make-shift rig to cover the many miles to land; then the dinghy's folding anchor with a very long line, with the idea of having a last defence against being swept into the Caribbean Sea should I miss the Islands, hoping, of course, that I would get close enough to shallow water for it to be of any use. Then my two flashlights with spare batteries; then my lifejacket; and finally my papers and the cash money I had in the boat, which I put in a watertight bag together with the spare batteries. I assembled all the gear by the cockpit, and as I walked up the companionway my eyes fell on the dinner-pot still on the stove. I had just been ready to eat when we struck, so not wanting to have had the work of cooking for nothing, took the pot along. When all was ready on deck, I pulled the dinghy alongside, quickly threw in all the gear, jumped in and pushed off.

I soon realized that I had grossly overloaded the little boat, as almost every wave shipped water into her, so I lost no time in throwing overboard part of the gear, as obviously even the most desirable piece of equipment would lose all its importance should the dinghy founder. The anchor with its line went over the side, then one of the two water bottles, then the lifejacket, as, come what may, I was not going to swim fifty-five miles. Then, thinking that I would either make land within a couple of days or not at all, I half-emptied the other water bottle.

This lightening made a tremendous difference, and if I now sat in the bottom of the boat instead of on the thwart, in order to lower her centre of gravity, the dinghy was both very stable and buoyant, lifting over every wave and hardly letting in any water at all. I let go the painter but held on the yacht's mainsheet for a while, looking at her with my torch, somehow reluctant to abandon her and to be on my own in that black night; but then a very strong squall came whistling down and I was unable to hold on any longer for fear of capsizing, even though *Dorothea* was hove to. So I let go the sheet and drifted off to leeward. About fifty minutes had elapsed since the collision and *Dorothea* was lying very deep in the water. I saw her lights for a while and then suddenly they disappeared.

I felt utterly lonesome, wet, cold and rather worried about the future. I was, however, soon relieved to see how well that little dinghy managed in the heavy seas. She really floated like a cork and even when the top of a crest was breaking and overtaking us in a white foam, making me at first think that "that one will swamp us," even then the little boat lifted bravely and the foam disappeared harmlessly below us.

I soon gained enough confidence to make the jury rig which I knew would be necessary if I did not want to spend days at sea before reaching the land. I then discovered that I had forgotten to bring the knife. I was extremely annoyed at myself for that, as I really had tried to do my best not to overlook anything. Fortunately I was able to tear the awning to the right size anyway by using my teeth to get the rip started. But I was entirely unable to cut the rope without a knife so I had to make the whole rig with one continuous length of rope, lashing one side of the "squaresail" to the gaff which was to serve as square yard, then lashing the middle of that gaff to the end of one of the oars which was to serve as mast. From that same

intersection I got out two lines to act as shrouds and then two more lines to the lower part of the sail as sheets.

When I had everything ready, I hoisted the "mast." The sail filled immediately but before losing control I was able to tighten the shrouds by taking up the turns around the thwart. I let the mast lean forward, thus not needing any forward stay which would have been very difficult to rig. Then by adjusting the sheets and steering with the remaining oar, the little boat scooted right along at a fair speed. Before I was able to rejoice much, however, I was suddenly dismayed by seeing the water rise in the bottom of the dinghy at a frightening rate. I then understood that it was the pressure of the sail which depressed the bow enough to let the water wash above it. The sail hiding the bow from where I sat had prevented me from seeing the danger. By moving quickly right aft and leaning over the stern thwart, then bailing out the dinghy, everything seemed under control.

At about 0130 I was startled and overjoyed to see a steamship coming toward me. This was almost unbelievable luck as these were little-frequented waters and this ship was, in fact, the first ship I had seen on the voyage since leaving Cayenne, not counting a few fishing boats along the coast of French Guiana. I flashed continuously the international distress signal, S.O.S., S.O.S., with my very powerful long-range torch which I trained straight at her. The ship came slowly closer and in my thoughts I prepared how I should board her. I presumed that the steamer would come alongside me at very slow speed and then throw me a rope for getting on board. I decided that I would make no attempt to save either the dinghy or anything in her except my papers and money. I would as quickly as possible tie the rope around my chest right under the armpits and make fast with a bowline. This knot never slips.

The ship was now very close and I could see her moving through the seas and I expected to see her slow down and set the course straight for me; but to my dismay the minutes passed without the ship altering course at all, then her bright red port light faded, as did her two masthead lights only to be replaced immediately by a single white light; her stern light. She had not seen me after all!

As the steamer's lights disappeared below the horizon, I stopped thinking about her and told myself that, after all, if the dinghy had managed these many hours, there was no reason why she should not continue doing so until I reached land. My thoughts wandered over to the new dreamship I was going to build and I decided that I would incorporate two strong, water-tight bulkheads so that I would not again be put too easily in such an awkward situation. I also secretly thought that next time I would have a bigger dinghy and a real sailing dinghy at that, but I did not dare linger too long on any criticism of my present dinghy for fear it would bring me bad luck. After all, she was doing her best to save my life.

The night was long, sleep was impossible and I was shivering with cold, all my clothes being soaking wet. At last daylight came. And best of all, about an hour after daybreak, I saw land in the distance. It was a most comforting sight, but I soon realized that my makeshift sailing dinghy, which seemed only able to sail with the wind aft, could not point high enough to reach it.

An hour later two more spots of land appeared, so with three peaks from which to take cross-bearings with my compass I soon found on the chart the only three places it matched and could thus determine my own position. Then to my great joy I realized that the land I was seeing was not at all the closest land to me but that a lower land still below the horizon was much nearer and was furthermore much easier to reach as it was almost straight downwind. All I needed to do was to alter the course by a few degrees.

I became very cheerful, despite my tiredness from the lack of sleep, the cold, the uncomfortable position in the bottom of the dinghy, the strain of steering and having to counteract every wave, and now the glare and the heat of the tropical sun, not to speak of the emotional strain. After a few hours land did indeed appear dead ahead of us as expected and I then could steer straight for it, using the compass for checking cross-currents which soon proved to be so strong that, had I not had the compass, I might not have realized their force until too late and then missed the island.

When I got close to the island and felt safe, I became careless and sat up on the middle thwart in order to get a better view to choose the best place to land. Immediately the bow plunged under the sea and the dinghy began to fill up. In a desperate move, I grabbed the "mast," uprooting it and let it fall over the side. The dinghy was at once relieved but already so full of water as to have lost all stability and threatened to capsize or fill up completely. I was close to land but still much too far to swim for it. As quickly but also as carefully as possible, I undid all the ropes holding the rig to the boat, then threw over the side the remaining bottle of water to give me more room for bailing and then bailed for dear life while all the time I kept shifting my weight to counteract the effect of the surging water. I breathed a sigh of relief when the dinghy was dry and had regained her stability. Without the rig I felt it was safe enough to sit up on the thwart and at long last stretch out my legs.

The island I had come to was called Canouan and was a small island in the Grenadines group. Its northern part was steep cliffs and impossible to land on, but its southern part seemed to be low sandbeaches. Unfortunately that part of the coast was bordered by a long reef on to which the whole Atlantic broke heavily. I was well aware of the danger of trying to land through such breakers and the sensible thing to do would, of course, have been to land on the island's lee side; but I was just too tired to even consider sculling all that way and I was also worried about the current perhaps being stronger than I and making me miss the lee-side altogether. Thus I preferred to take the chance on shooting the reef.

As I came closer, an islander high on the cliff signalled to me not to come any closer but to go round the island; however as I disregarded his advice and he realized that I really intended to go through the surf, he directed me to the best place where the rollers were not too big. I tried to time it so that I would get over the critical spot between two rollers but my dinghy was not fast enough and a huge breaker came foaming against me. I expected to be capsized but hoped to have enough strength to swim the rest of the way.

Much to my surprise the brave little dinghy just popped up on top of the broiling mass of water and shot forward at great speed. When the wave died down I found myself in smooth water. In the meantime, the islander on the cliff had jumped into a rowboat and was now coming toward me. He then towed me into the bottom of a quiet bay and helped me up the beach to lie down as my legs were so weak as to hardly be able to carry me. I was so tired I felt sick, but I knew that once more the words of the fortune teller who had told me at the age of fifteen that I was like the cat, born with nine lives, were still right. In fact, I should have two or three more to go!'

—————— ,, ——————

From: *Yachting World*, September 1967

30: Whalestrike

Yacht: *Guia III* (44ft ocean-racer)
Skipper: Jerome Poncet
Crew: George Marshall (navigator)
      Giorgio di Mola
      Claudio Cuoghi
      Giovanni Verbinni
      Francesco Longanesi
Bound from Rio de Janeiro, Brazil to Portsmouth, England
Time and date of loss: 1215, March 9th, 1976
Position: approximately 500 miles SW of Cape Verde Islands

The Italian-owned *Guia III* had sailed for Australia in their 1973 Admiral's Cup team under the name *Ginkgo*, but under her new ownership she had subsequently taken part in two of the three legs of the 1975–76 Atlantic Triangle races, the last one of which was between Rio de Janeiro and Portsmouth.

The third leg started on February 22nd, 1976, and until March 9th the race continued without incident. Thereafter, George Marshall, navigator and sole Englishman on board, tells the story:

———————— " ————————

'We started from Rio de Janeiro with a very good chance of winning the "Atlantic Triangle"; and after everything required to make the boat a winner had been checked and replaced where necessary. One item that needed doing was the liferaft; its certificate was out of date and only the eagle-eyed scrutineers spotted this. Like most long-distance sailors we had only made sure that we had one. The raft arrived back only hours before the start and was placed in its customary position in the centre cockpit.

The race soon became the usual long-distance ocean racing routine. Up to the equator we averaged 150 miles a day, hit the Doldrums on 6th

March, but during the night 8/9 March wind increased to 35 knots moderating as the sun came up.

At 8 o'clock the watch changed and I, with the other two on watch, went below for what was normally the best sleeping time. A very quick breakfast of hot chocolate, cookies and cheese, then wrap a sheet around myself and into the land of nod.

From the middle of a deep sleep I was awoken by a sudden crack and lurch upwards, and all the watch below sat up on their bunks. From the deck came the cry of "Orca" "Orca" – even my limited Italian was enough to translate this as whales. The head of Jepson appeared in the hatch and pointing forward he shouted "water in the boat."

I put my feet onto the cabin sole and found that indeed there was water in the boat, over the tops of my ankles.

Looking forward through the tunnel joining the forepeak to the main cabin I saw water rushing back. Diving forward into the forepeak I saw that the water was coming from the port side through the sail bins. I went back to the main cabin, got the knife that was always available on the galley, and went back to join Jerome our skipper and Giorgio from the deck watch. We cut the sail bins free and found what to us looked like an enormous hole. It was about 2 foot below the waterline and just abaft the fore bulkhead. It was an egg-shaped hole 3 ft long and 2 ft deep. The planks had been forced from the bottom to the top and it was very obvious that whatever had done the damage had hit the boat with great force.

The water gushed in, and for a second or two we just gaped at the damage in disbelief. Jerome and I then tried to force the wood back into the hole but the strength of the remaining fibres of wood were too much for our combined weight.

As we were doing this the remainder of the crew were handing the sails to take way off the yacht, the initial inrush of water making it impossible to tack or heave to. As it became obvious that we were not going to get the damaged portion of the hull back over the hole, Jerome told Giorgio and me to go on deck and try to get a headsail over the hole. He continued to try and plug the hole from the inside with spinnakers and anything else to hand. The water was waist deep at this time and as fast as he pushed a sail in the gap it was forced back.

Giorgio and I went up on deck and freed the No. 2 genoa from the lifelines. I took the head of the sail and stepped over the lifelines with the idea of jumping down past the hole and carrying the sail with me under the hull so that the water pressure would suck the sail into the hole.

Looking down into the very clear water I could see the jagged hole with long cracks, fore and aft. Also lying alongside the yacht about 2 to 3 ft down I could see a very big fish which was at least half the length of the yacht and appeared about 6 ft wide. Giorgio also saw it and very emphatically told me to stay on deck. In truth I had already changed my mind as I didn't fancy making a snack for whatever it was.

We then tried to take the sail around the bows, but by now the deck was awash and this proved impossible. Jerome then appeared in the main hatch and said it was time to abandon ship. The rest of the crew had already started to get stores up from the cabin and I went down below to start my part of the abandon ship drill. As I waited for the hatch to clear I looked around *Guia* and saw on the port side a pod of killer whales circling around about 50 ft from the beam. They are unmistakeable with their white patches and tall fins, and for the first time I realised what had happened. On the starboard side a school of dolphins, fairly large and with a mottled green and black skin, were sounding.

Down below I found that the water was thigh deep and the boat rocking swishing the water from beam to beam. The radio had been switched on and I soon had the first Mayday out on 2182 kHz. I knew that there was very little chance of it being picked up as we were by this time too far from land for the set to reach. A quick switch to the race control frequency of 4136.3 kHz and again a Mayday. The output meter on the set showed that the power was rapidly going as the seawater came over the tops of the battery. The water all this time was rising rapidly and soon Jerome and I were chest high. I continued sending Maydays on alternate frequencies until it was obvious that the set was only working on a bare minimum of power. As I was sending the signals I was helping Jerome by passing anything that floated past. All our kit that we kept for emergencies had already been passed up on deck and we knew that the liferaft had inflated and was being loaded.

Jerome then gave a very Gallic shrug and said to me that we must say *au revoir* to *Guia*, and told me to go on deck and get in the liferaft. I pushed the emergency signal button on the radio and noticed that it was transmitting, but at a very reduced output from normal. As we waded back to the hatch through the now neck-high water we managed to save a few more items – cans of fruit – a bag of mine that contained my camera and personal washing kit and a note book and some cans of condensed milk.

A shout from outside said that *Guia* was going. This made us move up on deck just in time to see the bows dip and in about 10 seconds from a boat awash there was only the stern and the top of the mast out of the water.

I slid into the water and swam the short distance to the raft. As I clung to the side of the raft *Guia* gave a very loud prolonged sigh as the air trapped in the stern escaped and disappeared entirely.

I then attempted to board the dinghy and found to my alarm that something was holding me down in the water. Jerome and Pimperle tried to pull me in but their combined strength couldn't get me in. We soon found that the sea anchor had wrapped itself around me and that this was keeping me in the water. It then became a simple matter of hauling it and me into the raft.

On entering the raft I saw that it was just a heap of bodies, kit, food containers and clothing. Everyone just sat for the first few minutes and I am sure that they felt as I did. To see a fine yacht like *Guia* disappear so suddenly was a shock to us all. Also the realisation that we were many miles away from both land and frequented shipping lanes made us all a little unhappy about our chances of survival. Looking around there was no sign of anything; no boat wreckage, no whales; just the sea and sky. It was a very lonely feeling.

We started to organise the inside of the raft and take inventory of what we had, and after we had inspected everything decided that we were not too badly off. There was plenty of food, enough with care to last a month. A box of flares. Helly Hansen suits and waterproofs for us all. Three blankets, 800 cigarettes, matches, lighters, torches, lifejackets and three kitbags with personal kit, including mine, with all my spare pullovers and some sailing trousers.

All the food was in polythene casks and we were glad that we had decided that this system was used on *Guia*. We thought if it ever came that the raft was badly damaged then we might be able to make a float with the food containers.

Our only shortcoming was water. We only had 15 litres and we knew that we would be in trouble if we didn't get some rain or make some from a still. However, we were pretty sure that we could last until a rain cloud came along as the area we were in always produced some rain.

After sorting out the raft and the stores we all changed into the thermal underwear and on the advice of Giorgio rested and talked about our chances. After a long discussion we agreed that we were going to survive come what may, and that we had three chances of being picked up. It was clear that the only place that we could go was towards South America with the odds of ending up somewhere in Venezuela. On the way we thought that within three days we should be somewhere near the mid-Atlantic route between the North American ports and Capetown, then two weeks later on the shipping route between Panama and Capetown and finally the inshore routes along the coast of South America.

After two hours the sea anchor was hauled in and we set off from the scene at about 2 to 2½ knots. The sea anchor had made us decide to leave, as its violent snubbing was liable to damage the raft and we would sooner take our chance with a possible long trip than end up with a sinking liferaft.

A food container and two lifebelts on the end of a 20-foot line kept the back of the liferaft to the wind and sea. It also broke up the worst of the waves so that only very occasionally did water come onto the canopy.

The motion of the raft was fairly comfortable, the floating anchor keeping us from dropping too fast down the front of the waves. The only discomfort was from the damp on the bottom of the raft and from the conglomeration of legs in the centre. The oilskins and blankets made the floor comfortable but the only answer for the legs was to grin and bear it. Giorgio was told that he might be getting some practice in amputation if we had to spend too much time in the dinghy.

As night fell the night watches were set for everyone to do one and a half hours in rotation. During the day only whoever was near the door had kept lookout as we knew that the best chance of seeing a boat was during the dark hours.

The lookout was stationed at the entrance with the torches, pumps and flares to hand. Each lookout was allowed two cigarettes and a cookie to keep him going during his watch.

As my turn was not until midnight I settled down to get what sleep I could. This proved easier than I thought but not until all the legs had been arranged to our mutual comfort.

At midnight Claudio Cuoghi, the youngest member of our crew, woke me and told me it was my turn for Guardia. After a long complicated manoeuvre I extracted myself from the pile of bodies and sat at the entrance of the raft. A shared cigarette with Claudio and a chat about the sinking, then he wormed his way into the pile of bodies and I was left alone with the sea. The wind was still about 25 knots and the sea about 9 to 12 feet high, but the raft was behaving perfectly well. Without moving I soon realised that I could cover 360 degrees of the horizon every 2 to 3 minutes as the raft swung at the end of the floats.

I can't say that I thought any great thoughts during the time I was on watch except that I probably felt very much at rest. The sea is so huge that it is difficult to feel anger or sorrow at anything that it or its inhabitants may do to you. Like the jungle the sea is neutral, and all that man can hope to do is live with it and accept all its moods.

After sitting for two hours I gave Pimperle a shake and he took over the watch from me. It was more difficult to get a comfortable space on the floor and it took me a while to get into that half dozy state that precedes sleep. Just as I had got warm and comfortable Pimperle leaned across me and shook Jerome. "I think that I can see a light," he said, "but it could just be a star rising."

I was at the entrance before he finished speaking, as I knew that there were clouds all around the horizon and it was almost sure that he had seen a ship. The three of us sat in the entrance staring out over our limited horizon. After what seemed an age we spotted a light dipping to windward. I wanted to put up a flare straight away (I had been delegated the job of igniting them as I had more practice than the others).

However, Jerome said to wait until we could see what it was and what course it was on. This seemed to me an even longer wait but soon the second masthead light of a steamer showed itself. It was soon apparent that it would pass us about three miles downwind, and I put up the first parachute red flare. It went straight up and burst into a very satisfying red glow. After about 30 seconds it went out and we all stared at the lights of the ship willing it to alter course. We waited 10 minutes and then discharged two more para flares one after the other, aiming to send them across the bows of the ship. They both worked and as they drifted down we saw the ship flash an Aldis lamp at us and the angle of her lights alter. Moments later all her deck lights came on and within minutes she went past us at a distance of 200 yards and stopped about a mile away. All our torches were lit, the buoy lights set flashing and I set to igniting the hand-held flares.

The next two hours were probably the most trying of my life. The ship made four passes at us but seemed to have great difficulty in seeing us. We only had ten hand-held flares, and some of those proved useless. My chief memory of those two hours is of violent curses against the people who sell such unseamanlike objects and gratitude to the sane ones who made the ones that worked.

Eventually the ship stopped downwind of us and we tried to paddle the raft to it, but as the ship was drifting faster than us we gave up and waited to see what they would do. From round the stern a ship's liferaft appeared. It was only when we saw it that we realised what size sea was running. Most of the time it was out of sight and at first went away from our position. The last hand flare brought it back towards us, and soon we transferred to the lifeboat, taking all our kit from the dinghy with us.

The raft was secured alongside, and soon we found ourselves alongside the *Hellenic Ideal*. We still had to manage ourselves up the ladder but the deck officer in charge made us all tie a lifeline around us before allowing us to climb to the deck from the lifeboat: a very sensible precaution as it turned out. Not one of us after the climb was able to stand, and each of us collapsed against a bulkhead; I think it was more from relief than weakness. After a cigarette and a tot of something very strong we were led down below to the passengers' dining room. The captain then came down from the bridge, made sure that we were complete, and said that until New York the ship was at our disposal.

It is difficult to express your thanks to someone who saves your life, but to the seaman who spotted our flare, and the Captain, Dimitros Dimitri, and the crew of the *Hellenic Ideal*, thank you. Your skill, seamanship and hospitality will never be forgotten.'

———————— ,, ————————

From: *R.N.S.A. Journal*, Spring 1976

31: The Sinking of *Tern*

Yacht: *Tern* (36ft gaff-rigged yawl)
Skipper: H.S. Carter
Crew: P. Woodcock
Bound from the Beaulieu River, Hampshire to Poole, Dorset
Time and date of loss: approx 1200, April 11th, 1928
Position: in entrance to Poole Harbour

Tern, designed by Albert Strange, was homeward bound from the Beaulieu River to Poole during the Easter weekend of 1928. She had made a fast run before a strong south-easterly and, as she reached the Bar, the lumpy sea grew confused as they met the first of the ebb running out of the channel, so that the skipper was intent on keeping *Tern* on course and did not notice a coasting collier coming up astern:

———————— " ————————

'The mate, who had been below for a few minutes, now appeared in the companion.

"She's going to pass us pretty closely, isn't she?" he remarked.

The skipper glanced round. The collier was nearly up with them, a little on their port quarter. She was close, but would pass them at a distance of forty feet or so. There seemed to be no cause for alarm. She would probably give them a heavy wash which might slop aboard, but that would hurt no one.

She was a steamer and an overtaking vessel. It was her duty to keep clear, so the skipper steered tranquilly on, while the mate joined him in the cockpit.

Slowly but steadily the collier overhauled them. It was after high water and she was pushing along at full speed. She was, in fact, in a hurry to pass the Bar, for, in those days, it had not been dredged to its present depth and

203

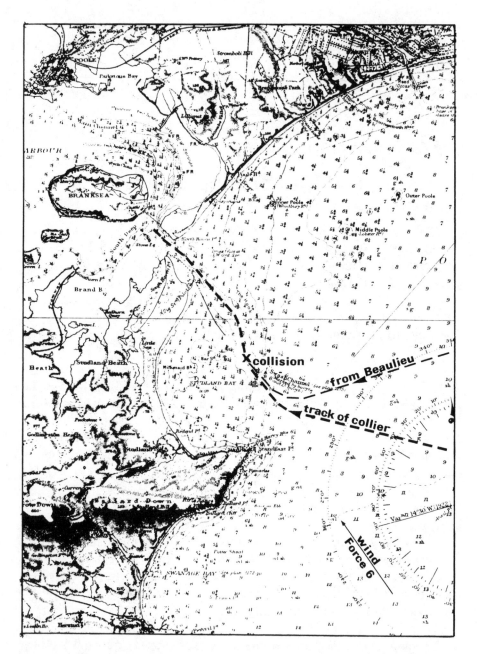

her draught was almost as great as the depth of water, so that the clearance under her keel could not have been more than a few inches.

She passed to leeward of the yawl, drawing out ahead until her counter was just clear of the end of the latter's bowsprit. Her bow wave rolled harmlessly under the canoe stern, a mere bucketful of water topping the rail

204

to fall inboard on deck. The danger, if any, seemed past; only the quarter wave remained to be negotiated.

Owing to the collier's draught and the comparatively shallow water, this wave was something of an outsize in waves. Very steep and with a curling foam-capped crest, it rushed along, an angry mass of drab-coloured, sand-filled water. This roaring quarter wave lifted Tern's stern. Higher and higher she reared and then she began to be carried forward with the wave.

Trouble at sea is apt to crop up at unexpected moments, and when things happen, they often happen quickly. They did so now. Like a bolt from the blue came disaster. From sitting at his tiller steering his ship before a big but by no means dangerous sea, the skipper suddenly found himself in the midst of a smother of foam which boiled up and slopped aboard on either quarter, while the tiller, from being a live thing under his hand, lost all feeling and became dead, a useless bit of inanimate wood, as the yawl, her rudder buried in a mass of moving water, tobogganed along on the face of the wave.

Faster and faster she went, so fast indeed that the mainboom came right inboard with the back draught. In a wild burst of speed she charged ahead, rushing up on the collier and overhauling her until she was once more level with the bridge.

Though from the beginning of her wild rush she had been entirely out of control, she had run straight, but now, under the influence of some irresistible power of suction and in spite of the hard-down helm, she suddenly sheered in towards the collier. There was a fearful splintering crash as the bowsprit snapped off short like a carrot; then, with a sickening thud, the bow drove home against the steel plates.

For a moment there seemed a lull. The collier drew ahead, the yawl fell astern. Then events again moved swiftly in this mad minute of misfortune.

"Are we leaking?" asked the skipper.

The mate started to run forward to see what damage had been done. He did not get far. Between the fore end of the self-draining cockpit and the companion was some five feet or so of deck. As the mate passed the hatch, he glanced below to see to his amazement and consternation the water already over the cabin seats and level with the table.

"By Jove, we're sinking!" he cried.

"Launch the dinghy, quick," ordered the skipper.

The dinghy was lashed on the small cabin top and, whipping out his knife, the mate started to cut the lashings. The skipper sprang to help, but in vain. There was no time. Even as they worked there came a long-drawn whistle as the invading water drove the air from the lockers round the cockpit, and less than half a minute after receiving the fatal blow, the little ship took her plunge.

Just before she sank the skipper tried to tear loose the lifebuoy which was lashed in the rigging, but the seizing was too strong and he found himself struggling in the heavy seas. He very quickly realized that, hampered as he was by his heavy coat, he had not the strength to keep afloat for long. As he struck out, he felt something solid, grasped it and held on. It was the head of the mizen mast which supported him, but in such a position that he was completely submerged by every wave.

The mate, intent on freeing the dinghy, worked on her till the last moment and was sucked under when the vessel sank, but, young and strong, he quickly bobbed to the surface again and, getting rid of some of his clothes, swam close to the skipper and encouraged him to hold on.

The crew of the collier had not seen the accident and the skipper and the mate had the mortification of seeing her cheerfully steam way up the channel while they fought for their lives. Luckily for them other eyes had been more observant and a motor launch was driving at full speed to the rescue. The skipper had almost resigned himself to the end when the mate sighted her approaching.

"Hang on," he cried to his skipper. "There's help coming. They'll soon be here."

Between his duckings the skipper also caught a cheering glimpse of the launch, but even then doubted his ability to last out.

The launch approached and stopped, fearing to strike the wreck and knock a hole in her bottom. Her crew threw a lifebuoy. It fell short by a dozen yards, but the mate retrieved it and swam with it to the skipper who, abandoning the mast, dropped thankfully into it and was towed to the launch. The mate clambered aboard and, with the help of the solitary youth who formed the launch's crew, managed to haul the skipper over the rail into the well where he subsided on to the bottom boards – exhausted, but safe.

Tern sank in the afternoon. She lay right in the fairway on the Poole side of the Bar. During the night another steamer entering the port steamed over her in the darkness, snapping off her hollow mast and crushing in her hull.

A few days later the wreck was raised and taken to Newman's yard at Hamworthy. Her mainmast and bowsprit were gone; the stem was practically torn out of her, the butt ends of the planks gaping wide on either side to the forefoot, while the hole in her port side made by the keel of the steamer reached well below the waterline. On survey she was pronounced a total constructive loss and her name disappeared from the Register of British yachts.'

———————— ,, ————————

From: *Yachting Monthly*, September 1931

32: *Easting Down's* Last Cruise

Yacht: *Easting Down* (38ft ex-R.N.L.I. gaff-ketch)
Skipper: J.S. Robertson
Crew: Mary Robertson
  Andrew Robertson
  Rachael Robertson
  Alexander Robertson
  John and Ruth (two friends of the children)
Bound from IJmuiden to the river Humber
Time and date of loss: 1300, August 24th, 1965
Position: approx. 45 miles W of IJmuiden

Easting Down was built for the R.N.L.I. in 1903, by double-diagonal construction. She was intended for service in the Portland Bill area and had a large centreplate, because sail and oar were often the only methods of propulsion in those days.

However, when the Robertson family and their two young friends set out in 1965 to cruise in Holland, she had been re-rigged as a gaff cutter, twin diesel engines had been installed and her spacious accommodation allowed three separate cabins.

They left South Ferriby Sluice on Sunday August 15th, and reached IJmuiden at 2100 on the following day. After visiting Amsterdam they locked through into the IJsselmeer, calling at Enkhuisen, Vollendam and Marken before returning to Amsterdam a week after arriving in Holland.

At 1200 on Monday August 23rd they left IJmuiden to commence the return passage, having heard Scheveningen Radio forecast southwesterly 4–5 becoming northwesterly 4–6 later.

——————— " ———————

'With a wind of Force 4 we were able to point our course for the Corton Reef L.V. closehauled on the port tack, making 4–5 knots. Gradually the

207

wind freshened and headed us slightly. By 1600 hours we were logging five knots under mains'l and stays'l and jib only. The wind continued to freshen. At 1800 we furled the jib. The wind was now Force 7. Shortly after handing over the watch at 2000 I was called out on account of some puzzling lights. At this time all seemed well. The ship was sailing and behaving very well. An hour later, however, we heeled so far that I could not remain in my bunk, and was horrified to find water where the cabin floor should be.

Dressing hurriedly I went out, to find my crew enjoying the sail, and quite unaware that anything was wrong. With the sum-log reading between six and seven knots, and the lee rail awash for the first time in its career, the ship was creaming along and a joy to handle. The wind was now very strong, and the sea rough, and we had a struggle to stow the mains'l, but we had to do so to reduce our list and allow the pumps to work. Starting the Thorneycroft engine we maintained our course and pumped. The water level did not fall. The standby pump was rigged, but soon both pumps became blocked by shavings left by the shipwrights. From 2200 hours onwards the bucket brigade laboured intermittently, filling buckets in the cabin, passing them out to the cockpit for emptying. Once we had got the level down we were able to keep it down to floor level by bailing alternate hours only.

Seasickness took an increasing toll. At first the duty watch continued to sail the ship while the others bailed. By 0100 GMT, however, it was impossible to steer the ship owing to the wind and sea. Engines were stopped, and we lay ahull.

A Consul fix placed us at Lat. 52° 40′ N Long. 03° 00′ E at 0600 hours, but we were drifing back towards the Dutch coast at an unknown rate. The wind was very strong, and still increasing. Daylight disclosed an impressive scene. The ventimeter showed a wind speed of 35 knots only 5 ft above sea level. Big breaking seas bore down on us, but the ship rode them magnificently. To reduce inflow of water through alongside the lifting cable, I had pulled up the centreplate just before dawn. Lying beam on to wind and sea we slid sideways down the face of each sea, leaving a slick of smooth water to windward. This protected us from the worst of the seas. By now the wind had moved towards the NW and cross seas produced occasional pillars of water which blew down onto us, crashing onto the deck, and finding hitherto unknown ways round the edges of closed hatches.

Charts and log had deteriorated into a sodden mess. Dividers and parallel rules, flung from the table, disappeared in the bilges.

I experimented, trying heading into the seas with both engines on, but this proved hard work, uncomfortable, and impossible to maintain. At the crest of each sea the wind caught our bows and blew them off to port or to starboard, and way was only regained as the next sea approached. Running downwind towing warps was also useless, creating risk of pooping and broaching to. I know now, beyond doubt, that in a vessel of shallow draft it is safer to lie ahull broadside to wind and sea, even with a non self-righting hull like *Easting Down's*. It is safe and relatively comfortable. Our only fears were that by the time the gale abated we might be too exhausted to sail the ship or we might have drifted onto the shoals of the Sheldt estuary. We had to keep the water bailed down to floorboard level lest it reach the unprotected "Nife" batteries and short out our power, so that we would be unable to use radio or engines in time of need.

At 0805 I attempted to send a "Mayday", but there was no answer. The aerial relay was jamming. At 1105 I tried again, and was answered by the British ship *Etterick* and by Scheveningen Radio. I estimated that by now we must have drifted near to Browns Ridge, and gave an estimated position of 52° 32' N 03° 10' E. A Consol count on Stavanger put us 05' further east, and I then advised *Etterick* of our corrected position. The distress frequency was busy, and we had to wait for signals concerned with the German timber ship *Tanenberg* in distress 25 miles SW of us, near the Outer Gabbard, to finish before we could talk. We maintained radio contact with *Etterick*, who was heading for our position at the time of the signal. A submarine passed within a mile to the north of us, but failed to answer our signals; but *Ossendrecht*, a 16,000-ton ship bound for Hudson Bay, picked up our call relayed on the LF distress frequency by Scheveningen Radio. Her master estimated our probable rate and direction of drift so well that he sailed straight towards us. Due to the height of the seas he did not see us until very close. At 1300 hours he steamed round us and hove to a cable to windward. We started the engines and motored alongside his pilot ladder. As the shipping forecast now promised further gales, and Hurricane Hilda was also approaching to our north at over 30 knots, it seemed wise for an exhausted crew to leave a leaking ship. Our position was now Lat. 52° 30' N, 03° 23' E, and we had drifted seven miles in the two hours since our distress call.

I was grieved to learn that *Ossendrecht* could not take *Easting Down* in tow. John volunteered to stay aboard with me and try to sail the ship to shelter, but I considered the risk too great. The children, who had been confined to their bunks for safety, climbed the ladder, followed by the ladies, while I attempted to salvage clothes, binoculars, cameras and radio. Then John and I also climbed the ladder.

While we were abandoning *Easting Down* she dropped into a trough, pulling the bow rope tight and wrenching a mooring cleat from the foredeck. Then, as *Ossendrecht* got under way and started to leave the yacht, a big sea rolled *Easting Down* and her mainmast struck *Ossendrecht's* hull and broke. With sorrow we watched her, with the broken mast drooping to starboard, as we steamed away. In a few minutes she was lost to view, her white hull hidden among the white breakers.

Next morning we learned that *Easting Down* had sunk only 15 minutes after being taken in tow by a tug – 4½ hours after we had left her.

Whether she could have been saved had I stayed aboard to bale we shall never know. The cause of the leak was never found. It may have been from the centreplate case, but the North Sea was full of baulks of jettisoned timber, and we had struck several pieces. One of these, thrust against the hull by a propeller blade a few miles from IJmuiden, may have damaged the hull.

While such hazards abound it would plainly pay to fit an engine-driven pump. Had we had one this tale would have had a happier ending.'

———————— ,, ————————

From: the *Journal of The Humber Yawl Club*, 1965

33: There She Blows

Yacht: *Pionier* (32ft sloop)
Skipper: Gordon Webb
Crew: Jennifer Webb
      Tony Keeney
      Peter Flockemann
      Willi Schutten
Bound (racing) from Cape Town, South Africa to Rio de Janeiro, Brazil
Time and date of loss: 0030, January 23rd, 1971
Position: approx. 1600 miles W of Cape Town

A few years before the loss of *Guia III*, the south African yacht, *Pionier* had also sunk after striking a whale while racing across the South Atlantic, and although there is much similarity between the two incidents some of the experiences of the crew of *Pionier* are of particular interest. The following extracts are from an account written by Anthony Hocking after interviews with the survivors from *Pionier*. The 1971 Cape to Rio race had started on January 11th and the 'strike' occurred when *Pionier* was eleven days out from Cape Town.

—————— " ——————

'Tony Keeney was on watch, sitting among the cushions in the cockpit behind the wheel as midnight approached. It was a dark night, with only a sliver of moon and a few brave stars appearing through the cloudy haze. Tony had been there since 10, alone while the other four rested below, reading, sleeping, plotting. Since the second day *Pionier*'s crew had been watching alone, two hours at a time through the day and night. Gordon Webb, *Pionier*'s skipper, was due to relieve Tony at midnight.

    Gordon took control, standing with one hand on the wheel looking out into the blackness ahead while Tony eased himself from the cushioned seat beside him, *en route* for his bunk. He had been at the wheel most of the day. There was not much to say. Both Gordon and Tony knew the implication of the position report. *Pionier* was placed to win, the wind was right, they were heading in straight for Rio. Almost, though neither of them would have dreamt of suggesting it out loud, the race was in the bag.

Suddenly there was a shuddering crash. *Pionier*'s bow shot high, arching out of the water in the darkness ahead, pointing to the stars as she crashed into some terrible obstruction. As she plunged down again, a fraction of a second later, there was a second bang, a sickening smash, this time from under the hull, as *Pionier* was hurled bodily to starboard.

The men struggled to keep their balance; there was not much light around. The binnacle light was on, there was light filtering from the cabin, a token glimmer from the sky, the stern light. Gordon looked aft, as *Pionier* fought gamely to recover from the cruel shock. In the glow of the stern light he saw the huge tail fin of a blue whale, 2½ metres across and forked, strong, majestic and now disappearing into the deep.

Tony had seen it too, just. Halfway into the cockpit, he had turned at the two crashes, and though he was low in the boat, he could see the end of the tail over the dodger and the life-rings, as it dipped slowly out of sight.

The boat lurched crazily as dazed wits gathered. Gordon still held the wheel, Tony was standing in the hatchway. Down below, Willi in the fo'c'sle had taken the full force of the first blow, Jennifer of the second. Willi had thought the boat had hit rough weather and wondered where it came from. Jennifer had felt the impact of the second blow under her head. She was thrown up and half out of her bunk, and she let her feet fall to the deck to steady herself.

It was then she felt the water. Creeping up through the deck planks, from down somewhere by the keel, she could feel it lapping her ankles as the boat heeled over under full sail. She screamed her discovery up to Gordon on deck. Gordon and Jenny eased up the deck planks to see if they could find the hole admitting the water. But it was coming in too fast. Gordon told Peter Flockemann to get on to the radio.

Peter tuned the transmitter, 2182, the international distress frequency. It was supposed to be left free for emergencies like this one, and all ships were supposed to keep a watch on it. But there was the usual cacophony of messages broadcast in abuse of the international agreement. Peter could hear a conversation going on, by the sound of it not far away. He switched on the transmitter and began broadcasting the Mayday. *Pionier* was sinking, he called. He gave the position they had calculated most recently, 24.30 S, 07.06 W. Again he repeated it, appealing for rescue. But when he switched on the receiver to see if anyone was responding, he drew a blank.

Gordon had abandoned any plans to save the ship from the inside, though Willi had begun to bale with a bucket. The water was swirling knee deep in the saloon by this time, the ship was sinking to the gunnels. Gordon had read somewhere of a way of saving a holed ship with sails, by draping them over the side and allowing suction to pull them into the hole and seal it off. He outlined the plan to Tony and Willi, and they set about the job. There were two spinnakers in the cockpit, and they took one from its bag and draped it over the port side. The boat had lost way by now, and they draped the second spinnaker in its place.

But still the water poured in. Now it was waist deep in the cabin. Gordon was out in the cockpit, taking the life-raft from its cover. He pulled the inflation trigger, it opened with a loud hiss, and he put the raft over the side. He shouted down to Jennifer to cut free the plastic jerrycans of water lashed to the legs of the saloon table below, the extra water *Pionier* was obliged to carry in addition to the water in her tanks, to comply with the race rules. She tossed four of the jerrycans to Willi up in the cockpit. They weighed 22½ kg apiece, but she hardly noticed.

Jennifer's next thought was of food. She scrambled to collect all she could find in the provision lockers and pass it to Willi on deck, who by this time had hold of the life-raft alongside. Anything she could find, most of it floating around her, tins, cereals, eggs in their boxes, vegetables, jars, anything within reach. As she passed the provisions up to Willi, Gordon remembered they would need the tin-opener. He reminded her, and Jenny turned to open the door where it was kept. But it was jammed. Peter left the radio to wrench it open for her, then went up on deck to help Tony with the spinnakers. Jenny took over the radio, and had time to shout out two more Mayday signals before the radio went silent as the flooded batteries died.

Willi had remembered to grab flares before going up on deck. He took a full box of them, ordinary night flares, unfortunately, rather than the parachute flares he had been looking for. And he grabbed an heirloom from the days when he had sailed his first yacht, *Falcon*, years before. His one and only smoke flare. It had sailed with him on *Falcon* and his second yacht *Sprinter*, without a moment's anxiety, and now it was with him on *Pionier*. He threw it into the raft.

Tony's thought was of clothing. He had read an article on life-raft survival before the race. It had pointed out that though water was a high priority in survival at sea, almost as high was – not food or flares – but shelter. It had advocated clothing as protection both from heat and cold, and it was this thought that drove Tony to the nearest clothes locker, his and Willi's. He grabbed armfuls of whatever came to hand. Sodden jerseys and trousers, anything, he passed them to Willi in the cockpit. Peter, equally practical, found a sleeping-bag and a bottle of whisky.

Gordon ordered everyone on deck. The boat was sinking fast. Willi was in the life-raft, holding it to the gunnel of the yacht in the heavy swell, still wearing nothing but his underpants. Gordon told Jennifer to climb in with him, after her Tony, after him Peter. He looked down the yacht. The bows were under but the stern was still above water. He wondered if there was a bubble of air keeping her afloat and if there was a chance of saving her after all. He began bailing, but only for a moment. He knew there was no hope, and he thought of something else. Their passports. He knew they were in a wallet down below. He went down, the cabin almost full of water, and dived down to the locker where they were kept. He found them, surfaced, and found too his precious sextant and navigation books floating by. He took them in his arms and himself climbed into the life-raft, able to step straight from the gunnel into the shelter, so low was the yacht.

The life-raft stood off some way, for the yacht was rolling over. Slowly she dipped at the bows, further under water as the pulpit disappeared, and as she heeled over, as if in final, tragic salute, a short somewhere on the electric panel produced the last cruel joke. All *Pionier*'s lights flashed on, her masthead lights, the navigation lights, the lights on her spreader, and over she rolled, her bared poles sinking under the waves as like a whale herself she showed her underside, deep fin keel with rudder still intact on the skeg – and the long, jagged rip in her hull which told *Pionier*'s crew what they needed to know: that they could never have saved their ship. And the yacht disappeared, and they were alone.

There they sat, in the dark. They had a torch, but to conserve its batteries they used it only sparingly. They had brought one packet of cigarettes, and a box of matches. But the matches were soaked in sea water and would have to be dried out. Some tried to sleep, ignoring the cramp of legs intertwined uncomfortably with four other pairs. And every so often came an unnerving hiss of escaping air from the raft beneath them, the only sound besides their close breathing and the lap of the water. There was nothing to say.

The dawn found them. With light to see what they were doing, they began to organize their raft. It might be their home for weeks. The sail they had brought as a sea anchor was already trailing overboard. Gordon decided the three white plastic jerrycans should be trailed as well once he had made sure their plastic caps would not let in sea water. Fresh water being lighter than salt, they would float. So the jerrycans were tied together with a rope, and gently let into the water.

While they were securing the jerrycans overboard, conversation turned to food, and the five investigated the contents of the sail-bag. Tins galore, boxes of dehydrated vegetables, broken eggs in their boxes, muesli breakfast cereal, the sodden packets spilling their contents; even a hunk of

Christmas cake wrapped in tinfoil and a jar of honey. Jennifer set about preparing something. Her eye fell on Gordon's sextant box and she commandeered it. The sextant was ejected, and the box became a serviceable pot. She mixed the muesli cereal and some broken eggs into a tasty paste, with Christmas cake to follow. Nobody noticed the tang of salt water.

Breakfast over, they opened the emergency survival pack they had found in the raft. Nobody had any idea what might be in it, so it was like opening a Christmas parcel. First, they found a handpump for the raft, with instructions which among other things explained the disturbing hisses of air they had heard in the night. These had come as air was let out of the raft to counteract its heavy load. There were sponges, to help in drying out the raft, which was itself ankle deep in water from the night before. There were six 3-pint tins of water, and a can-opener, with a measuring cup. Instructions with the water advised regular rationing. No random drinking, but instead a cupful early in the morning, one at noon, and a third at night. Though they had plenty of water in the jerrycans, Gordon decided they would follow the directions. Glucose sweets, an emergency medical kit and a funnel to catch rainwater completed the provisions.

There was not much conversation. Gordon had told them at the outset they were in quite a spot. They were way off the normal shipping lanes, and it would be a miracle if their Mayday signal had been picked up. The rest of the fleet would not miss them as a number of yachts had not been heard of in days, in most cases because of the failure of their generator plants. So it might be weeks before anyone thought of mounting a search for them. On the other hand, they had plenty of water, the means of catching more, and clothing and covering enough to shelter them. They knew that even without food they could survive for weeks on the water alone.

What was suggested openly was that it would not be long before a few legs were amputated and thrown overboard. All were in agonies of cramp, unable to move their legs without dislodging the whole arrangement of the raft. But nobody complained.

Noon arrived, and it was getting hot. Somebody had tossed a sodden sheet into the raft, Jenny's tropical sleeping-bag – an ordinary sheet sewn double along three-quarters of its length. They had a couple of large sombrero hats with them too. It was found one way of keeping the watchkeeper cool during his twenty-minute agony was to soak the sheet in sea water and drape it over his back and neck, while he wore one of the hats. Noon was the time for more water rations, and each received his measure from the cup. Nobody wanted food.

So the watches went on through the afternoon, twenty minutes turn and turn about, the raft bobbing to the top of the swell and giving a view for 3 miles around, and then dropping back into a hollow. The watchkeeper wearing his sheet and his hat, the other four cowering in the shelter, without speaking. On the raft's canopy, all the clothing there was room for, drying in the sunshine. And the precious matches, being dried for the pleasure of the packet of cigarettes still to be smoked.

Tony was sitting outside again, passing in to the others the clothes that had been drying in the sun.

Then someone asked for the matches. Tony did not smoke, but he looked for the matches and found they had disappeared. It looked as if they had gone over the side as they had been threatening to all along. With disgust the others resigned themselves to survival without cigarettes, and the apparently useless packet was thrown over board. Two minutes later the matches turned up – among the dried clothes in the life-raft.

Scanning the horizon for a sail, the shapes of clouds had played cruel tricks with the hopes of the watchkeepers, so much so that they had taken to looking many times before daring to believe their eyes. And each time it had turned out there was nothing there. But when Tony noticed a movement on the horizon, as the life-raft rose to the top of a swell, he felt a curious burst of excitement. It was a new shape, to the north-west. But it was far distant, and he knew he could be wrong. He looked to the south, to the east, looking for a sail, anywhere but to the north-west. But he had to look again. This time he was sure there was something there. What looked to him like goalposts, the derricks of a big bulk carrier, or tanker, perhaps. But he wanted to be sure.

He carried on watching as the life-raft rode the swells, watching as the ship came closer. He could see his "goalposts" clearer now, and he was sure it was a ship. But still he said nothing. He watched as the ship emerged clearer from the mist on the horizon, and looked again at the approaching rain squall, getting dangerously close. He could see the ship's bows and her bridge. His heart was beating fit to burst, but he stayed quiet, until he was confident there was hope of rescue, and his eyes were not betraying him. He called Gordon.

"I think there might be something over there," he said, leaning towards the opening in the canopy.

"What, a ship?"

"I don't know. It might be."

The atmosphere was electric as Gordon slowly crawled across the craft, its bottom heaving, and knelt in the opening to see what Tony had spotted. He was not over-optimistic. Clearly there was a ship, but he estimated she would pass 3 miles away.

Tony had been watching it some minutes now. He told Gordon he felt she had changed course. Gordon did not allow his hopes to ride too high.

The three left inside the shelter were hanging on to every muttered word that passed between the two men. The ship was 5 miles away.

Gordon thought quickly. How could he attract the ship's attention to the tiny ball of orange adrift between swells? He was revising his ideas of how far away the ship would pass. As she came closer, he thought it might be something like 2 miles. But she was still far away.

There was suddenly pandemonium on board. The box of flares Willi had saved was useless in daylight, and this was a blow. The white flares in the box would not be spotted if they were fired now. The only hope rested with the orange smoke flare, but it was years old. Gordon read and re-read the instructions on its side, to make sure he made no mistake in firing it. And while the five waited in a tension of fright for the approach of the ship, the flare was passed from hand to hand as each strove to find a new significance in the simply listed instructions.

There could be no doubt now that the ship would be passing close by even if she had not seen life on the raft. But she was still miles away, and it would be too late to fire the flare when she came abeam. As Gordon knew well, in a lonely ocean like this there might be no one on the bridge. So Gordon read the instructions on the flare for the last time, and all wills were with it as Gordon pulled its triggering mechanism and flung it through the air. It landed 9 metres away and worked, scattering bright orange smoke over a wide area of ocean. But hearts on the life-raft sank to their lowest ebb. The wind scattering the smoke kept it only half a metre or so above the sea's surface, and for all but a fraction of the time it was as invisible to the ship as the raft itself. If they could not see the ship, how could it see the life-raft?

But the ship kept coming, and Gordon was beginning to agree it might come close after all. Peter and Tony grabbed two bright orange jackets which had been salvaged with the clothes, Jenny's and Willi's, part of the crew's uniform. They stuck them on the two short paddles that had come as part of the life-raft kit, and began waving them furiously through the opening of the shelter, waving till their arms refused to work more and dropped in exhaustion. And it was then the ship responded with three long blasts of her whistle.

There was pandemonium on that life-raft. Jennifer Webb burst into tears and flung herself at the necks of each man in turn, her husband first and then Willi, Peter and Tony. and on each face there was a smile as big as it could take. They were cheering, everyone was talking at once. Everyone realized they had been rescued without going through any ordeal at all, only 16 hours in the water when they had feared they might be there for ever.

Up came the ship, more than 13,000 tons of her, rusted and wave-worn. A ship they would not have spared a second glance if they had seen her in harbour. But now she was the most beautiful ship the five had ever seen. A bulk grain carrier, and on her bow they could read her name: *Potomac*. She manoeuvred to within 100 metres of them, as they wriggled eagerly in what seemed eternity, waiting for their deliverance. On deck they could see the crew making ready. A pilot's ladder was lowered over the side, and deck-hands were standing ready with a rope. Others were swinging a lifeboat overboard, still on its davits. On the bridge stood several officers, one of them with a loud-hailer. He tried to shout down instructions to them, but his words were carried away on the wind. Those of the crew not involved with the preparations were standing at the rail, many of them with cameras.

The *Potomac* came up close. A line was thrown across, but missed the raft. As it was thrown the rain squall which had been threatening all afternoon arrived. Driving rain forced them back under the canopy, even finding its way through the air vents. The sky grew dark, the sea green and the swells white-capped. The *Potomac* lost way and had to start her engines. Their wash swept the tiny life-raft astern to her, and away into the gloom. The *Potomac* disappeared, ahead, over the swells half a mile away.

"They'll lose us," cried Jennifer. The smiles disappeared as new anxious thoughts crowded in. The squall was dangerous. It was as if the sea had reacted in fury as it saw its victims all but snatched from its clutches, and was taking its revenge on them. But they could see the *Potomac* circling round, and she came up from behind, this time further away. They watched as the lifeboat on its davits was lowered into the water, with its crew of seven aboard. And they watched as it crossed the swells separating them from the ship. On the ship, the crew were rigging a scrambling net forward.

The sea was rough and it was a dangerous manoeuvre and the lifeboat chugged in to relieve the excited survivors. But soon it was alongside and brawny arms helped first Jennifer, then each of the men into the lifeboat. Peter carried the bottle of whisky with him, still all but full as they had consumed only a part of it on the raft. The other things were left on the raft, which was towed to the ship behind the lifeboat. And the survivors met their rescuers.

They were Americans. The *Potomac* was from Portland, Oregon, on America's west coast, and was on her way to Cape Town. In command of the lifeboat was the man they had to thank for their deliverance, Third Officer Roy Newkirk. He had been on watch on the bridge, soon to be relieved, when he saw the tiny orange dot in the distance, 3 miles off the port bow. He thought it might be a buoy drifting. But he did not want to take chances, and told the *Potomac*'s master about it. Vernon Hansen, from America's deep South, had been asleep in his cabin, but climbed to the bridge immediately. Through binoculars it was obvious the orange dot was a life-raft, and Hansen ordered a change of course. But there was no sign of life aboard. Just then Hansen spotted the trail of orange smoke from Gordon's flare. It drifted over a wide expanse of water.

"There's life all right," he told Newkirk.

He ordered a lifeboat to be prepared and Newkirk himself asked to be put in charge of it. He wanted to find out what people were doing out in the middle of nowhere where nobody ought to be, he explained.

The lifeboat pulled alongside the ship, heaving in the swell, and the crew helped the survivors grab the scramble net and clamber up the deck, a vertical climb of 24 metres. Jennifer and Gordon went first, Jennifer a little worried about the bikini bottom she was wearing as its elastic had broken. She had tied a piece of string to it taken round her neck as a kind of suspender. Willi went next, hampered by his injured leg and clambering up with the strength of his arms. Peter and Tony brought up the rear, and the lifeboat was winched back on deck.'

———————— ,, ————————

From: *Yachting in Southern Africa* (1972),
Purnell & Sons (S.A.) (Pty) Ltd

34: The Mudhook Disaster

Yacht: *Valkyrie II* (117ft gaff-rigged racing cutter)
Skipper: Capt. William Cranfield
Crew: 35 paid hands (mostly Essex men)
Others on board: Lord Dunraven and his party, including the
yacht's designer, Mr G.L. Watson, and two ladies
Time and date of loss: 1018, July 5th, 1894
Position: in 17 fathoms off Hunters Quay on the Clyde

It was estimated that one hundred thousand people were trying to watch the start of the first race on the first day of the Mudhook Regatta on July 5th, 1894. The reason for such a vast crowd, many of them aboard steam yachts and river steamers, was that they hoped to witness the first appearance in British waters of the famed Herreshoff designed *Vigilant*, following her victory over *Valkyrie* in the America's Cup series of 1893.

Overnight, the British yachts *Britannia*, *Satanita* and *Valkyrie* had lain in the mouth of the Holy Loch, while *Vigilant* had been on the other side of the Clyde in Gourock Bay.

The course was from a line off Hunter's Quay, round flag-boats off Skelmorlie, Ascog and Kilcreggan and back to Hunter's Quay – twice round, a total of 50 miles. The wind was southwesterly and the visibility poor, in rain.

One of the best contemporary descriptions of the scene and the events before the start appeared in the *Yacht Racing Calendar and Review* for 1894 and was written by a journalist/observer, James Meikle.

——————— " ———————

'The *Lutra*, which was flagship, was lying just clear of the fleet at anchor, and, immediately before the start, the *Valkyrie* was coming on starboard tack with a clear line to skim close to the flagship and secure the highest weather berth possible. The *Satanita*, which was reaching in on port tack (at some 14 knots) with *Britannia* in her wake, was bent on standing on past

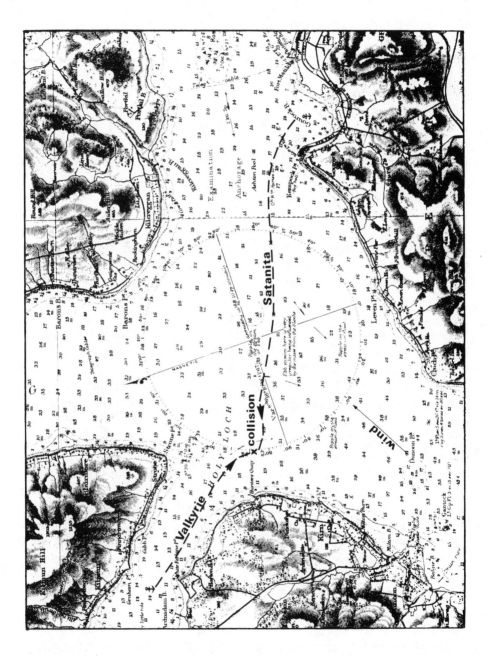

Lutra until she could stay on on *Valkyrie*'s weather quarter. A small craft, however, with four men in her, blocked *Satanita*'s course and in common humanity the helm was eased to clear them; this was barely accomplished as the bow wave of *Satanita* washed one of the men overboard, and the boat was no sooner cleared than *Satanita*'s amateur helmsman found it physically impossible to get the vessel off. The skipper of *Satanita* helping at the tiller could not avoid the inevitable, and she smashed stem on into the *Valkyrie*, cutting in two her port side between rigging and runners to below the water line and about 6 ft into the deck. *Satanita*'s bowsprit broke off and came back in board, and the force of the collision drove *Valkyrie* right round until she gybed one way and *Satanita* the other, and ultimately drove *Valkyrie* broadside on to the *Vanduara* steam yacht, with the result that a lot of bulwarks of the latter were carried away and her large steam launch smashed up. At the time of the collision a number of *Valkyrie*'s men jumped overboard, fearing the probable falling of gear, while others got on *Satanita*. It was providential that the foredeck of the latter rose and thus eased the forestay, for, had the latter burst, as it was feared it would, the mast and everything would have fallen aft. The vessels remained locked and *Satanita* thus kept *Valkyrie* up, but when she blew back clear, *Valkyrie* at once began to take a port list, and directly after the stern rose in the air and *Valkyrie* went down head first.

   Lord Dunraven, who had guests on board including two ladies, was late in leaving the vessel, but with so many yachts near, there was plenty of help at hand. Neither owner nor crew were able to save anything, and a good many valuables went down with *Valkyrie*. It may be said that just as she was settling down the topmast broke off, and at low water she was showing her masthead some ten feet. The vessel is lying on the fishing bank just inside the deep water of Holy Loch, yet is in about seventeen fathoms. *Satanita*'s damage was a great gaping chasm, from about ten inches above the copper upwards, and back to about six frames on one side and three on the other, while several deck beams are broken. *Satanita* lost no other spars than bowsprit, but her topmast was at one time bent like a bow through some of *Valkyrie*'s gear hooking the backstays. It was 35 sec. before the starting gun that the collision occurred, and the match between *Britannia* and *Vigilant* commenced unperceived by many.'

————————— ,, —————————

Valkyrie was subsequently raised and towed to Greenock, but the underwriters regarded her as a total loss and she was broken up in 1896.

From: A report by James Miekle in the *Racing Calendar and Review*, 1894

PART VI: FIRE OR EXPLOSION

35: *Strumpet* was Gone!

Yacht: *Strumpet* (28ft GRP copy of a Morecombe Bay prawner)
Skipper: Henry Irving
Crew: Barry Speakman
      Jondo Irving
      Joe Irving
Bound from Wainfleet Haven, Lincolnshire to Wells, Norfolk
Time and date of loss: 0845, August 3rd, 1980
Position: 1 mile S of Gibraltar Point, approx. 6 miles S of Skegness

Henry Irving, author of the pilots' guide *Tidal Havens of the Wash and Humber*, has sailed those waters, summer and winter, for many years, usually in his own boat *Venture*, but this time in a friend's yacht, *Strumpet*.

They had set sail from Wainfleet Creek at the northern corner of the Wash and were bound for Wells, some thirty miles away on the north Norfolk coast. *Strumpet* was a reinforced glass-fibre replica of a Morecombe Bay prawner – a strong and sea-kindly vessel. Besides Barry, an old friend and experienced cruising companion, Irving had his two young sons, Jondo and Joe, on board. In company, some two cables astern as they left the creek, was another friend, Peter Tomlinson, in his steel yacht *Temptress* with a crew of four.

The mood was merry, Skegness had been good, the day promised to be good and Wells promised to be even better.

Fifteen minutes later, all eight of them were aboard *Temptress* and *Strumpet* was a blazing inferno.

———————— " ————————

'Tide time arrived that morning in the middle of ablutions, so it was necessary to postpone breakfast, start the engine and cast off lines. Wainfleet permits little dallying on the ebb. As I steered *Strumpet* down the tortuous creek between the withies, Barry prepared breakfast and served

up to Jondo and Joe. Since we were nearing the haven mouth, I suggested that he kept our breakfasts warm in the oven whilst raising sail. A leisurely breakfast under sail appealed to me much more than something crammed down astern of a noisy diesel engine. Jondo, fearing that he was missing something of interest, bolted his breakfast and rushed on to the foredeck to assist. Joe, unwilling to abandon his carefully-prepared bread soldiers, stayed below to savour his food. Something, however, was spoiling his childish pleasure:

"Dad, there's an awful smell of fumes."

"Oh, shut up. It's only the diesel. Eat your breakfast. I'll switch it off in a minute."

The sails went up, I bore off, and switched off the engine.

"I can't stand these fumes. I'm going to eat my breakfast out there."

By this time, I could smell something, so I summoned Jondo to the helm and scrambled below. A quick glance at the galley showed me that Barry had left no pans on the gas, and a peep into the oven revealed a reassuring pile of bacon, mushrooms and tomatoes, warmly awaiting the arrival of the as yet uncooked eggs. I looked at the engine temperature gauge. All fine. To check, I lifted the engine cover and smelled fumes, but the engine did not feel excessively warm. Thinking it must have been an oily rag on the exhaust, I climbed into the cockpit to check this, unhurried because the engine was now quiet and presumably cooling. Nothing amiss in that department so I looked at the sails and sea scene once more, assuming that the smell would soon go.

Joe finished his breakfast so I asked him to go below and start cooking the eggs for Barry and myself. He disappeared, only to re-emerge immediately to say that black smoke was now pouring into the cabin from the foc's'le. I seized the large CO_2 extinguisher from the cockpit locker and scrambled below, but the dense black smoke prevented me from getting anywhere near the foc's'le. I held what breath I had and directed the extinguisher into the smoke for a few futile seconds then rushed out on deck. The hatch boards were stowed in the aft locker so I could not quickly fit them. When I got my breath I realised that Peter had come close alongside and had hurled his extinguisher at Barry. We went on to the foredeck and I opened the hatch so that Barry could direct the extinguisher on to the source of the smoke. Immediately a roar of black smoke and flame shot out of the hatch, igniting the staysail and causing us both to stagger back with black faces and singed eyebrows.

My thoughts then turned to saving life rather than fighting fire. *Temptress* was still at hand so I called Peter to come alongside and take off crew. The sea was quite choppy, but the manoeuvre was well executed and the boys and Barry got safely on to *Temptress*. I attempted to unfasten the inflated dinghy from the cabin roof, but as I did so the forward section burst into flame so I abandoned the attempt. I called for a tow rope and managed to make it fast to the forestay, thinking that a sandbank was a better place to sink than a swatchway. By this time, the heat was becoming so intense that *Temptress'* sails and rigging were endangered, and the boys were clearly in distress, so I jumped aboard. We towed *Strumpet* on a long line, which finally burned through as we were atop the Outer Dog's Head. The maelstrom that ensued was awesome to behold: sails burst into flame, the mast tumbled, the Calor cylinder exploded in the aft locker making an insignificant contribution to the overall scene and finally the hull slowly melted away till she sank. *Strumpet* was gone.

Speculations and lessons
Naturally the insurance company required a full explanation. As the nightmare subsided, to be replaced by a dull, numb feeling of loss, I spent hours trying to sift through the events in order to provide one. I could only think of one possibility. There was no natural light in the foc's'le of *Strumpet*, so the boys, who were sleeping therein, used a Camping Gaz lamp which the owner had left hanging on a hook for this purpose. That morning, they had used it to dress and had put it out before emerging to accompany me to the toilet. As I have previously said, our ablutions that morning were hasty, so it was only a matter of minutes before we had cast off and were motoring down the creek. At the haven mouth there was a chop in the water which caused the boat to dance about. I can only think that this motion caused the lamp to jump off the hook and fall with a still-hot glass on to one of the sleeping bags, causing it to burn. The sleeping bag must have ignited the Dunlopillo mattress (which I subsequently simulated with horrifying results) and the mattress in turn generated sufficient heat for the GRP and plywood of the foc's'le to catch fire. The speed of these events was of an order that I would never have imagined possible. From Joe's olfactory misgivings until the evacuation of the boat was no more than fifteen minutes.

It is certainly possible, and perhaps useful, to make the usual set of recriminations – the checklist of guilt and the vows for the future. Camping Gaz lamps on hooks are out; Dunlopillo mattresses are suspect (though they continue to be temptingly comfortable, and I still sail with one on *Venture*, albeit with a robust cover on it); GRP boats have never been my favourite kind of craft and I would now hesitate to undertake a serious cruise in one. So much for materials; what of human action and inaction? I will always remember to seal up a boat on fire rather than to mess about with silly extinguishers. I have always preferred to cruise in company for social reasons. This incident revealed practical ones. But at the end of the day, the basic lesson to be learned is that disaster can strike a small cruising yacht very quickly and cause loss of life. If you can't cope with this, then don't go to sea. But don't get into a car either, and don't cross the road to get your morning paper.'

———————— ,, ————————

Written for this book by Henry Irving

36: A Chance in a Lifetime

Yacht: *Freedom To* (34ft motor-sailer)
Skipper: C. Binnings
Crew: J. Warrington
Bound from Hamble, Hampshire to Newport, South Wales
Time and date of loss: 0530, May 20th, 1981
Position: 5 miles S of Eddystone Lighthouse

Freedom To, a Westerly Vulcan, was brand-new and on her way from the Solent to Newport, South Wales, which was to be her home port.

———————— " ————————

'We left Hamble at 1100 on Tuesday, motored down to the Solent and took our departure from the Needles. As we came on to 260 degrees, the wind came up dead astern and with the roller headsail full out and the revs down to 2,200 we made 6½ knots – pleasant sailing.

A week previously I had sent a CG66 to Swansea and accordingly informed Solent Coastguard of our departure as well as Portland and Brixham as we passed. We had planned for Dartmouth, but changed our plans when the afternoon brought a blue sky and the evening a good moon. We decided to make for Penzance.

At 0100 we saw flashes of lightning way to the south. By 0400 it was raining and the flashes were getting nearer. Visibility was by now down to about two to three miles. We continued to run under full headsail and 2,200 revs.

Jim had the 0200–0600 watch and at 0530 he joined me below in the main cabin, saying that he would steer from the inside position for a while. He had done more than his fair share of helming on the previous day. Feeling sufficiently awake I said I would take over and settled myself into the helmsman's seat with a glance at the compass.

I would liken it to a television tube exploding. Our first thoughts were

230

"the engine", but it appeared to be running normally enough. We raced to the cockpit to look for visible damage and as I looked I noticed the aerial had gone. Jim switched off the engine and gas bottle in the nearby locker. A thick tanny brown smoke was rolling up the companionway to be straightened and carried away by the wind. It's still raining, I thought, I'm going to get wet out here without oilskins. I quite believed that it was only a matter of waiting for the smoke to clear. I had other thoughts. If the situation deteriorated further, sending a Mayday was impossible now with the aerial gone. Top priority was the dinghy, flares and lifejackets.

I took a deep breath and leapt down the companionway. Visibility nil. The lifejackets were in the hanging wardrobe and the flares under the settee berths, but access was still a stranger and familiarity not yet an ally. The attempt was aborted, but I did manage to grab a fire extinguisher which was clipped under the saloon table.

By now Jim was in the cockpit with a full bucket of water, but with smoke issuing from every quarter it was difficult to know where to start the attack. We lifted the cockpit locker to get at the dinghy – more dense smoke. This is a big 7 ft deep locker with the dinghy at the bottom under a mound of carefully stowed warps and fenders, the outboard motor and five gallons of spare diesel. I came out gasping for air. The dinghy was firmly lodged. We climbed to the weather side to avoid the toxic fumes, while *Freedom To* continued to turn. As we came up on to the starboard side we saw the first lick of flame from the main hatch. It was impossible to believe, the possible avenues of retreat were rapidly being whittled away, we had no VHF, flares or lifejackets. A stuck dinghy and two horseshoe buoys were all that was left.

With Jim making a last ditch effort to free the inflatable, I grabbed at the horseshoes, freeing one. Still no flames in the cockpit locker as the dinghy finally freed. We yanked it clear, the rubber warm and sticky. By now the flames were at Jim's sea boots as we hauled the dinghy down the weather side outside the lifelines. By now the cabin roof was melting, with flames breaking through to leeward. We stood in the pulpit together desperately trying to inflate the dinghy by mouth. The heat on our backs was appalling, as all deck features folded in before taking on a mantle of flame.

Flame and heat quickly precipitated our departure from on deck and with the dinghy only perhaps 20 per cent inflated we followed it into the water. "That's it, we can stand it no longer."

With the partially inflated dinghy folded like a clam we searched with our mouths for the inflation holes which were some way under water. The dinghy by now was alongside the starboard beam, although I have no idea why. We continued to inflate – it was taking shape, holding air. Then down came the mast immediately above us. Six or seven feet from the hull and it would have hit us, but we were close enough to the side for safety as it lay at right angles into the sea. Seconds later the boom came tumbling into the water alongside the dinghy. It was still, however, attached to the gooseneck and lolled, burning, inches from the rubber. The mainsail which had been left wrapped on to the boom had burned and the metal was molten with heat. I remember clearly that for about 12 inches the inside of the boom was revealed and the waves were throwing up against it.

Jim was still busy blowing air. I thumped him for his attention and four hands sent water flying to douse this our latest hazard. This was followed by our next concern, the danger of explosion from the 40 gallons of diesel on board and the two gas cylinders. Using our hands as paddles we made some distance from the wreck. Ten, fifteen, twenty feet and I looked astern.

She lay in the water, her superstructure gone, a floating cauldron with her spars dangling. We could still make out her Vulcan lines. We paddled further and as I lifted my head on the next crest I saw the coaster, maybe 700 yards off. You're not safe yet, I thought, she's probably on autopilot. As she neared we could see figures on deck and heard the sounds of reversing engines. Through salt drenched eyes I could read the name on her bows. Will I ever forget that name *Moray Firth*? Never.

As we were helped up the side and up on to the bridge, the first of two explosions wracked *Freedom To*. She was last reported burnt to the waterline. We informed the Coastguard of our safety.'

——————— ,, ———————

From: *Yachting Monthly*, September 1981

37: One Touch of the Button

Yacht: *Ladybee* (30ft gaff-rigged double-ender)
Skipper: James Houston
Crew: Margaret Houston
Bound from Puilladobhrain, Argyll to Tobermory, Isle of Mull,
   Scotland
Time and date of loss: abandoned 1310, June 10th, 1972
Position: 2 miles S of Duart Point, Sound of Mull

Ladybee was a double-ender of the Colin Archer type, heavily built by
Weatherhead of Cockenzie in 1929. She was originally called *Lady Bridgella
of Rhu* and was well known on the Clyde. *Ladybee* had served well as a slow
but comfortable family cruiser for James and Margaret Houston and their
children. The engine was a petrol/paraffin Kelvin, and in the spring of 1972
it was giving a lot of trouble.

———————— " ————————

'Our cruise this year commenced with the Lamlash Race when we took up
our customary position of being last. The Sunday was an absolutely perfect
day for soaking up the sun, not to mention Jimmy Gillespie's cocktails
before lunch. It came as quite a disappointment, however, to find that the
absence of wind was soon to be joined by the absence of engine. It seemed
that nothing short of oars would get us past the old wreck on Holy Isle until
we secured a welcome hitch from one of these common white yachts!

Despite regular attention by notable engineers our engine had given
trouble all spring, and we were more than a little despondent to find that
things were still not right and that the palliatives like stripping and cleaning
the carburettors, renewing the plugs, etc., made little or no difference.

We thought it better to have the engine examined properly even at the
expense of losing another precious day of our fortnight. We found that a
manufacturer's engineer was coming down to Fairlie the following day in

233

any case, and so we were able to secure his services at quite short notice. We finally got away on the Tuesday morning, and had a fine sail all the way to Ardrishaig. The engine started reassuringly as we approached the breakwater. But it packed up again as we circled around to await the opening of the sea lock gates! We ended up having to rush at the lock from some distance with plenty of impetus to carry us in. Help!

The next day a very competent and helpful young man from the garage fitted a shining new starter switch, starter button and solenoid. He tested and re-aligned the starter motor and it was reassuring to see that everything at long last appeared to be functioning perfectly. One touch of the button – marvellous!

It was with confidence and perhaps with a touch of bravado that we demonstrated our skill in gliding our ten-foot beam serenely through what looked like a nine-foot half-gate! At the sixth lock we found a small fishing boat having engine trouble and as the skipper was quick to notice our great power and manoeuvrability, he actually requested a tow! I really couldn't help laughing. Later on I felt quite superior by being able to diagnose the fault of his engine, and instantly produced a proper-sized jet-spanner to remedy it. I could see he was quite impressed by my knowledge of the engine and I secretly hoped that Margaret wouldn't spoil my act by revealing to him that his engine was exactly the same as ours anyway.

Last year the first two weeks of June were just sublime and we had fond memories of cloudless skies, sparkling water and warm southerly winds keeping the eternal swell crashing into the depths of Fingal's Cave. We drifted round the Mull in bikinis to arrive home the colour of Indians and stating knowledgeably that everyone should take their holidays in June when the weather is always at its best.

This year the cold northerly wind blew through the buttonholes of our oilskins as we pounded our way with the tide up the Sound of Luing. Tacking back from the Mull shore found us near enough Puilladobhrain to have us thinking of the warm pub over the hill at Clachan Bridge, so we fairly tore into that well-known sheltered lagoon. The cold wind dropped in the evening so that we could sit comfortably in the fading light and admire the nice new woodwork and homely interior of our saloon. But it rose again with us in the morning so the ham and egg breakfast was not to be enjoyed in the exposed cockpit.

We set off for Tobermory, choosing our time for wind and tide to be in the same direction, making for a flatter sea, but unfortunately, as you will gather, these elements were coming almost exactly from the direction of our destination. Before leaving the shelter of Kerrera on our third tack, we brought the grey inflatable dinghy on board as it had been snatching at the painter while out in the Firth. Although it does spoil the view we always like to keep it inflated, not so much for its immediate availability for use as a liferaft, but more because it is such a tiresome task having to blow the thing up again! Anyway, the air valves had been leaking a bit in the spring, and although it had been serviced by the agents in Glasgow we noticed that sudden deflation was less frequent when the full pressure was maintained. Several thoroughly secure lashings kept the dinghy a good three inches clear of the boom, and I managed to get some good cine shots for the Club Trophy as we left Bach Island rapidly to port, but it didn't look as though we had a hope in hell of leaving Duart Point to port! The best we made in fact was a couple of miles south of that, and we felt rather tempted at the time to motorsail up the coast to save another tedious tack into the Firth.

But there was no particular hurry, so we went about as usual and turned our backs to the fresh wind and hauled the sheets in tight. Soon, however, a combination of good ideas like having coffee now, and perhaps reaching the Mishnish before closing time, prompted a reconsideration of the motorsail idea. The coffee was therefore extracted from the cupboard on the uphill side of the boat and I reached forward from the cockpit for one touch of the button. The boat blew up.

Margaret was shouting something about her leg and I couldn't understand where she had disappeared to, or why I could now see the whole engine which had hitherto been concealed by the heavy plywood covers: or where all the flames suddenly appeared from; or where was the companionway that used to be bolted over the engine covers.

Ladybee must then have been given her head for I remember using both hands from a crouching position to tear, I think ineffectively, at a red jersey levering itself up into the cockpit. We were absolutely stunned. I remembered a fire extinguisher decorating a bulkhead at each end of our boat so here was the chance to try one out as I have always wanted to! It wasn't necessary to open the fore-hatch because it had already disappeared and fragments of plastic could be seen clinging to the wet deck around the windlass against which the hatch had undoubtedly smashed. The extinguisher had fallen from its bracket to the floor and in searching quickly for it I noticed the bulkhead was slightly deformed and the doorway which used to open into the saloon was now opening slightly into the fo'c'sle.

Anyway the extinguisher was a bit of a disappointment. The wind carried some of the white stuff into the sea and the remainder was soon to be exhausted. The jet seemed to choke a bit when directed towards the flames surrounding the engine and I wished that I had another extinguisher to try out because it looked like the petrol in the tanks would soon be on the boil. We forgot about coffee.

Meanwhile we decided that it was now an appropriate time to secure a line of retreat. The lashings on the dinghy suddenly became fused to the rails and the fingers began to fumble frantically until we saw that the bow of the Avon had a great hole in it. The shock of this observation must have caused us to take stock, because we began to tackle the lashings in a more orderly manner; and perhaps we realized that despite the decompression of one half of the dinghy, the other half was miraculously staying fully inflated so we wasted no time in launching the dinghy which was tethered by Margaret while I collected oars, and the bellows! By this time we had agreed that it might be prudent to actually use the line of retreat before the petrol tanks blew up. As with fire extinguishers, we had also wondered about flares. A hasty return to the fo'c'sle confirmed that the flares along with the life jackets were unobtainable in the saloon, but in any case there was as much smoke trailing across the Firth of Lorne as any flare would have made. I caught a glimpse of the fenders which we had been using to go through the Canal and it occurred to me that they would have made quite good emergency floats when tied together.

I also hesitated to consider the new outboard motor but decided against that. We were getting a bit fed up with engine trouble anyway and surely nothing much could go wrong with a pair of oars. So we cast off at 1310 and *Ladybee* pulled rapidly away. Margaret gathered the deflated loose part of the dinghy around her waist to keep the water out as we began to row towards the Mull shore and we suddenly felt very sad indeed.

A second explosion perhaps ten minutes later confirmed that we were now in the safer vessel. While it had seemed that we were alone on the Firth of Lorne we suddenly noticed the steamer abeam of Lady Rock lighthouse, presumably on her way from Craignure to Oban, and we saw her alter course. Perched on each successive wave crest we could see *Ladybee* sailing now on a more southerly course back towards Puilladobhrain and away from the steamer. A flash of white light, followed a second or two later by a loud report, must have been the gas cylinders blowing up, and we wondered what the skipper of the steamer would be thinking. It looked as though he was getting quite close to *Ladybee* – if only we could let him know there was nobody on board. We did worry in case someone would get hurt trying to find out, but we were now miles away and a half-sized grey rubber dinghy is not the most conspicuous object on a dark grey sea. We discovered later on that a report was issued at Southend (Argyll C.R.H.Q.) at 1331 hours from Oban radio to the effect that the car ferry *Columbia* was going alongside a yacht with a blue jib and white main sail about one mile south-west of Kerrera Island. No one could be seen on board. It seems that Mr Devine, the Coastguardsman in charge at Oban, was immediately informed and within a few minutes he had put to sea in the f.v. *Callum Cille* and was making for the position.

We had, however, been spotted by someone on Mull, and it seems that

Captain Leslie, the Coastguard Reporting Member at Grasspoint on Mull, was soon able to inform the *Columbia* that we were safely ashore. We didn't know this at the time of course, but we did notice the arrival of other vessels in the area and saw with some relief that *Columbia* was able to depart.

I had been informed as a child that if I ever fell out of a balloon (which I could never understand) I would be sure to land on a feather bed.

It was only to be expected therefore that the rocky shore we suddenly gaped at as we made our diagonal journey should give way to the most beautiful sheltered sandy bay precisely at the point where it seemed we would fetch up. Margaret dissolved in tears as we walked up the beach. She had left her make-up case behind!

Looking around the hillside revealed no immediate signs of life until two figures appeared standing in the bracken some distance away. I approached them to be informed (believe it or not) that "some boat was in trouble out there." As I followed the sweep of the gentleman's arm I screwed up my eyes incredulously. Perhaps people had a habit of coming ashore there with blackened faces and singed eyebrows.'

—————— ,, ——————

From: *Yachting World*, September 1972

PART VII: BEING TOWED

38: *Mischief*'s Last Voyage

Yacht: *Mischief* (45ft Bristol Channel pilot-cutter)
Skipper: Major H.W. Tilman
Crew: Charles Marriott
     Simon Beckett
     Kenneth Winterschladen
     Ian Duckworth
Bound from Jan Mayen Island to Norway (under tow)
Time and date of loss: 2400, August 4th, 1968
Position: off east coast of Jan Mayen Island

Between 1954 and 1968, when he lost her off Jan Mayen Island, Bill Tilman sailed *Mischief* some 110,000 miles. *Sea Breeze*, her successor, also a Bristol Channel pilot-cutter and even older than *Mischief*, was lost in 1972 on the south coast of Greenland. Her going is described on page 121.

Tilman sailed mostly to places where there was snow, ice, mountains and very few people. In 1968 he chose Iceland and Jan Mayen Island as his goals and *Mischief* left Lymington on May 31st, after the crew had subscribed for the hire of a liferaft. Having called at Thorshavn in the Faeroes, they were in Akuryri on the north coast of Iceland by June 26th, where they stayed for a few days, leaving on July 7th, bound for Jan Mayen, some 300 miles to the north.

The long axis of Jan Mayen Island runs from south-west to north-east, the middle of the island being barely two miles wide. Almost the whole of the north-eastern half is filled by Beerenberg's massive bulk. This 7000 ft peak was of course Tilman's climbing goal. Because the chart agent had mistakenly told him that there was no Admiralty chart of Jan Mayen, Tilman was using a chart on which the 30-mile-long island occupied little more than one inch. —————— " ——————

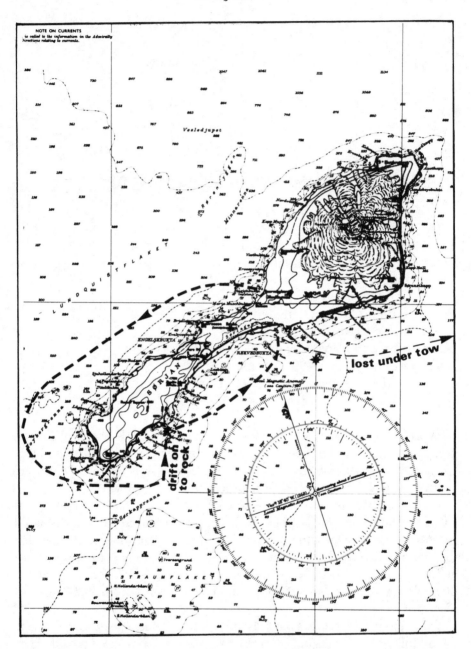

'Variable winds and too much fog marked our passage to Jan Mayen. On the 17th we luckily got sights which put us some 10 miles from the island, so we steered, once more in fog, to clear South Cape by 5 miles. In fact, that afternoon some very impressive rocks suddenly loomed up only 2 cables away. These we identified as Sjuskjæra, a group of seven rocks a mile off the cape. Next day we anchored off the old Norwegian weather station at Mary Musbukta on the west coast.

What few anchorages there are on either the east or west coast of Jan Mayen are wide open, but the west coast is preferable as it is free from dangers. Nor was there any ice in the vicinity of Mary Musbukta, though 3 miles to the north we could see pack-ice extending westwards. However, I thought we ought to let the Norwegians know that we were there, with designs on Beerenberg, so after anchoring I went in search of their new base. On the east coast, south of Eggoya, where the beach is very wide, and thick with driftwood, originating probably in Siberia, I found a party at work. We had no common language and, except that I had no beard, they must have thought I had been left behind, possibly under a stone, by some earlier expedition. I got a lift in a truck 5 miles to the present Norwegian station where we were just in time for supper. It is a large installation comprising some fifty men, mostly technicians. The Commandant was surprised to see me, for a Norwegian naval vessel, approaching by the east coast, had been turned back by ice. He showed me a small bay close by which they used for landing stores and suggested that we lie there. We were, so to speak, uninvited guests, so I thought it best to comply, though the bay was more than half covered with ice floes. From this mistake all our troubles stemmed.

We started round on Saturday 20 July, a brilliant morning on which we enjoyed the only view we ever had of the ice slopes of Beerenberg, the mountain we hoped to climb. The brilliance soon faded, and once more we rounded South Cape in thick fog, having to tack twice to weather it. The wind died at night, and having steered east for 2 miles to get an offing we handed sails and let her drift, waiting for the fog to clear. The coast runs SW–NE so that by steering east we had not gained that much offing, and although the ship had no way on, it was a mistake to think she was not moving. I had the midnight to 0200 watch and on the false assumption that we were not moving sat below, taking a look round on deck every 15 minutes. It was, of course, fully light, but miserably cold and damp, visibility less than a quarter mile. Accordingly I told my relief Ian that he need not remain on deck all the time provided he went up at frequent intervals. He interpreted this liberally and must have remained below most of his watch.

At about 0350 a terrible crash roused me. We were almost alongside a lone rock pinnacle lying about half a mile off the coast – I could have touched it with a boathook – the slight swell bumping us heavily on its plinth. This result of his neglect seemed to have unnerved Ian who had already pulled the cord of the liferaft without troubling to launch it, so that a huge yellow balloon now filled most of the starboard deck. To make

243

doubly sure of getting off he had also cut the dinghy lashings. Once the engine had started she slid off easily but not before having struck hard at least six times. She proved to be leaking a lot but the Whale pump and deck pump together kept it under control. To hit this rock we must have drifted in the course of the night some 3 miles to the north at a rate of nearly half a knot.

Owing to fog and a lot of ice close inshore we had trouble in finding the bay. About 0700 we anchored off it while I went ashore to tell the Norwegians what had happened. They said, and I agreed, that the only thing to do was to beach her to get at the leaks. So we brought her in through the floes until she grounded on a beach of black sand. In order to float her further up we started taking out the ballast (some 5 tons of pig iron), drained the water tanks, and put ashore the anchor and cable. The rise and fall of the tide was only 3 ft (*Mischief* draws 7 ft) and the beach shelved quickly towards her stern, so that we could not get at the garboard strake or the planks above it except at the forefoot. On heaving her down with a bulldozer and examining what we could of the port side at low water we saw no sprung or started planks; in places the caulking had spewed out, and aft about 10 ft of the false keel had broken away.

With the help of the Norwegians, who generously supplied anything needed, we covered the likeliest leak sources with tar, felt, and copper. Then we turned her round and hove down to get at the starboard side where, too, there were no obvious signs of damage. The leaks had been reduced though not cured but I thought that we could easily sail her back to Iceland or even home. Ian thought otherwise and had already arranged a passage to Norway in *Brandal*, a sealing vessel chartered to bring stores, due about 2 August. Charles, I knew, would stay with *Mischief*, while the two younger crew, though apprehensive, were willing to try.

Meantime the ice, which the day after our arrival had moved in almost to fill the bay (thus helping us by damping any swell) began to move out. Preparatory to refloating her we put back the ballast, all but a ton – no doubt, another mistake. By Saturday, 27 July, there remained only an unbroken line of massive floes close to the beach, most of them probably aground. The Norwegian who had been helping me realized better than I did that *Mischief* was now in peril. By means of a wire led from the stern to a block slung on an adjacent rock and thence to a bulldozer we tried to haul her off. She moved a foot or two but anyway there was no forcing a passage between the floes and no means of hauling them away.

Next day, Sunday 28 July, the Commandant came down and managed to break up with dynamite a floe threateningly close to our rudder. A floe lying only a yard or so from our port side was too big and a series of underwater explosions close aboard might have damaged the ship. That morning it began blowing hard from the south, causing the ice to surge forward, bumping *Mischief* heavily on the beach, and edging her higher up. I rallied the crew for a last effort to get her off by means of a warp to the anchor winch and the engine. She would not budge. With a couple of bulldozers we might have succeeded, but when I ran to the base for help there was no one about. By the time I got back the ice had battered a hole in her hull below the engine water intake and started several planks. That evening, in despair, I wrote her off. She was one-third full of water so we took ashore the gear below deck. Charles, who had not been well, now collapsed and retired to a bed in the base sick-room. On first beaching *Mischief* we had all lived in a small hut close to the beach.

Next day a powerful red-bearded Norwegian whom I called the Viking, who had taken to heart *Mischief*'s plight and was as anxious as myself to save her, suggested that she should be hauled right out so that in the winter he could repair her. I doubted the feasibility because it meant hauling her at least 50 yards over very soft sand sloping up at about 15 degrees. Clutching at straws, I agreed. Once more we took out the ballast and that evening the Viking and a bulldozer moved her about 2 yards. She still lay among the breakers, the wind continued blowing, and the swell rolling in lifted and dropped her heavily on the sand. A big float with an outboard engine used for bringing ashore stores, on which we had deposited the ballast, lay hard by on the beach; and the next night *Mischief*, driven ever higher by the seas, had her bowsprit broken on the float in spite of our having reefed it.

The idea of hauling her right out seemed to be tacitly abandoned. Instead, on 30 July, we put a big patch over the hole, having arranged with *Brandal*, then about to leave Norway, to tow us to Bodö. She was also to bring out a small motor pump to cope with the leaks which by now were well beyond our two hand pumps. With another gale on 1 August the breakers tore off *Mischief*'s rudder, but *Brandal*, with whom the base spoke by radio telephone, reckoned they could still tow. *Brandal* arrived on 2 August, fetching up north of the island in spite of radio beacons, radar and Loran, and that morning the big patch we had put on was torn off by the seas. Upon this the Viking and I reverted to the idea of leaving her there for the winter hauled right out, but the Commandant to whom we appealed thought little of it and said she must be towed. So on 3 August the Viking and I again put on a patch, a wet job since waves were sweeping the stage we had slung overside to work from. That evening I went on board *Brandal*. To make all safe they agreed to lend us a small electric pump to reinforce the petrol pump they had brought which we had already installed in the cockpit. I had to sign a guarantee against the loss of this pump. The Commandant also arranged for a walkie-talkie set and a field telephone to keep *Brandal* and *Mischief* in touch.

Overnight we rove a 3-in wire through a big block slung on the nearby rocks and passed a length of 6-in nylon rope twice round *Mischief*'s hull. At 0700 on Sunday 4 August, a fortnight to the day since we first limped in, the Norwegians rallied in force to get us off. Although the ballast was out it took some doing. Either the sand had piled up or she had dug herself in, so the biggest bulldozer, a real monster, dropped its scoop into the sand and using the sand as a cushion advanced on *Mischief* and pushed her bodily sideways. The two bulldozers in tandem then coupled on to the wire, a big dory with an engine pulled from seawards, and *Mischief* slid slowly into deep water. Simon and I were on board with the pump going. It needed to be for she leaked like a basket.

Having secured astern of *Brandal* lying half a mile out we remained there, tossed about in a rough sea, until late afternoon. Meantime the float made two or three trips out to *Brandal*, the last with seven men from the base and the remaining three of our crew. Charles was to travel in her while the other two helped in *Mischief*. Since we were to be closely attended Ian had consented to come. Our only contact with *Brandal* was by the float, and in the evening it came alongside with three of her crew to arrange the tow-line, the electric pump, field telephone, walkie-talkie set, and a liferaft. Our own had no gas cylinder, that having been expended when Ian prematurely pulled the string a fortnight before. He and Ken now joined us, and was promptly seasick. For the tow they used a nylon warp shackled to 10 fathoms of our anchor chain on which they hung three big tyres to act as a spring. The remaining 35 fathoms of our chain with the 1-cwt anchor attached we led to *Mischief*'s stern to drop over when the tow started. This served in place of a rudder and kept her from yawing. The heavy electric cable to supply current from *Brandal* to the pump they merely dropped loose into the sea. Its own weight imposed a heavy strain, no current ever passed, and immediately the tow began *Brandal* told us it had broken. Had it been hitched to the tow-line or to another line *Mischief* might have survived. This meant that the little petrol pump must function for 3 days without fail. I did not think it would. Since early morning Simon and I had been running it for 5 minutes in every 10 to keep the water at bay.

At about 2000 in a rough sea the tow began. At 2100 Simon and I lay down leaving Ken and Ian to carry on until 0100. With the water sloshing about inside sleep was hardly possible and for food we made do with hard tack and a cup of tea. Just before midnight I learnt that the pump had given up; the engine ran but was not pumping. Three of us were ready enough to quit and I confess that the skipper and owner, who had so much more at stake, had no longer the will to persevere, a fortnight of trouble, toil, and anxiety having worn me down. *Brandal* had already been told. She lay to about a cable away and told us to bring off only personal gear. So we collected our gear, launched the liferaft, and abandoned *Mischief*. She had then about 3 ft of water inside her. Paddling over to *Brandal* we climbed on board while three of her crew returned in the raft to salvage the two pumps and the telephone. The electric pump, which weighed a lot, we had already hoisted on deck through the skylight. The pumps met with scant ceremony, being thown overboard on the end of a line to be hauled through the sea to *Brandal*. While *Brandal* got under way I remained on deck watching *Mischief*, still floating defiantly, until she was out of sight. We were then 30 miles east of Jan Mayen.

As I have said, ice conditions in 1968 were unusually bad; in a normal year Jan Mayen is clear of ice by the end of May. And, apart from human failings, ice was the principal cause of the loss of *Mischief*. For me it meant the loss of more than a yacht. I felt like one who had betrayed and then deserted a stricken friend, a friend with whom for the last 14 years I had probably spent more time at sea than on land, and who when not at sea had seldom been out of my thoughts. Moreover I could not help feeling that by my mistakes and by the failure of one of those who were there to safeguard her we had broken faith; that the disaster or sequence of disasters need not have happened; and that more might have been done to save her. I shall never forget her.'

——————— ,, ———————

From: *Roving Commissions 9* (1969), published by the Royal Cruising Club

39: The Wreck of the *Dragon*

Yacht: *Dragon* (25ft centre-board yawl)
Skipper: C.C. Lynam
Crew: Maurice Crouch
Bound from Overstrand to Yarmouth, Norfolk
Time and date of loss: soon after dawn, August 26th, 1891
Position: 4 miles NE of Happisburgh (Haisború), Norfolk

Dr Gairdner of the Cruising Association discovered this account, by C.C. Lynam, of the loss of his first *Dragon*. Unlike the *Blue Dragon* which Lynam subsequently owned and wrote about, this little yawl was painted yellow – surely a very unusual choice for those days, but perhaps one that made her easier to spot in those grey seas off the Norfolk coast. Of 'The Skipper', Douglas Gairdner writes:

——————— " ———————

'C.C. Lynam was a colourful figure in the yachting world for many years from the 1890s onwards. In 1892 he had built a 25ft centre-board yawl *Blue Dragon* which he proceeded to sail down through the Thames Locks to the estuary, from where he was said to have kept on turning right until he reached the west coast of Scotland! This remained his cruising ground for the rest of his life, and in effect he may be said to have invented cruising in that part of the world. He returned to the west coast regularly each school holiday including Christmas, sailing sometimes single-handed, and only hanging up his boots when he reached the age of 77 in 1934.

Lynam was possessed of a marvellously genial nature, while as a sailor he was decidedly happy-go-lucky, a quality which is discernible perhaps in The Skipper's log which follows. Be that as it may, he sailed his boat to the North Cape of Norway, and for this he was awarded the RCC Challenge Cup.

In the first of his three books describing cruises in *Blue Dragon* Lynam

248

alludes briefly to the fact that in 1891 he had been wrecked in a previous boat, the *Dragon*. An account of this appeared in the school magazine *The Draconian* of that year. It gives an interesting picture of the east coast yachting scene more than 90 years ago.'

—————— „ ——————

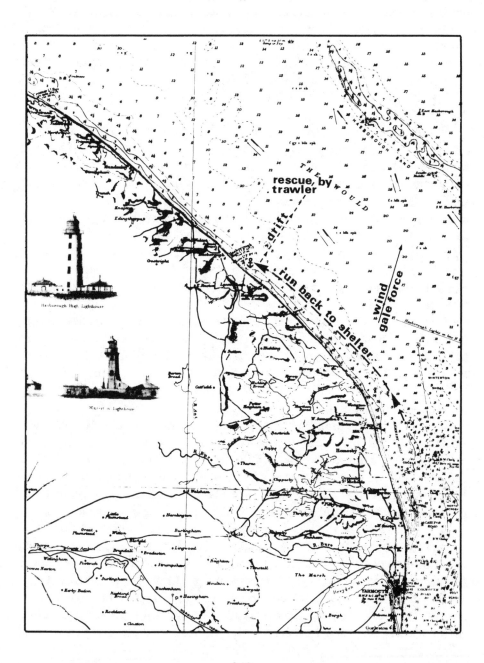

Being Towed

The cruise had started from the Thames:

––––––––––––––––––– " –––––––––––––––––––

July 26, 1891. 'In our hasty departure (prize-giving and speechifying only 4 hours ago) we left charts and guide-books, also hamper of provisions, behind. Moored off some barges near Woolwich for the night. When tide turned our moorings got foul of barge's bottom, and we found ourselves in middle of night thumping against the barge's side with our bowsprit jammed between hull and leeboard, roused the sleepy bargemen who, grumbling, turned out and gave us a sheer off.

July 27. No wind, drifted with tide to Gravesend, landed, explored Tilbury Fort, waited for ebb; wind sprang up from E and freshened, passed Holehaven as the night came on; touched the Blyth Sands. At about 23.00, cold and weary and wet, dropped anchor in Sheerness harbour. In morning found ourselves adrift, crew not having secured anchor cable; cable and anchor remained at the bottom! – drifting towards steamer at anchor, set sail in a hurry but it blew hard from the NE, rain, very dirty weather; so after trying hard to find our way from the mouth of the Estuary we thought best to run back to Sheerness; lunched on bread and water. Later in day it cleared a little, so started off, foolishly hoping to make Harwich; wind went round to NNW, crept along Essex coast over Maplins, hoping to cross Foulness Sands and shelter in the Colne, but tide was running out and we were soon thumping on Foulness Sands in about 1½ foot of water; up centre-board, breakers all round except seaward, so up jib and flew before it; sea got high and nasty, wind increasing to a gale, saw Swin Middle lightship right ahead, gave a blast on foghorn and burnt blue light. Skipper of lightship let out a rope which with difficulty in a heavy tumbling sea we secured and hitched round mast with chain and rope cable, and we were tossed about in gruesome fashion all night.

July 28. Near morning bowsprit cap carried away and mast fell on deck, smashing in part of cabin top and ventilator. Skipper gave us capital breakfast and entertained us hospitably whilst his carpenter repaired damages. Off we sailed with wind from WNW and we kept it up for 13½ hours; in the growing darkness, the wind falling, we groped along the coast past the strange old ruin of Dunwich and moored off Southwold.

July 29. Fair wind, ran past Lowestoft and into Yarmouth with tide. Had an exciting time getting into the harbour round the pier, tide running out like a mill race; tug with mud barges entering; we failed at first attempt; almost run down by tug, tide swirling us round across her bows. Tried again; got a line from S pier and were hauled round; got to bridge at dead low water but carried away cap of mizzen mast in getting through; put up at Brown's. Left *Dragon* to be cleaned up, cushions dried etc, and had a much needed bath. Went by train to Wroxham, where we found the canoe yawl *Snake* all ready for us.'

————————— ,, —————————

There followed further sailing on the Broads, and the cruise was resumed 3 weeks later, with, it appears, a single crewman and the skipper.

————————— " —————————

August 19. 'Started from Yarmouth for Cromer, but carried away bowsprit while beating down harbour, so returned to moorings off Brown's, Cobholm Island.

August 20. Made fresh start: leaving dinghy behind, plenty of provisions on board. Ho! for the North Sea. Sailed before a nice SE breeze past the Caister shoals, through the Gateway, past Winterton, past Eccles' desolate church tower on the beach, whose Norman doorway is washed by every tide; Eccles church has long since been washed into the sea with the continued erosion of this coast (author's note). On to Happisburgh, Mundesley, and the lovely tower of Sidestrand, Garden of Sleep; moored off Overstrand. Found friends there; asked them to breakfast with us on board in morning. Anchored further from shore in accordance with beachman's instructions; turned in, but at 12.30 found that the wind had veered round to ENE and that we were bumping on the sand; got into water up to our necks, hauled *Dragon* up as far as possible, left lying on sand as tide ebbed. At 02.30 roused again by a voice shouting to us that we should be smashed to pieces when tide came in. Grumpily turned out, got beachman, and after 3 hours of infinite labour dragged *Dragon* up the beach to foot of cliff. Wind now blowing strong from NNE and heavy swell getting up.

August 21 to 24. Weather bound ashore. The *Dragon* was hauled up a zigzag path on the cliff side, as the spring-tides, with the strong northerly wind, caused the sea to wash right up to the foot of the cliff. We often had friends in the *Dragon*, though her keel was tilted up at 30°, and we had to drive nails into the table to keep the dishes on. It was great fun, a constant picnic; we wandered far along the lonely shore. Visited the ghost-haunted Garden of Sleep, photographed groups of weatherworn fishermen, and all our friends, bathed, climbed, philosophized, hob-a-nobbed with the yarning old beachmen, and on the evening of the 24th were right sorry to launch out into the blackness.

The surf was still angrily beating on the shore, but the wind had died down from the N; the glass had fallen, however, and we were strongly dissuaded from going, but we hardened our hearts and hastily launched the old *Dragon* for what proved her last voyage. We confidently expected to make Yarmouth with the tide, but the launching through the surf kept us longer than we thought; saying farewell was bitter, and somehow we had

melancholy forebodings. We remembered how we had shot a poor gull on the voyage hither, and thought of the Ancient Mariner, for the winds had seemed against us ever since. Keeping in a line the Cromer and Mundesley lights we sailed on and on; passed Happisburgh and Winterton and thought our voyage over notwithstanding all presentiments, but at 11.00 the tide failed us, and the wind began to blow in gusts from the SW. Tacking in the Gatway between the Barber and Caister shoals was (though we tried hard) not to be achieved that night, so we ran back to Winterton and anchored. All night we tossed on an angry sea keeping watch by turn. One bad heave of a sea smashed our water jar, and we had no liquor on board.

August 25. In the morning the wind was rapidly rising to a gale right in our teeth, hour after hour we tried to beat against it; again we were close to Yarmouth, but the *Dragon* would not go about in the heavy seas, and we could not get through the shoals. One huge sea burst over us and soaked our loaf of bread and biscuits, our only provisions. We ran back about 10 miles to Happisburgh, hoping that there we should be more sheltered. Anchored again and passed the night in weary watching, for the tempest never abated but rather increased in force, and sleep in such a pitching sea was impossible.

August 26. Morning dawned but with very little light. All round driving rain, sand and spray, no sight of land! Our anchor had dragged and we were about 4 miles from land, drifting, drifting whither? For there to leeward of us seemed a great churning, boiling cauldron. One look at the chart showed we were drifting right towards the Happisburgh (Haisborough) sands; there no vessel could live a moment in such a wild sea. Nothing for it but to try and get some sail on the struggling *Dragon*. We put up the storm jib reefed and the mizzen with three reefs down, but the mizzen mast carried away and the jib was torn to tatters, for it was now blowing a hurricane. Then, rolling in the trough of every sea, we hoisted half-mast high a white flag as a signal of distress. A steamer passed us but took no notice. A great 70-ton trawler under reefed main and foresails soon after bore along close by us, her skipper asked if we would come aboard, we shouted would he tow us to Yarmouth? He hove a line and (now dangerously near the breakers on the sands) we hauled it in and found a strong wire rope attached; this we hastily secured to the bowsprit chocks and round the mast. Suddenly the rope they were paying out tightened, the trawler was dashing through the water at 9 knots, the strain was terrific, the bowsprit snapped off, carrying with it the forestay. Down came the mast, and now all the strain was amidships and over went the *Dragon*, rolling on her cabin in the great waves; we managed somehow to cling to her and scramble on her bottom. The skipper shouted to his crew to back foresail and down mainsail as he luffed the trawler up, but there was a moment's inevitable confusion, as all the crew expected to see us struggling in the water, and how the old *Dragon* floated and was towed rolling bottom uppermost I know not. After a perilous moment or two the trawler lost her way; the *Dragon* righted, and we with even greater difficulty got on her deck again.

We then had had enough and I shouted "we'll come aboard". Waiting our opportunity when heaved up on the top of a wave, we got on the trawler's deck. She was the *Prima Donna* of Lowestoft, skipper Henry Setterfield. He sent us below to a warm fire and hot cup of tea, but soon we heard a shout and saw the mere shell of the *Dragon* a quarter of a mile astern; we had dragged the mast and cabin off her, and there she lay half waterlogged, every wave breaking over and into her.

The trawler's skipper asked whether we should try for her: I said "yes" fearing that if she was found derelict we should be considered drowned.

So after missing stays the *Prima Donna* jibbed and in jibbing carried away her gaff, a great spar as thick as a man's body broke right in two. However, the skipper was not to be beat, and setting mizzen and foresail and clearing away the wreck, he shot up alongside the hulk of the *Dragon* and threw a grapnel on board, dragged her up alongside, and with the aid of winch and tackle on mizzen mast hauled her right aboard.

We got some of my personal property (including school reports! that had been stowed beneath the side decks) out of her. We landed at Lowestoft, sold the wreck, and paid the salvage.

Sailed a race in the trawler two days afterwards in the Lowestoft smack Regatta, and not without melancholy feelings parted with the poor old *Dragon*, our home so often and for so long.'

—————— " ——————

From: *Cruising Association Bulletin*, December 1981

PART VIII: EXHAUSTION OR ILLNESS

40: *Odd Times* at Sea

Yacht: *Odd Times* (23ft gaff-rigged cutter)
Skipper: Peter Rose
Crew: Paul Sheard
Bound from St Pierre Island, Nova Scotia to Cornwall, England
Time and date of loss: 0655, July 28th, 1967
Position: approx. 200 miles SE of St Johns, Newfoundland

Odd Times was designed by John Leather and built for Peter Rose in 1958. Having sailed in her 'from her native Essex shores to the Aegean and from Scotland to the Antilles', *Odd Times* was in Barbados in January 1966. During that year, Peter Rose, sometimes with a crew and sometimes single-handed, sailed up the east coast of the U.S. as far as Ivesterly, Rhode Island, where *Odd Times* remained for the winter of 1966/67.

The return voyage to England was to be made during the summer of 1967, with Paul Sheard as crew, but a few weeks before their departure from Nova Scotia, Peter Rose began to suffer serious seasickness:

——————— " ———————

'At Sydney we topped up with provisions before sailing for St Pierre. The fogs that had delayed us earlier caused us to omit southern Newfoundland from our itinerary as we wished to be on our way from St Pierre by about the middle of July. It seemed to me that it would be wise to be away from the north Atlantic Ocean well before the end of August so as to have a better chance of avoiding gales and even the odd long-distance wandering hurricane. On the other hand, to be much earlier would mean increasing the chance of encounters with ice on the western side of the ocean. So we sailed for St Pierre, and I was afflicted by seasickness of a worse sort than I had ever previously experienced except perhaps in the worst of conditions. But our conditions were good and it was not only unpleasant, it was also very worrying. I was able to help Paul with the navigation, but other than that he sailed *Odd Times* on his own, and made a very good job of it too. We arrived at St Pierre on the afternoon of 14 July (a big day there, of course) and, off the heaving swell, I recovered.

The French government runs a small but well equipped hospital on the island and I was examined by a competent young doctor who had various tests and X-rays carried out to try and find the reason for the extreme sea-sickness. The result of this was that I seemed quite healthy but that there was strong circumstantial evidence that I was allergic to a particular type of drug contained in some anti-seasickness tablets – the type that I had taken on the crossing from Maine to Nova Scotia and then again on sailing from Sydney to St Pierre. This was a great relief and we prepared to sail from St Pierre, this unique and isolated bit of France in North America, eight days after our arrival. We were both feeling much more confident and we jettisoned all anti-seasickness tablets: Paul, lucky chap, doesn't need them anyway, and I would cope with the "ordinary" dose of this affliction and get over it in the normal way after a day or two.

After lunch on 21 July we sailed. It was a fine day, though, as usual, the fog was hovering a short way out to sea. The wind was light to moderate and fair and we easily sailed our course, a little east of south away from the island. For the first twenty-four hours progress was good and all seemed to be going well in favourable conditions. I was slightly seasick but this caused only minor discomfort and I got over it rather more rapidly than usual. And yet all was not as well as it seemed.

It is, of course, normal to have some fatigue on the initial stages of a long passage; getting one's system used to four hours on, four hours off, watch and watch, is bound to be a bit of a strain until one becomes acclimatised. Previously this had taken me two or three days to achieve. On this occasion I just did not begin to get there, and as the days went on the fatigue increased and changed to exhaustion for no apparent reason, conditions remaining generally favourable other than the all-pervading fog. It was not even particularly cold.

Paul coped splendidly with the increasing burden as I became less and less capable of doing anything at all other than remaining supinely horizontal.

One week out from St Pierre came the time for a momentous decision. Up until then we, or rather Paul, had carried on; either letting the boat self-steer when he needed rest, or heaving to when conditions were such that *Odd Times* would not hold to a reasonable course. Until then we both hoped and rather anticipated that I would recover but, as time passed, this hope seemed increasingly remote. Fog had prevented the possibility of obtaining sun sights as, although it was sometimes sunny, the horizon was never visible. I could have instructed Paul how to obtain a noon latitude sight at least; though, normally, at this stage of the crossing a lack of knowledge of our exact position would not have mattered. As it was we discovered later that we were considerably in error in our dead reckoning as we had not passed from the west-flowing to the east-flowing current despite the very considerable increase in water temperature which we had thought of as signalling the change from the Labrador current to the North Atlantic Drift.

There seemed to be three possibilities open to us. To carry on, to turn back towards Newfoundland, or to seek assistance. If we carried on our next assured possibility of obtaining help, assuming we did not meet a ship, was ocean weather ship "Delta", stationed near our projected course about five or six hundred miles ahead and on to which we could home by means of our radio direction-finding equipment when within about one hundred miles. Beyond "Delta" the Azores lay about the same distance ahead but a couple of hundred miles to the south of the course for England. This possibility seemed all very well providing that conditions remained fair – a possibility but, in those waters, very far from being a certainty. What would Paul's position be if called upon to cope single-handed with bad conditions as well as with an invalid who seemed to be getting weaker every day?

The next possibility was to return to Newfoundland. This would have entailed a probable continuous beat to windward against the prevailing wind, back in cold conditions. At this stage I felt hardly able to trust my own judgment and made the decision that I will long continue to ponder. We would seek assistance if possible.

Now the fog cleared and we had overcast skies with intermittent rain squalls. The barometer was going down and this doubtless had its influence. We both felt very depressed but there seemed to be no alternative to the decision.

A few hours later, shortly after noon, Paul sighted two trawlers. He started the engine and motor-sailed towards them; they were proceeding very slowly with a net strung out between and astern of them. Somehow I managed to crawl up on deck and into the cockpit. Paul took in all sail. The trawlers turned out to be Spanish and we had some initial difficulty in making ourselves understood. Eventually they realized that something was wrong and we manoeuvred under the lee of one of the vessels and managed, despite the heavy swell, to get *Odd Times* close enough for Paul to jump aboard the trawler and to get clear again without touching.

Then commenced a few hours that I hope never to repeat. I was not at all sick, just exhausted; and I was finding great difficulty in maintaining my equilibrium, both physically and mentally. Whilst Paul explained the problem first to an English-speaking Spaniard and then by means of their radio to the St John's, Newfoundland, coastguard, I tried to keep *Odd Times* in the lee of the slow-moving trawler, without getting too close. Recurring spells of dizziness did not help.

Paul eventually got into direct communication with a ship carrying a doctor that was about 15 hours from us, and with a Dutch survey vessel and ocean-going tug that was only about 4 hours away and which was bound for St John's. It seemed that immediate rest rather than a further night followed by medical aid would be wiser and the tug was diverted to come to our aid.

When the tug, the *Smit Lloyd II*, hove in sight Paul rejoined *Odd Times*, somehow or other again without damage.

Soon after 2000 in the failing light we went alongside the *Smit Lloyd*. It was now that *Odd Times* received her first damage, superficially. The noise as we struck in the large swell was utterly heart-rending, with splintering wood predominating as part of the rubbing strake and the starboard navigation light was wrenched off. A heavy nylon warp was passed from the tug and made fast round *Odd Times'* mast with a bight taken round the samson post. Paul passed up an emergency bag that he had earlier packed containing irreplacable papers, the photographic slide record of the voyages of the *Odd Times* and our various cameras. I was hauled aboard the tug, and would have lost some fingers between the rigging and the tug's side in the process but for some quick thinking and shouting by a member of the tug's crew. Paul jumped and *Odd Times* was taken in tow. I was half led and half carried below.

Odd Times, still perfectly sound except for the already mentioned superficial damage, fell into position astern and the tug proceeded at about 5 knots. *Odd Times*, with her helm lashed amidships, followed docilely.

At about 0200 the line to *Odd Times* was seen to be chafing and was replaced with a wire rope by a member of the tug's crew. Apparently at this time she was in good shape and completely dry down below. All seemed to go well for the next few hours but the wind freshened to 30 knots or more and the swell increased – both coming from a couple of points of the port bow. The *Smit Lloyd II* slowed to about 4 knots, the minimum speed at which she could maintain adequate control.

At 06.55, at 45° 00′ N. 51° 41′ W. the disaster occurred. Either the bight of the wire rope had come off the samson post or else, under the enormous strain of being towed in the then heavy swell, the samson post had carried away; but, either way, the strain of the tow was taken directly on the mast and before anyone on the tug could do anything about it *Odd Times* started sheering wildly and was pulled right over; she filled, and sank. All of this in little more time than it takes to say it. The master of the tug had done all that he could and had no option but to sever the tow line and proceed.'

—————— „ ——————

From: *Yachting World*, April 1969

This dramatic sequence of photographs shows the rescue of Harry Ormiston from the doomed schooner *Halcyon*. Although a first-hand account was not available, the series is included to show sea conditions

1

Photos 1 and 2: *Halcyon* is spotted and *Alert's* inflatable races to the rescue.

3

Photos 3 and 4: The schooner capsizes before they reach her, and her skipper is thrown overboard.

5

Photos 5 and 6: His head can be seen between the two craft just before the rescue crew pick him up.

encountered in a 70 knot Atlantic gale. The photographs were taken by Lieutenant D B Perkins from the US Coast Guard Cutter *Alert*, 300 miles off Cape Fear, North Carolina.

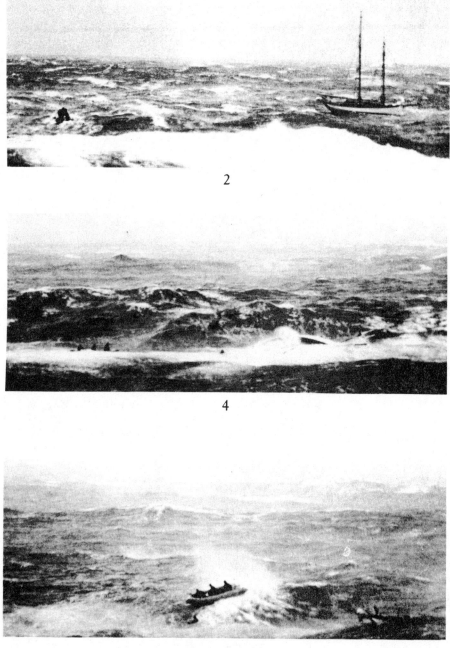

2

4

6

PART IX: LESSONS AND CONCLUSIONS

INTRODUCTION

The choice of first-hand accounts to be included in this book was governed by two main considerations: first, each story should provide a 'good read'; and secondly, apart from one exception, which I will leave to the yachting historians to discover, none of the accounts should involve loss of life.

Because of these criteria, it would be unwise for anyone to draw generalised conclusions from this particular collection of stories. Yet it would seem to be wasteful and even unfair to those people who wrote their accounts because they believed they might prove instructive, if their views were not summarised and compared.

CAUSES OF LOSS

As the preceding pages tell, there are many ways in which a yacht may become a total loss, but broadly the causes can be grouped like this:

- Stress of Weather
- Faulty Navigation
- Failure of Gear or Rigging
- Failure of Ground Tackle or Mooring Lines
- Collision
- Fire or Explosion
- Being Towed
- Exhaustion or Illness

The accounts were arranged and will be considered in much the same order as this list.

STRESS OF WEATHER

Starting with the decidely happy-go-lucky account of the cruise of the *Dragon* in 1891, the collection of incidents spans more than ninety years; thus enabling us to appreciate how vastly different our sailing now is from the tough, almost primitive game it was nearly a century ago. Radio communication, position indicators, life-rafts, and many other facilities have greatly improved the chances of survival in cases of emergency; yet none of these things has altered the fact that, when faced with really bad weather, the same difficult decisions have to be made today as skippers have faced since sailing began.

In that sense, nothing has changed. Will she heave-to, or would she do better lying a-hull? Would a sea-anchor help and, if so, should she be held by the bow or the stern? Or should she run down wind, perhaps with warps out astern? These and many other questions can only be answered by the skipper at the time, and it will give him little comfort to know that, whatever he decides to do, someone (who was not there) will certainly tell him that he would have fared better had he done something else.

Heaving-to

The first of the two boats that W.H.A. Whitworth lost was the very old Dixon Kemp designed 'plank on edge' yawl, *Alektor*, and with her draft of 7ft 3in and overall length of 34ft, she could hardly be more different from today's beamy, light-displacement yacht.

Nevertheless, there is something to be learned from Whitworth's story, for surely even McMullen would have approved the good sense and courage that *Alektor*'s skipper showed by keeping the sea. It was McMullen who in 1886 advised the young Claud Worth that 'If it looks like blowing hard onshore, get in somewhere in good time or else give the land a very wide berth.'

Whitworth had intended to approach St Peter Port in the dark, but only if the weather conditions were good; and, since they were not, he decided to heave-to for the night. By the morning, he reckoned that they had increased their offing and were about 20 miles NNW of Les Hanois, and, as he saw it, they must either run before the NW wind to St Peter Port, risking the dangerous seas that could be expected as they rounded Les Hanois, or increase their offing while they could still sail. The latter course was taken and after getting under way they found they should easily clear the Casquets.

But then, first the lacing of the mainsail to the gaff gave way, and soon after that the jib split in two. Under staysail and mizen *Alektor* would sail nowhere near the wind and they were suddenly in trouble. They tried to heave-to, but now she would not come up into the wind and the only other thing was to use the sea-anchor. In this, Whitworth had previous experience to guide him, for as he said, 'I had ridden to this sea-anchor for some eighteen hours in mid-Channel the year before and I had no doubts about being able to ride out a harder blow than this.'

Sea-anchor to Slow Down Drift

By now the wind had backed N of NW, and although Whitworth believed he had some 20 miles of sea room, he also knew that he could not go on drifting through another night; and so after seven hours riding to the sea-anchor he 'informed the crew that we could not clear the Casquets and that I was afraid we were in a bad way', and then a statement that is difficult to believe today – 'There was nothing more to be done except hoist a signal of distress.' That signal was simply an inverted ensign; which by the greatest of good fortune was seen within half an hour by the S.S. *Tairoa*, a 10,000-ton ship bound for London.

While there have always been wide differences of opinion about the behaviour of yachts while lying to a sea-anchor, they must be useful in slowing down the rate of drift towards a lee shore, as in this case.

Damaged While Hove-to

Not many people were sailing small yachts east to west across the North Atlantic in 1927; but W.E. Sinclair was a seasoned cruising man, and he and his crew, Meredith Jackson, managed to keep the *Joan* afloat and still moving in the right direction even after being dismasted and badly damaged while hove-to.

That Sinclair knew very well how to heave-to in the *Joan* is apparent when he says, 'After seeing Greenland we ran into ten days of nearly continuous gale. For most of the time we were hove-to either on the sea-anchor or trys'l. It was not as uncomfortable as it sounds – and I have even made use of a spell of sea-anchor work to do some arrears of typing!' But unfortunately this method of dealing with the storm failed them at about 10 p.m. on September 1st, 1927, when 'There was a tremendous crash' and Jackson 'found himself in a place he did not recognise.' It was Sinclair who managed to get out of the cabin first and announce that the mast had gone.

At this point in the story of the *Joan*, it is interesting to note that the immediate concern was to keep the boat afloat: 'The wreckage had to be cut away before it stove us in, and the foot of water above the floorboards in the cabin had to be returned to the Atlantic. Sinclair did the first job and I did the second.' Such matter-of-fact statements certainly belied the magnitude of the tasks they each undertook. Yet there was not much they could do except tackle those jobs, since there was little chance of their being rescued as they had no means of alerting anyone that could not see them and they knew they were to the north of the steamer track.

They bailed all night – often the two of them working together because the pump had failed – until next morning, when they managed 'to caulk the worst leak with a sock.'

There is a lesson here for any skipper whose boat is suddenly damaged or holed. First, pump or bail continuously with whatever means possible, until it can be decided whether the inflow of water can be countered. Then try to locate the main cause of the leak. This may well mean tearing away linings and fittings, but it will be no time to worry about that. The use of crowbar and saw may well be necessary.

After bailing and working on repairs for two days, they set a staysail on the *Joan*, between the stem head and the top of the mizen mast, and then 'limped away to the south-west.'

These experiences of the *Joan* tell us that, while lying to a sea-anchor may be safe in wind strengths up to gale force, beyond that, in a North Atlantic hurricane for example, when even liners are forced to heave-to, a small boat like the *Joan* will be 'laid right over until both masts are in the water with the keel in the air.'

Sea-anchor Streamed from Bows

The *Un-named 5-tonner* first tried lying to a sea-anchor just south of the Kentish Knock lightvessel, 'So now, if ever, was the time to try out our beautiful new sea-anchor.'

It was rigged on a new springy warp (probably coir rope in those days) of some twenty fathoms and they paid it out slowly over the weather bow. Around the same time they lost the jib while trying to furl it with what was almost certainly a Wyckeham Martin gear, but they did manage to stow the mainsail safely. Then they awaited the result – 'For an incredibly short space of time she lay quiet enough, until a huge breaking sea smote her and threw her over almost on her beam ends in the trough. She righted at once, but lay broached to, rolling to an alarming extent, shipping a lot of broken water and resolutely refusing to budge from that really dangerous position.'

So much for using a sea-anchor from the stem head of a 5-tonner in a gale in the short seas of the Thames Estuary.

Some experienced ocean racing and cruising men would say that the skipper of the 5-tonner was wrong to try to bring his boat head to sea, and that he would have been better off rigging his sea-anchor from a bridle made fast at bow and quarter so that he could adjust the relative position of the sea-anchor until the boat rode in the slick formed by her sideways drift. Others, including Hiscock and Roth, consider that the right place for a sea-anchor to be, when attached to a modern yacht, is astern, because then she will lie with her stern or quarter to the sea and present a smaller target.

But still believing that their boat must somehow be 'brought up to meet the seas', the crew of the 5-tonner let an anchor go, not expecting it to hold but hoping that it would provide sufficient drag to bring her head to wind and sea. 'But in this case it proved of no effect, as she towed the anchor and twenty fathoms of chain without a sign of looking up in the right direction.'

Strain on Sea-anchors

The way in which the ground tackle was towed through the water as if it were not there, should serve to illustrate the forces that are at play with a yacht in heavy weather. If a further reminder is needed, picture the effort that was involved to recover that chain and anchor:

'Having no windlass, it was not an easy job, as we could only get an inch or two at a time as she fell into the troughs, while we clawed at the cable till the blood spurted from our finger nails.'

The Alternative

But they got it on board at last, hoisted a reefed staysail and 'put her before it'; shaping a course between the Kentish Knock lightvessel and her watch-buoy and then keeping as much to the north as they dared. They also did something that is almost always recommended when a yacht is running before a gale of wind; they towed a rope astern. In fact they had to use the end of their mainsheet and it 'had a surprising effect, as the most threatening seas would divide on the warp, and, breaking, cream away under the counter without doing any harm.'

They ran on in this way for several hours, but realised that, even on the most northerly course they could manage, they would miss the land off Lowestoft by five or ten miles and without charts they only knew that there were sands off the Norfolk coast and that the slightest touch on them during the long night would spell their end.

So, when a tramp steamer came up astern they ran up a couple of dish-cloths rolled into a ball with another below as a square flag, and awaited results. The internationally recognised signal consists of 'a square flag having above it a ball or anything resembling a ball.'

In those days the sighting of visual signals was common enough for the message of distress to be spotted and understood, and, after an abortive attempt to be taken in tow, all three of the crew of the 5-tonner managed to get aboard the freighter just before the little cutter went down.

Types of Sea-anchor

Few chandlers seem to stock sea-anchors nowadays, although the official Department of Trade types are listed in the catalogues of both Simpson

Lawrence and Davey & Co.; but these are clearly intended for use with ships' lifeboats. There is little doubt that shallow-draft openboats of that kind will need a sea-anchor to prevent them capsizing in really rough seas, and it also seems clear from the recent work that has been done on the behaviour of inflatable life-rafts that they too need to be tethered to a drogue if they are not to capsize in big and breaking seas.

Claud Worth, in his classic book *Yacht Cruising*, describes in some detail the construction of a canvas sea-anchor of the truncated cone type and recommends a mouth diameter equivalent to at least one-tenth of the waterline length of the yacht.

Some people prefer a different kind of sea-anchor – the para-anchor, which, as the name suggests, is shaped like a parachute but made from coarsely woven nylon.

Another Opinion on Sea-anchors

Peter Combe of the *Windstar* admitted quite frankly that 'I was certainly not eager to construct a sea-anchor' and goes on to add 'Later we were told we should have done this, but even had the ship's company been more up to it, the gear easy of access, and conditions more sympathetic to efficient and seamanlike movements, I think it would have been an error. There is something so very helpless about being at the mercy of a sea-anchor, and our hull would have taken a worse beating holding into the seas.'

After having lost the use of their large diesel engine to propel the boat, further troubles came quickly. First the jib blew out and then a lower mast shroud parted; after which Combe asked his skipper 'What do we do now?' and the irrepressible Bertram Currie 'with a ring of trumpets in his voice' answered 'Run before the wind under bare poles.' Which they did; expecting to be badly pooped, but in the event 'only once did a large wave break over the stern, which rose wonderfully to each following sea.'

Running Downwind in the Thames Estuary

That it was really blowing we know because of what was happening to all the other craft that were caught out by that July gale in 1956.

It is said that the short seas and drying shoals of the Thames Estuary make that area more dangerous than any ocean. Certainly the stories told by the skipper of the *Un-named 5-tonner* and by Peter Combe of the *Windstar* graphically describe the dangers that beset a yacht caught in a gale while among the channels and swatches that lie between the coast of Essex and the north coast of Kent. But there is one lesson that is common to both of these stories and peculiar to the Thames Estuary: if the gale is from the south-west, which it so often is, and a yacht can clear the Kentish Knock, then it may be able to run away safely into the deeper water of the North

Sea. Both of these yachts, quite different in size, seemed to manage quite well once they had made the decision to run before it.

Auxiliary Power in Heavy Weather

Adlard Coles says in *Heavy Weather Sailing* that 'the average auxiliary engine would be useless even in Force 7'. Peter Tangvald goes further, in that he would never sail a yacht with an engine in it, believing that misplaced dependence on auxiliary power has resulted in more losses than any other cause. Nevertheless, it must surely be true that a reliable engine driving an efficient propeller will sometimes spell the difference between being blow ashore and managing to hold off.

Maaslust was not a motor-sailer in the modern sense, but even devoted owners of such traditional Dutchmen would not claim that these picturesque flat-bottomed craft sail well to windward. So, when a sequence of gear failures occurred while they were near the Nab Tower, Margaret Wells knew that they then depended for their lives on 'the gallant Porbeagle with its limited fuel supply' – partially submerged though it was.

Advantages of a Diesel

No petrol/gasoline engine would have kept going under such conditions, and there is no doubt that modern marine diesel units have greatly improved the dependability of auxiliary power in yachts – particularly when the engine is installed so that it can be started by hand when the batteries are flat.

But further troubles quickly followed for *Maaslust*, because after dropping her two anchors just off the Hayling shore both chains parted within a few minutes. Somehow they managed to get under way again and win sufficient offing to clear the Chichester Bar buoy, when the sound but difficult decision was made to keep to sea rather than make what would surely have been a suicidal attempt to enter Chichester Harbour.

The 48ft ketch *Island Princess* was also depending upon her engine in winds of over 100 knots, and her skipper Finbar Gittelman remembers that he was not particularly worried as 'even under bare poles she felt stable and the engine was driving her to windward controllably.'

But when the wind got up to somewhere around 150 knots – Gittelman admits he was guessing by this time – 'The boat didn't feel stable any more – and all thirty tons of her were being lifted off the crests and thrown sideways into the troughs.' Gittelman now thought it was time to try trailing warps, but in those seas it took a long time to get the necessary gear, including lines, chain and 45-pound anchor, from the forward lockers and to stream them over the stern. 'It took me about two or three minutes to realise it just wasn't going to work,' Gittelman said. 'She was doing 8 knots and broaching, rolling her sides under. She was squirrely as hell and we were getting pooped.'

Without their powerful engine it seems unlikely that they could ever have got *Island Princess* heading into the wind again.

After that, the yacht was knocked down repeatedly, and when eventually the inside ballast shifted, the skipper knew that it was time to abandon her.

Lying A-hull

Easting Down was over sixty years old when she was lost, and had undergone many alterations since being built in 1903 as a sailing centre-board lifeboat for the R.N.L.I. At the time she was abandoned in the North Sea in 1965, she had twin diesel engines, and her skipper 'experimented, trying heading into the seas with both engines on, but this proved hard work, uncomfortable and impossible to maintain. At the crest of each sea the wind caught our bows and blew them off to port or starboard, and way was only regained as the next sea approached. Running downwind towing warps was also useless, creating risk of pooping and broaching-to. I know now, beyond doubt, that in a vessel of shallow draft it is safer to lie a-hull broadside to wind and sea, even with a non-self-righting hull like *Easting Down*'s. Our only fears were that by the time the gale had abated we might be too exhausted to sail the ship or we might have drifted into the shoals of the Schelde estuary.'

It is not clear from his account whether Robertson actually tried running downwind and 'found it useless', or whether this was simply his belief based on earlier experience. In any case, it was the realisation that they could not keep the water at bay and that when its level reached the batteries it would short out their power and they would then be unable to use the radio, that made Robertson decide to send a Mayday.

Although none of the yachts taking part in the 1979 Fastnet Race would have had large auxiliary engines or propellers, the fact remains that the Report on the disaster includes these comments: 'Several damaged yachts retired safely under power. There is also some evidence that the use of engines improved the manoeuvrability of yachts in picking up survivors and in some cases in maintaining steerage way in storm conditions. The R.O.R.C. should consider whether engines should not be mandatory for safety reasons and whether alternative methods of starting engines should be required when the starting battery is flat.'

The crew of the R.O.R.C. boat *Griffin* may well owe their lives to the fact that the French yacht *Lorelei* was able to use her engine – a twelve horse-power diesel with a variable pitch propeller – to manoeuvre alongside their liferaft before taking them all on board.

Multihull Yachts

The wide divergency of opinion on the best thing to do when facing heavy weather in a monohull yacht is certainly matched when it comes to the advice or preferences of experienced multihull sailors. The late Mike McMullen was probably wisest when he wrote, in his *Multihull Seamanship*, 'It is very easy to be too dogmatic about the course of action to be followed by a multihull in bad weather.'

Many accounts have been written of the losses of both catamarans and trimarans, but I have been at some pains to strike a reasonable balance in the number and nature of the reports I have included, not wishing to aggravate the longstanding differences that exist between supporters of monohulls and the multihull enthusiasts.

Lazy Daisy was a modified Catalac catamaran; modified in that 7ft by 12in keels had been fitted to her hulls. During her west–east passsage along the Scottish coast between Inverness and Frazerburgh she had done pretty well with a Force 6 from the NE, but as the course gradually changed, first to the S and then to the SE, the wind came more and more aft until they were travelling at 6–8 knots under jib.

Surfing

Lionel Miller seems to have been unaware of any risks and remembers that 'The waves were now giving us some fast sleigh rides as we boiled along; despite the darkness and cold, we were having a great sail.' Then the warning came: 'Suddenly I found the boat going downhill at an alarming angle, the high flared bows were almost underwater despite their enormous reserves of buoyancy, and the hulls vibrated with a deep humming sound as we tore through the water at 12 knots plus.'

There followed some trouble with the dinghy, which, in view of subsequent events, they were fortunate to solve. Then the inevitable happened – 'Looking round now, all thoughts of the dinghy problem vanished. The wave coming up was big, perhaps 30ft, but the threat of destruction was in the 5ft-high breaking crest which was commencing its avalanche down the long slope towards us.' The enormous thrust of that wave lifted *Lazy Daisy* 'into a vertical position, and the press of water under the bridgedeck completed the capsize in a matter of 2–3 seconds.'

It is very tempting to say that in this case the catamaran was capsized because of its excessive speed. But can one be sure what would have happened to her had she lain a-hull as the trimaran *Boatfile* did in the Atlantic while on her way back from the U.S.? Nick Hallam, skipper of *Boatfile*, reports that they were lying a-hull in Force 8 winds, a procedure they had followed in other gales, and although they had a drogue and warps ready in the cockpit, they were not in use. The trimaran was lying quietly with the dagger board retracted and the helm lashed down so that she was drifting to leeward, leaving a well-defined slick upwind. They never heard the wave that caused their capsize, but they were 'picked up by something very big, and in a rush of broken water *Boatfile* was rolled rapidly over to starboard and settled into an irrevocably inverted position.'

Breaking-up

Too large a number of multihulled yachts have been lost as the result of breaking-up. One of the reasons for this kind of loss was recognised by Rob James in the book *Multihulls Offshore*, written just before his death. James pointed out that, in the sixties in particular, multihulls gained a bad reputation because of 'a lot of amateur designed, amateur built and amateur sailed craft, many of which foundered, causing unwanted and unwarranted adverse publicity for multihulls in general.'

On the subject of multihulls in heavy weather, James considered it is best to keep sailing as long as possible, 'as I am firmly of the belief that it is the correct thing to do, even to windward'; but he also added: 'The most likely event that may cause one to give up the effort, is damage.'

That is what seems to have happened to the 35ft trimaran *Livery Dole* when she was well on her way to Newport, R.I., in the 1980 OSTAR. Peter Phillips reported 'doing 6–7 knots but slamming and dipping the lee float well under water. The weather float is another problem. The seas are so big that every now and again a wave hits the up float with alarming force.'

Having taken the fourth reef in the main so that speed was reduced to 4–5 knots, Phillips seems to have decided to 'run off under storm jib', because later he says 'I then heard a roar behind me and I looked back to windward. There is a big wave, much bigger than the others, coming towards me with a vicious, already breaking, top. It hits the windward float and throws it in the air. The tri is virtually standing on its starboard float with the mast along the surface of the water. I am convinced we are going right over and will capsize. The wave picks up the main hull and then moves upright, but the down float goes on up and the windward float gets slammed back down on to the water to windward with an almighty crash. I hear a crack, and to my utter surprise the whole front section of the windward (port) float has just snapped off and is gone.'

It is worth noting that all three of the preceding accounts blame extraordinarily large waves with breaking crests for their disasters. Some of the competitors caught in the Fastnet storm also reported that 'there were some waves which were of a size and shape such that there was no defensive tactic which would prevent them from rolling or severely damaging a yacht caught in their path.'

The Crew Matter Most

Perhaps a good way of concluding this section, with its widely different opinions on the behaviour of yachts in heavy weather, will be to quote the words of Claud Worth, who in his classic book, *Yacht Cruising*, had this to say on the subject: 'No agreement is ever reached, or ever can be reached, because the points under discussion are not the most essential. By far the most important factor in determining the seaworthiness of a yacht is the crew, next comes the gear, and last of all the form of the yacht.'

Keeping Her Afloat

R.N.L.I. coxswain, Trevor England, once said that 'The time to abandon a small boat is when your navel starts getting wet, and not before.' Certainly the number of yachts that remained afloat after being abandoned during the 1979 Fastnet storm was notably high. Of the 24 craft left to the mercy of those seas, only 5 are believed to have sunk.

Unsinkable Yachts

There are ways in which a monohull yacht can be rendered unsinkable, either at the time of construction or by the subsequent addition of extra buoyancy in the form of expanded polyurethane or inflatable buoyancy bags. But these precautions necessarily involve the loss of useful space within the hull, since the addition of some 3000 litres of closed-cell polyurethane foam is required to make a 26-footer 'unsinkable' and even inflatable bags must have room to expand. Not many yachtsmen choose to pay the price of such insurance against what they presumably consider to be the remote possibility that one day their boat might sink.

To say that a yacht is unsinkable is not to say that it will remain tenable after being flooded. It seems likely that some of the yachts abandoned during the 1979 Fastnet will have remained afloat only in such a waterlogged state as to make them quite untenable for any crew. On the other hand, it is possible that other boats may have filled slowly enough for a determined crew to have been able to keep the water at bay long enough to discover the principal cause of the leak and either to staunch it or to prevent its recurrence.

While reading about it at leisure it is not difficult to understand that after a boat has been holed or a skin fitting has failed, the rate at which water will enter the hull depends upon the size of the hole and its depth below the external water level. It is equally easy to comprehend that as the level of the water inside the hull rises, so the rate of flow into the boat will slow down. But these basic truths will be very difficult to bear in mind when your yacht has just collided with a rock, a whale or some other submerged object.

Getting at a Leak

It must be terrifyingly difficult for a singlehander aboard a badly-leaking monohull to decide whether to attempt to divide his efforts between pumping and searching for the cause of the leak or to abandon while there is still time to launch the raft or dinghy and collect a few essential things. When Peter Tangvald's *Dorothea* collided with something at night while they were about 40 miles south-west of Barbados, he knew that the leak was serious because water was above the floorboards almost immediately. He also realised that his heavily ballasted ship would soon sink unless he could quickly locate the damage and make temporary repairs; but 'this proved to be impossible because of the inside ceiling which hid the planking.' He also comments that 'to look for the leak from the outside would no doubt have been possible in a calm sea and in daylight, and I might then have been able to nail over a piece of canvas; but as it was, with a rolling ship, in heavy seas and pitch darkness, it was an impossibility.'

Unlike many wooden boats, G.R.P. craft are not usually lined with an inner skin that would prevent ready access to the hull in emergency. Even so, bulkheads and lockers may have to be ruthlessly torn away if a leak is to be found and staunched before it is too late. One disadvantage of a glassfibre boat is that an external patch cannot be nailed to the hull as can sometimes be done with a wooden boat.

Capsized Multihulls

One of the arguments in favour of multihull yachts is that they are unsinkable. This may not invariably be true, as Nick Hallam found with *Boatfile*; but it is certain that they are capsizable – and, once capsized, they seldom offer a safe refuge in their upturned state. In fact those who have experienced the capsize of a cat or a trimaran usually have something to say about the difficulties of remaining with the yacht, let alone regaining entry to the hull or hulls.

Livery Dole had a safety hatch in her main hull, and after taking to his liferaft Peter Phillips tried to use the hatch to enter the cabin to get more food and water, 'but the big seas break and wash me off'; and later: 'I pull myself in and climb back on the bits of crossbeam – try as I can I can't get in the hatch. I just get washed off by the seas.'

Nick Hallam and Nye Williams were caught below when their tri, *Boatfile*, capsized, and with the 'surging mess of loose gear washing back and forth with every wave' they 'began laboriously to cut a hatch in the hull above our heads – on the assumption that, like other capsized trimarans, she would stay afloat.' However, 'when the boat's stern was plunged into the trough of a wave twice within 20 minutes, both times trapping us under water in the cabin, we began reluctantly to suspect that the trimaran was starting to sink.'

The Big Decision
Just when to abandon a yacht will always be a matter of judgement, but the fateful decision must always be made by the skipper.

Peter Tangvald was almost certainly right to leave the *Dorothea* when he did, for although he remembers seeing her still afloat some 50 minutes after he left her, she was by then 'lying very deep in the water. I saw her lights for a while and then suddenly they disappeared.'

Just as Tangvald believed that *Dorothea* struck a submerged log, so J.S. Robertson thought it was her collision with a baulk of jettisoned timber in the North Sea that caused *Easting Down* to leak so dangerously. But in that case, *Easting Down* did not sink until 4½ hours after being abandoned, and even then she sank as a result of being taken in tow. Learning of this subsequently caused her skipper to ask himself 'whether she could have been saved had I stayed on board to bail.'

But even an engine-driven pump is fallible, particularly if it is driven from the propeller shaft and the stern gear becomes damaged. When this happened to *Windstar*, her crew could only resort to pumping by hand, a job that was made the more difficult because the pump was installed 'hard against the port side of the engine space.' This is a reminder that careful attention should be given to the positioning of bilge pumps.

Siting and Number of Pumps
Peter Haward, who pioneered the business of yacht delivery at a time when almost all the boats he delivered were wooden and many of them old and prone to leak, has said 'never should it be left to chance whether water invading the bilges can be pumped back to the sea.' It should be easier to comply with this wise counsel now that we have so much more reliable pumps than the semi-rotary and piston types that were common when Haward was making his first delivery trips. Almost invariably, matchsticks, shavings or labels from food cans found their way into the valves of those earlier bilge pumps, once the violent motion of the bilge water had swilled them from their hiding places.

Clogged Pumps
The *Un-named 5-tonner*, with her leaking topsides, would have undoubtedly been dependent on a piston-type bilge pump which 'after spurting feebly once or twice would produce nothing but a coughing sound and a little air. The pump was cleared and reassembled, only to fail again for the same reason – a matchstick in the valve.' Eventually, when the job of taking

down and reassembly became impossible, 'we had to give up the struggle and rely on such bailing as we could do with a bucket.'

Margaret Wells also tells how in *Maaslust* 'The bilge pump was not man enough for the job, and priming was virtually impossible with the motion of the ship, so we set to with a bucket and basin, bailing alternately.'

Sailormen in Thames spritsail barges also knew what it meant to stand on deck pumping for their lives with heavy vertically operated piston pumps. Bob Roberts tells of this when describing events after the *Martinet* began leaking badly off Orfordness: 'Both the big pumps aft were got working, and the three of us settled down to regular spells, two pumping while one rested. After half an hour of this I went below to see how much was in her. To my horror, there was no difference. There was only one thing to do – pump all night and get into some kind of harbour – anywhere – as soon as it was light. . . . The pumps were just about holding their own, then the starboard one choked. Eventually we took it to pieces and, lying flat on the deck, the seas breaking over and soaking through out clothes (sailormen seldom wore oilskins), attempted to reach down the pipe in a desperate attempt to clear it.'

No doubt Bruce Paulsen considered that he had done his homework so far as the pumps aboard *Mariah* were concerned, since before setting out to sail her south from City Island, N.Y., he had 'flushed out the bilges to see that each was functioning properly.' *Mariah* had no less than four pumps on board. 'Besides the 7 gallon-per-minute electric pump there was a Whale Gusher on the deck . . . Then there were our big guns: a 50-plus gallon-per-minute Jabsco that ran off the Lehman diesel and a 75-plus gallon-per-minute firehose/bilge pump that ran off its own one-cylinder diesel mounted in the lazarette.'

Despite all this, the fifty-year-old *Mariah* was soon in difficulties, because when she began to work and leak in a 40-knot wind, the 7 gallon-a-minute electric pump could not keep up, and when they 'turned to the engine-driven Jabsco, it worked for a minute or two, but then grew hot and stopped pumping altogether.' To reduce the water level so they could operate the Jabsco pump, they began to bail with buckets – and continued to do so for the next 30 hours, because when they were able to run it again, the Jabsco impeller once more burnt out. The monster firehose pump was supposed to be self-priming, but 'perhaps because of the 10ft waves', it never did, so they kept on bailing.

Bailing with Buckets

All of which lends support to the saying that 'no bilge pump is as effective as a scared man with a bucket.'

After the *Joan* suffered a knock down in the Atlantic, her mast tore a hole in her deck when it went by the board, so that they quickly had a foot of water over the floorboards, and, although they plugged the gap with blankets, the 'leaking was so hard that we had to bail with a bucket until evening', which meant that the two of them had bailed for 18 hours.

It has been estimated that a two- or three-man team working flat-out can take some 2000 gallons an hour out of a boat by bailing with buckets. This rate of transfer could not be matched by a relay of people working a single pump.

By way of a reference, it is worth remembering that when Des Sleightholme, editor of *Yachting Monthly*, carried out a 'live' experiment by opening a 2½in skin fitting in a 24-footer, he found that she took in 40 gallons in 2½ minutes – just about matching the capacity of most large diaphragm pumps.

Nevertheless, it is rather surprising that despite the obvious improvements that have been made in the design of pumps, no less than 20 per cent of the competitors replying to the Fastnet questionnaire reported 'unsatisfactory' bilge pumping arrangements, while 29 per cent used buckets to bail and found them 'effective'.

Time to Abandon

After striking a whale, the skipper and crew of *Guia III* did not leave her until they were compelled to do so. George Marshall recounts how they made desperate efforts to staunch the enormous flow of water coming into the boat – 'The water gushed in, and for a second or two we just gaped at the damage in disbelief. Jerome and I tried to force the wood back into the hole but the strength of the remaining fibres of wood was too much for our combined weight. . . . Jerome told Giorgio and me to go on deck and try to get a headsail over the hole. He continued to try and plug the hole from the inside with spinnakers and anything else to hand. The water was waist deep at this time, and as fast as he pushed a sail in the gap it was forced back.' The attempt to cover the hole from the outside also failed, because the bow of the yacht was awash by this time. 'Jerome then gave a very Gallic shrug and said we must say *au revoir* to *Guia*.'

At other times it is necessary to abandon without any delay. Michael Millar remembers that immediately after *Quiver* had struck a rock off the north coast of Brittany, 'a quick look below revealed a hopeless situation. Richard was already on the pump, but the water in the cabin was rising at an alarming speed. Water was gushing in both sides of the stem forward, under the port bunk and again under the cockpit – we had to abandon!'

Distress Signals

After making the decision to leave his ship, Millar's immediate concern was to get out of *Quiver* and into the 9ft Nautisport dinghy, which had been stowed fully inflated upside down on the cabin top; but he also knew that he must signal their distress. 'My main armament was some seven or eight (flares) of the "Roman Candle" type; they burn a steady red flame in your hand, while throwing up a succession of red balls to a very satisfactory height. They all went off beautifully, and the display must have lasted at least four minutes; the only snag was that there was no audience.'

Flares are just one of the many ways in which distress can be signalled, and although some methods are more likely to be useful than others, none of them should be ignored. As technology expands, so the list of ways in which distress can be indicated becomes longer; at present it includes:

1. a gun or other explosive signal fired at intervals of about a minute; continuous sounding of any fog signalling apparatus.
2. rockets or shells, throwing red stars fired one at a time at short intervals.
3. a signal made by radiotelegraphy or by other signalling method consisting of the group $\cdots - - - \cdots$ (SOS) in Morse Code.
4. a signal sent by radiotelephony consisting of the spoken word 'Mayday'.
5. the International Code Signal of distress indicated by N.C.
6. a signal consisting of a square flag having above or below it a ball or anything resembling a ball.
7. flames on the vessel (as from a burning oily rag, etc.).
8. rocket parachute flare or hand flare showing a red light.
9. a smoke signal giving off orange-coloured smoke.
10. slowly and repeatedly raising and lowering arms outstretched to each side.
11. the radiotelegraph alarm signal.
12. the radio telephone alarm signal.
13. signals transmitted by emergency position-indicating radio beacons (E.P.I.R.B.).

The last decade has seen the marketing of compact, moderately priced VHF radio transceivers, and their adoption by yachtsmen has been rapid. One only needs to count the number of masthead aerials in a marina to see that at least half the yachts can now communicate by radio. But many of the accounts in this book relate to times or occasions when simpler methods of signalling had to be used, and these older ways of indicating distress should certainly not be ignored, for they can assume critical importance when, for any reason, radio communication fails.

The dish-cloth signals used by the *Un-named 5-tonner* in the Thames

Estuary in 1924 provided a rudimentary but effective way of calling for help, but a hundred years ago an even simpler single white flag, hoisted 'half-mast high' was sufficient to bring help to the little *Dragon* when she was in difficulties off the Norfolk coast.

Signalling with Flares

At night some kind of luminous or pyrotechnic display becomes necessary, but there always seems to be a degree of uncertainty surrounding the use of flares. Even so, the sorry episode Peter Combe describes must have been due to the age of the flares they carried aboard *Windstar*: 'About 2100 hours I suddenly saw for a moment a large vessel bearing green 130 about three miles off, and yelled for the flares. Bertram, after a short argument with the cabin doors, leant out on to the seat with a red tin which had a screw cap on one side, and seemed to take an age to unscrew. He then tried to get out a flare through a small hole, and after a great deal of probing and pulling, produced a piece of rumpled newspaper packing. At last a flare permitted itself to emerge. We then had to discover what to do with it. "They are self-igniting," said Bertram. But how, neither of us knew . . . I could make out the far from striking printing, which said "Tear off cap and rub inside smartly against head of flare." This produced absolutely no result.'

Things went better for Bob Roberts, and when it became certain that the *Martinet* could not be saved, he 'lit a rocket, but it misfired, hit the mizzenmast and went straight down into the sea. We tried another which was more successful. It soared skywards in a graceful arc, leaving a trail of sparks behind it. Immediately afterwards we lit a flare so that if anyone on shore had seen our rocket, they could then determine the position of our vessel by bearings.' This was sound reasoning, and a similar procedure was recommended to Robin Gardiner-Hill by the captain of the German lifeboat that rescued him from the stranded *Pentina II* in the mouth of the Elbe. He advised that flares should always be let off in pairs, at an interval of about 10 seconds. Otherwise someone sees what might or might not be a distress signal, watches for a bit, and, if he does not see another flare, tends to assume that it was his imagination.

Importance of Flares

Five of the six-man crew of *Guia III* were trying to get some sleep during the first night in the liferaft, when the lookout said that he thought he could see a light, although it could have been a rising star. George Marshall wanted to put up a flare straight away. However Jerome (the skipper) said: 'wait until we can see what it is and what course it was on. It was soon apparent that it would pass us about three miles downwind, and I put up the first parachute red flare. It went straight up and burst into a very satisfactory red glow. After about 30 seconds it went out and we all stared at the lights of the ship, willing it to change course. We waited ten minutes and then discharged two more para flares, one after the other. They both worked, and as they drifted down we saw the ship flash an Aldis lamp and the angle of her lights alter.'

The Mayday Peter Phillips was able to send just before quitting *Livery Dole* had been successfully received and two S.A.R. aircraft were flying overhead when Phillips realised that his E.P.I.R.B. was not working, so 'I get three red flares ready and wait until one of the aircraft is flying straight at me. I light all three flares at once and stand up and wave at them. Nothing, and then . . . YES . . . something is dropped from the plane. It hits the water and goes off, a smoke marker. He has got me.'

The R.Y.A. recommends that star and parachute flares should be used in pairs – a second one following the first within two minutes.

How Many Flares and What Type?

The types of flares, rockets and smoke signals that should be aboard a yacht depends upon where she will be sailing. If a boat is always likely to remain within sight of the shore – say no more than 3 miles off – then a couple of red handflares and two hand-held orange smoke signals is probably all she will ever need. For craft likely to be a bit further out, far enough not to be seen from the shore, two red parachute flares should be added to the basic inshore kit. For those who will be far from land, while going foreign, ocean racing or even world cruising, there should be a predominance of red parachute rockets and red handflares – at least five or six of each. As a guide, the R.O.R.C. recommended offshore pack would include 4 red parachute rockets, 4 red handflares, 2 orange (floating) smoke signals and 4 white handflares for collision warn-off purposes. But some of the 1979 Fastnet competitors reported to the Inquiry that they had plenty of red handflares but not enough red parachutes.

Clementina Gordon, having had no success after firing three rockets and three flares from her Silhouette anchored inside Boulogne harbour, suggests that 'Perhaps one ought to carry a minimum of a dozen rockets and a dozen flares.'

Stowage of Flares

Flares must be kept dry and to hand – not under the settee berths, as they were on *Freedom To* when she was stuck by lightning. Manufacturers go a long way towards ensuring that their flares do keep dry, by packaging them in waterproof plastic containers, but they cannot decide where they should be stowed – that will always be down to the skipper of the yacht. Any container used for storing distress flares must not only be instantly accessible but must also be easily opened on the roughest, blackest night, so that the correct flare or rocket can be found without fumbling or delay. Flares will not remain effective for ever, and nowadays they are usually marked with an expiry date, so don't count on them to work successfully after that time.

Mini-Flares

Mini-flares can provide a useful back-up for larger flares and rockets, since a pack of them can be kept in a pocket and taken into a liferaft if it becomes necessary to abandon the yacht. Not all mini-flares are guaranteed waterproof – but make sure that yours are.

Robin Gardiner-Hill resorted to mini-flares after using up all his larger ones in vain attempts to attract attention in the mouth of the Elbe, when 'Despite the heavy traffic in the estuary it was about half an hour before I made contact with a ship; by that time I was down to mini-flares and flashing with a torch. I cannot really say that mini-flares are better than rockets and hand-held flares, but they produced results.'

Signalling with Lights

The distance over which a light can be seen obviously depends upon a number of factors, including the prevailing atmospheric conditions, the brightness of the light source, its height above the sea, and the efficiency of any optics associated with it. Given a clear line of sight, it can be taken that a point source of light of one candle-power (candela) will be visible for about a mile in clear conditions, but because the transmission of light follows the inverse square law, the brightness of the lamp would have to be increased to around 4 candelas for it to be seen over 2 miles and to some 100 candelas to be visible 10 miles away. However, the use of a suitable mirror behind a light source can greatly improve its efficiency – in one direction. So, if 12 volt ships' batteries can be used, hand-held lamps can be made to produce directional brightness of hundreds of thousands of candelas, while even a portable lamp such as the Guest Type 285, with a self-contained 6 volt battery, can yield 22,000 candle power, which exceeds the brightness of most flares – but it will not of course be visible in all directions.

After George Harrod-Eagles had wrecked his *Song* on a reef off the coast of Puerto Rico, he successfully contacted the U.S. Coastguard on his VHF radio, but then they had the problem of locating him in intense darkness among dangerous reefs. He recalls, 'At last there appeared a fast-moving light searching the area of the reef, but away to the north-west. Concluding it to belong to the Coastguard, we flashed her with the torch I always keep in the cockpit. This soon brought a reponse. . .'

The crew of *Island Princess* were rescued by the tanker *Jastella* only because Bob Harvey, who knew Morse Code, 'began to signal with the flashlight. Among other things he signalled S.O.S. and Out of Water.' The second mate aboard the tanker 'saw a blinking white light, someone was trying to signal him. He picked out the word "water" . . . It had to be, he reasoned, a raft.'

Peter Tangvald was not so lucky. Soon after leaving *Dorothea* in his little wooden dinghy and setting off on an attempt to reach one or other of the Grenadine Islands, that lay some 55 miles downwind, he was overjoyed to see the lights of a ship coming towards him. 'I flashed continuously the International distress signal S.O.S., S.O.S., with my very powerful long-range torch which I trained straight at her. The ship came slowly closer and in my thoughts I prepared how I should board her . . . The ship was now very close and . . . I expected to see her slow down; but to my dismay the minutes passed without the ship altering course at all, then her bright red port light faded, as did her two masthead lights, only to be replaced immediately by a single white light, her stern light. She had not seen me after all!'

What a terrible feeling to watch that light getting fainter and fainter and finally disappearing altogether.

Peter Combe had more reason to bless stern lights when he discovered that the one that had been swinging about on *Windstar* was still working. '. . . to my amazement, when I switched on the stern light it lit – although it had been banging about the deck on the end of its flex for most of the day. With one hand on the backstay I stood holding it as high off the deck as I could, and began to flash S.O.S. in a wide arc between the two ships.' His efforts were rewarded when in due course a ship flashed back.

Signalling with a Mirror
In sunlight a mirror can provide a very effective signal by directing light right into the wheelhouse of a ship or to people on shore. There is a specially made mirror or heliograph used by climbers and backpackers. It has a small central sighting aperture containing a grid by means of which the reflected beam of sunlight can be accurately directed. This is a very useful improvement over a plain mirror, but in emergency do not hesitate to remove and use the one from the cabin or the heads.

Signalling by Radio
Ever since 1901 when Marconi sent the first message across the Atlantic by 'wireless' telegraphy, radio telegraphy and telephony have played an ever more important part in saving life at sea. But it is doubtful whether even Marconi could have foreseen that eighty years later, the crew of an abandoned yacht, having taken to their liferaft, could reasonably expect to

be rescued within hours after their radio distress signals had been relayed to the nearest search and rescue services, either by plane or a satellite.

Medium Frequency Equipment

One or two of the accounts included in the book describe the sending of radio signals that must have required powerful transmitters using the medium frequency (MF) band. But not many yachts, and certainly not small ones, are equipped with MF sets because of their size, their cost, their heavy demand on batteries and, in the UK, the rigorous type approval standards required by the Home Office. This is unfortunate, since MF radio-telephones do have a far greater surface range than modern VHF transceivers.

That *Easting Down* had an MF set in 1965 is indicated by the fact that her skipper was using Consol beacons to determine his position, and his radio-telephone to send the Mayday that was eventually acknowledged by the British ship *Etterickland* and by Scheveningen Radio.

Guia III also operated on the 2182 kHz International Distress Frequency, but as George Marshall recalls, 'Down below I found that water was thigh deep and the boat rocking, swishing water from beam to beam. The radio had been switched on and I soon had the first *Mayday* out on 2182 kHz . . . The output meter on the set showed that the power was rapidly going as the seawater came over the tops of the battery.'

Anthony Lealand intended to send out a second priority PAN-PAN urgency call on 2182 kHz, but while his crew Annette was waiting for the next period of silence to make the broadcast, *Rushcutter* was capsized and lost her mast together with the backstay aerial. Their subsequent rescue from the Tasman Sea was almost certainly due to the emergency radio beacon they took with them into the liferaft.

Automatic Alarm

Medium-wave transmitters operating in the International Marine Distress Frequency can transmit a two-tone signal that will automatically alert any ship or Coastguard station within range, which can be up to 200 miles. All vessels fitted with equipment capable of receiving on 2182 kHz are *expected to* maintain a listening watch on that frequency during the three-minute silence periods commencing at each hour and half hour G.M.T. However, there is a body of opinion among ocean-going yachtsmen who often find themselves in very remote waters, that their best chance of having a distress signal picked up is to transmit an S.O.S. on the ship-telegraph frequency of 500 kHz. George Marshall, in a report written after the loss of *Guia III*, goes so far as to say that for long-distance races 'Each yacht must be equipped with radio equipment that sends out an automatic S.O.S. on 500 kHz. This is the *only* frequency that deep-sea ships keep watch on.'

At this point it may be useful to restate the 'Statutory Duties of Masters of Ships to Rescue', which require that: 'The Master of a ship, on receiving at sea a distress signal or information from any source that a vessel or aircraft is in distress, must proceed with all speed to the assistance of the persons in distress, informing them, if possible, that he is doing so.'

Mayday Broadcasts
Peter Phillips left *Livery Dole* in a hurry after she capsized, and he only had time 'to throw the liferaft over the side and operate the Panic button on the Argos satellite transmitter.' Fortunately he had already broadcast a Mayday on the 2182 kHz distress frequency, and this, together with the use of flares, resulted in his eventual location and rescue.

Bruce Paulsen, aboard the *Mariah* with her successively failing pumps, reported that 'by 0600 the water was a foot over the floorboards, something had sprung and it was getting difficult to keep up. At this point, the first of a long series of Maydays was sent and the tanker *Navios Crusader* relayed our message to the Cape May Coastguard.' The *Mariah* was then about 200 miles SE of Cape May, but their distress signals triggered off a remarkable series of rescue operations. First to find them was a transport aircraft carrying an emergency pump which was dropped by parachute too far upwind for the *Mariah* to reach it. Then, four hours later, the same plane dropped an orange drum containing a second pump, but this too eluded the crew of the *Mariah*. By this time the merchant vessel *Dorsetshire* was standing by, and after another seven hours a helicopter arrived with still more pumps; but after half an hour's manoeuvring, the pilot decided that 'instead of lowering a pump he would begin evacuation procedures'.

All this time the *Mariah* was able to maintain radio contact with the aircraft and the Coastguard cutter *Alert*, which was now standing by after taking ten hours to reach them from Cape May.

After a frightening 40 minutes during which only two of *Mariah*'s crew were winched into the helicopter, it was decided not to proceed with that method of rescue and to depend upon the *Alert* to complete the evacuation.

The *Mariah* incident not only illustrates the way in which help of many kinds can be initiated as the result of a justifiable Mayday call, but also shows how vital continuous communication by radio-telephone can be during the course of extended rescue operations.

Correct Procedure
When a yacht is equipped with a VHF radio-telephone but is about to be abandoned, it might prove to be vital that someone continues to broadcast

the Mayday distress call and message and to listen for any acknowledgement that might indicate what help could be coming and how long it will be. At such a critical time it is likely that the skipper of the stricken yacht will be busy launching the dinghy or liferaft or ensuring that emergency supplies are transferred to the raft, in which case any member of the crew should be capable of manning the radio up to the very last minute. One way of ensuring that the radio can be properly operated by any member of the crew is to give them the necessary instruction when they join the ship, and to back this up with a clearly typed or printed procedure card placed in a prominent position by the set.

While it is important that any member of the crew of a yacht should be able to make a distress call on the radio-telephone, the skipper must make it absolutely clear that the order to make such a call can only be given by him. This rule is necessary because a distress call must only be made when a yacht is in serious and imminent danger, and it is the skipper and he alone who must decide if and when this is the case.

Portable Radio-telephones

Failure of batteries, as occurred in both *Mariah* and *Guia III*, might possibly have been avoided if sealed batteries with waterproof connections had been installed. Alternatively, a portable radio-telephone can be used as a back-up for the main set. One such single-purpose portable transceiver, the Seafarer Callbuoy, is pre-tuned to 2182 kHz. Once its antenna has been extended and the earthing sinker has been thrown into the sea, the press of a button will broadcast a two-tone signal to automatically trigger any of the listening-watch Coastguard or ships' receivers that are within a 60–80 mile range. This radio-telephone can also be used to make speech contact with the Coastguard or rescuers. Although the Callbuoy is large by comparison with VHF transceivers, it is waterproof and can certainly be taken into a liferaft, where it will operate for 80 hours before its transmission falls to half strength.

Emergency Antenna

To guard against the possibility that VHF radio communications might be stopped because a mast is lost after a knock-down or capsize, a spare antenna should be carried on board. Some helically formed emergency antennae are packed in a watertight tube, small enough to stow in a handy place with the distress flares.

Many of those who have had to abandon a yacht in recent years would agree that the most important thing they took into their liferaft was an Emergency Position Indicating Radio Beacon, usually abbreviated to the awkward-sounding acronym E.P.I.R.B. In 1970 the U.S. Congress passed a law requiring aircraft to carry an Emergency Locator Transmitter (E.L.T.) to indicate their position in the event of their having to come down in the sea or some other remote region. When first introduced, the safeguard was not intended to be used by surface craft, but by 1972 the U.S. National Transportation Safety Board had recommended that the Coastguard should require ocean-going vessels to carry an emergency position indicating radio beacon. In the U.K., after a period of uncertainty, the Department of Transport issued a Merchant Shipping Notice (M982) in 1983, recommending the carriage of a suitable E.P.I.R.B. for owners of yachts.

In the U.S., two different types of E.P.I.R.B. have been officially established: Class A is intended for passenger-carrying craft and must be capable of floating free of a sinking vessel and automatically activating, while Class B can be hand-held and hand-operated. Both classes are required to transmit a modulated (wailing) distress signal simultaneously at 121.5 MHz and 243 MHz, the former being the International Distress frequency for civil aircraft and the latter used by military and search and rescue (S.A.R.) planes.

As matters stood between 1972 and 1982, the possibility of a distress signal from an E.P.I.R.B. being picked up was entirely dependent upon the chance of a plane overflying within 100 miles or so of the incident and within 48 hours of the commencement of transmission. In effect this meant that a yachtsman in trouble in the North Atlantic stood a reasonably good chance of being located, as several accounts testify; but elsewhere in the oceans of the world, an E.P.I.R.B. might be useless.

SARSAT

Recognising these limitations, in 1983 three countries – Canada, France and the U.S. – collaborated in a satellite assisted search-and-rescue (SARSAT) project designed to demonstrate and evaluate the enormously wider scope of a radio distress beacon operating via a satellite. Even then it was known that the 1983 programme would be only a stepping stone towards global coverage, since it will require an additional transmitting frequency (406 MHz) before signals from an E.P.I.R.B. can be received, processed and stored on-board a satellite, ready to be transmitted to earth when a ground station comes 'into view'.

The rapid progress that is being made in this field was dramatically demonstrated in 1983 by the wonderful rescue of the Frenchman Jacques de Roux by the British yachtsman Richard Broadhead when they were both in the Roaring Forties while racing single-handed round the world.

Improved Design

Because they operate on VHF, E.P.I.R.B.s can be much smaller and cheaper than an emergency transmitter using the 2182 kHz band, and some of them are now even small enough to be stowed with a liferaft. For these reasons it is not surprising that their use has increased rapidly in recent years. The latest E.P.I.R.B.s incorporate both power indicators and indicator lights, and often use lithium batteries with a storage life of 10 years.

The importance of having some assurance that an E.P.I.R.B. is actually working was stressed by Nick Hallam when inside the upturned trimaran *Boatfile* – 'Looking at its tiny indicator lamp, I prayed that its signal was radiating through the upturned hull.' From subsequent reports it is clear that those early signals were not picked up, but after Hallam and Williams had abandoned *Boatfile*, the distress signals from the liferaft were received by a British Airways jumbo jet, and this led to a successful search and rescue.

The emergency beacon the crew of *Island Princess* found with their liferaft was in two parts, and it soon gave trouble when the battery pack separated from the transmitter 'making the E.P.I.R.B. inoperable.' Recent improvements in design have resulted in E.P.I.R.B.s becoming more robust and easier to use, some of them even having their antenna integral with the body of the unit so that it is not exposed to rain or sea and cannot be damaged.

Emergency Kit

In future one of the most important things for an offshore yachtsman to take into a liferaft will be an E.P.I.R.B. of some kind; but there are also other things of potentially critical importance.

What will be needed in a liferaft or dinghy will depend upon the conditions at the time of the abandonment and of course where it takes place. If a yacht has to be abandoned in The Solent or in Long Island Sound, it is unlikely that its crew will need to take food and water for many days or that an E.P.I.R.B. will be necessary to signal their distress. On the other hand, when the ocean-racing yacht *Guia III* sank while about midway between South America and Africa, her crew reckoned: 'It was clear that the only place we could go was towards South America, with the odds of ending up somewhere in Venezuela.'

Guia's skipper and crew were very experienced ocean-racing types, and it was to be expected that they would be pretty well organised so that even while some of them made last-minute attempts to keep *Guia III* afloat, others 'had already started to get stores up from the cabin.' So by the time their skipper had to make his decision to abandon, 'All our kit that was

291

kept for emergencies had already been passed on deck, and we knew that the liferaft had inflated and was being loaded.' After recovering from the shock of seeing *Guia* go down, they 'started to organise the inside of the raft and take inventory of what we had, and after we had inspected everything decided that we were not too badly off. There was plenty of food, enough with care to last a month. A box of flares. [These were to prove their saviour.] Helly Hansen suits and waterproofs for us all. Three blankets, 800 cigarettes, matches, lighters, torches, lifejackets and three kitbags with personal gear . . . All the food was in polythene casks, and we were glad that we had decided to use this system in *Guia*.'

As it happened, they were rescued by a ship within twenty-four hours, but when they took to the raft they were not to know how lucky they would be.

When they had to abandon *Quiver* in the middle of the night, Michael Millar and his grandson Richard were not quite as well prepared as the crew of *Guia III*, but then *Quiver* was only sailing between Guernsey and Brittany and they were no more than three or four miles offshore. Millar describes the scene: 'We started loading the dinghy: oars, rowlocks, pump, bailer. Food? A big plastic gash-bag, shove in cakes, biscuits, tarts, tie a knot in it; water? All in the tank, tiny galley pump, no container to hand! At that moment, six long-life milk cartons conveniently floated out of their locker, in they went; what next? I grabbed my wallet and travellers cheques; personal kit – one large travel bag each; next? My second bag with all the ship's and personal papers – in it went (it wasn't until two hours later that I realised it was the wrong second bag, all I saved was a lot of useless hardware). We grabbed a few more bits and pieces, but then decided we had better get out in case she took a wave into the cockpit and plunged suddenly.'

Rushcutter had been well prepared for her voyage across the Tasman Sea, and when she had to be abandoned, Anthony Lealand 'cut free our water bottles and bag of emergency gear, passing them to Annette, who lashed them into the liferaft.' Of the items of food contained in the emergency kit, Lealand comments on two: 'Lunch was tinned peaches. And I can thoroughly recommend them. Easy to swallow, sweet and wet. Later we tried a lifeboat biscuit. Scientifically designed they may be, with no protein and high in calories, but they are such a foul brew, forming a great sticky glob in our mouths, that we gave up eating them.'

Peter Phillips was lucky when his Mayday on 2182 kHz got through, so that he was able to give an accurate position, since his emergency beacon failed to work and he had no food or water in the liferaft with him. He had hoped to get back on board *Livery Dole* to collect supplies, but was unable to do so.

Peter Tangvald had no liferaft, but simply a 7ft plywood dinghy. Nevertheless, he aimed to sail downwind in that tiny craft until he reached one of the Grenadine Islands, some 55 miles away. Fortunately he did have a little time 'to assemble all the gear I considered desirable for increasing my chances to make land alive. First of all I took the two plastic bottles containing 2½ gallons of fresh water each, which I always keep as emergency rations should *Dorothea*'s single tank spring a leak, then I half filled a sail bag with food, the second sail bag with some clothes, then the chart and the compass; then an awning, a short gaff and some rope with the idea of a makeshift rig to cover the many miles to land . . . Then my two flashlights with spare batteries, then my lifejacket, and finally my papers and the cash money I had in the boat.'

Importance of a Knife

Tangvald soon found that he had to jettison much of this gear since he soon 'realised that I had grossly overloaded the little boat'. Having lightened her he found that the dinghy 'floated like a cork' and he set about making a jury rig – 'I then discovered that I had forgotten to bring a knife.'

Finbar Gittelman also tells how important a knife was to him when he finally abandoned the *Island Princess*: 'As soon as I climbed onto the raft I realised that something was tangled with it and that the boat was pulling it down. I needed a knife, but couldn't get to mine because it was inside my foul-weather gear. So I shouted for a knife and before the words were out of my mouth, Doc slapped his into my hand. The blade was already open.' To which 'Doc' St Clair added – 'I'd lost my good-luck hat in the first five minutes, but that knife saved our asses!'

When *Lazy Daisy* capsized off the north-east coast of Scotland, Lionel Miller and his crew took to their rubber dinghy, but afterwards realised that although the catamaran was upside down, she was not going to sink immediately; so they 'decided to climb onto the bridgedeck and take the dinghy with them. Unfortunately the dinghy painter was impossible to untie and none of them had a knife.'

Liferaft Emergency Packs

There are differences between the recommendations made by relevant authorities in different countries, but in the U.K. the yachtsman has a choice between two 'official' lists of items to be included in the 'short-term' emergency pack that will be supplied with his liferaft. The R.O.R.C. pack, which is basic, contains the following items, *but no food or water*:

- 1 knife
- Rescue quoit and 100ft of line

- Sea-anchor
- Bailer
- 2 paddles
- Repair kit including leak stoppers for rapid repairs to the raft
- Bellows
- Instructions on how to survive
- Rescue Signal Table
- A signalling torch
- 3 hand flares
- Anti-seasickness pills (6 per person)

The contents of the Y.M.('E') short-term emergency pack include all the items provided in the R.O.R.C. pack as well as the following:

- 1 first aid outfit
- ½ litre of drinking water per person
- 2 safety tin openers
- 1 graduated drinking cup
- 1 plastic bag per person, to be used to collect rainwater or hold remnants of food, and similar items
- 2 resealing lids, to reseal water cans
- Fishing kit
- 2 parachute distress signals
- 2 sponges
- Spare batteries and bulb for torch
- Signalling mirror

Food and Protective Clothing
Obviously both of these lists need to be augmented by food and clothing, the quantity and choice of which will depend on the judgement of the skipper, who must consider all the conditions he might meet on the intended voyage or race.

One or two practical ideas do emerge from the accounts that describe the use of a liferaft. For instance, emergency water containers should not be quite filled, but enough air left in them to ensure that they will float if accidentally dropped into the sea. Whatever food is taken into the liferaft or dinghy should be stored in watertight plastic containers.

Survival in Liferafts or Dinghies
Inflatable liferafts were developed during World War II to give airmen some chance of rescue after their aircraft had been brought down in the sea. Before that time liferafts or floats were rigidly constructed, as were the

dinghies used by yachtsmen, and it is interesting that none of the accounts in the book which relate to incidents before World War II involved the use of a dinghy or a liferaft.

That a small wooden dinghy can, under favourable circumstances, serve as a lifesaving craft is clear from the story told by Peter Tangvald of his successful 55-mile voyage to safety in a 7½ft plywood pram. But Tangvald himself admits that 'I was like the cat, born with nine lives'.

Keith Douglas Young had a different story to tell. In 1949 when *Merlan* was lost on a reef near Melbourne, it was usual to have a wooden dinghy as a tender to a yacht, but few people had much faith in them in emergency, as Douglas Young makes clear: 'We had barely left the stricken *Merlan* when our cockleshell dinghy was swamped and we were left struggling in the powerful sucking rip tide.'

After World War II, yachtsmen began slowly to appreciate the advantages of using an inflatable rubber rather than a rigid wooden dinghy, and they also saw that under certain conditions a rubber dinghy could serve a secondary purpose as a liferaft. Those accounts in the book which describe the use of an inflatable dinghy as a liferaft, following the loss of a yacht, all relate to 'inshore' incidents in which the time spent in the dinghy was relatively short and the conditions not too severe.

Although she did not have far to go, Clementina Gordon was very well aware that she probably owed her life to the fact that she had inflated her rubber dinghy just before the Silhouette, *Mary Williams*, was turned bow over stern with her skipper underneath. She managed to hang on to the dinghy and was then blown ashore in conditions 'that no other dinghy would have had the buoyancy to bring me through'.

Even when only half of it is inflated, a rubber dinghy can serve as a small liferaft – provided there is no rough water to contend with. When James Houston's *Ladybee* caught fire in the Sound of Mull, he found that the lashings of the dinghy had fused to the rails and 'we saw that the bow of the Avon had a great hole in it.' But the other half was still fully inflated, so they lost no time in launching it and then cast off and pulled rapidly away while 'Margaret gathered the deflated loose part of the dinghy around her waist to keep the water out'. In this manner they reached the safety of the shore.

When a boat is on fire and the fire cannot be got under control, there is absolutely no time to hang about. But if the inflatable dinghy has been stowed in a locker the situation will be really frightening. Just such a crisis occurred aboard the brand new Westerly Vulcan, *Freedom To*, as her owner describes: 'We lifted the cockpit locker to get at the dinghy – this is a big 7ft-deep locker with the dinghy at the bottom under a mound of carefully stowed warps and fenders, the outboard motor and five gallons of spare diesel. I came out gasping for air. The dinghy was firmly lodged . . . we had no VHF, flares or lifejackets. A stuck dinghy and two horseshoe buoys were all that was left.' When they did eventually manage to yank the dinghy clear it was warm and sticky, so it must have been a very close thing. Then: 'We stood in the pulpit together desperately trying to inflate the dinghy by mouth. Flame and heat quickly precipitated our departure from on deck, and with the dinghy only perhaps 20 per cent inflated, we followed it into the water.'

Somehow they managed to get more air into the dinghy to keep her afloat until they were rescued by a passing coaster. They were extraordinarily lucky and the story must surely persuade anyone not to keep a dinghy in a locker while underway.

Michael Millar had a fully inflated 9ft Nautisport dinghy on the deck of his little 21ft *Quiver* on the night she struck one of the Triagoz rocks off Brittany, and within a few minutes they were ready to cast off from the sinking yacht. Ten hours were to elapse before they were seen and rescued, and as Millar says, 'It was a hell of a long time.'

Dinghy or Liferaft

Liferafts differ from dinghies in a number of significant ways. Firstly, they inflate 'automatically', if by that one understands that they simply require a tug on the painter to operate a valve on the compressed gas cylinder. When thrown overboard with its painter made fast to provide the necessary tug, a liferaft should inflate within 30 seconds. Secondly, all modern liferafts incorporate ballast pockets or chambers to reduce the risk of capsize, while most of them have self-erecting canopies, although some must have their supporting arch inflated by means of a pump. Rafts can also have inflatable floors to insulate their occupants from the chilling effects of sea water. Additionally, all liferafts are equipped with some form of emergency or survival kit, although the contents of the kits differ considerably, as does the design of the sea-anchor or drogue that comes with each raft.

Launching a Liferaft

Rushcutter's liferaft was swept overboard when the yacht was rolled in the Tasman Sea, but it was attached by a line, so Anthony Lealand 'pulled yards of string from the liferaft, till it popped open and was full in an instant. Annette leapt in gratefully.' A good start, but later Lealand tells of the troubles they experienced when the raft was capsized.

Peter Phillips had no trouble when launching his raft, and simply says 'I grab the liferaft painter and pull it several times. It inflates right way up.' But they did have trouble with their raft on *Boatfile*, as Nick Hallam relates: 'In the struggle to release it, I must have failed to cut one lashing,

296

because it had great difficulty in escaping from its valise, and when finally it did, it had lost so much CO_2 via the relief valve that it was perilously soft.'

Valise or Canister

Liferafts can be supplied packed either in a soft valise or in a rigid glassfibre container. The advantage of a valise-packed raft is that it can, in fact must, be stowed in a protected place such as a cockpit locker, whereas a rigid canister-packed raft can and should be kept on deck at all times. The lacing used to close a liferaft valise ought to be strong enough to keep the raft protected while stowed, yet weak enough to be broken when the gas cylinder is fired. Judging by the *Boatfile* experience, this delicate balance may be difficult to ensure.

Susceptibility to Damage

The susceptibility of liferafts to damage in really rough seas was highlighted during the Fastnet Race in 1979, but this problem should be assessed on the understanding that there are in fact two categories of liferaft:

1. Those intended for use by merchant vessels and passenger ships. These must in the U.K. conform with government-imposed Safety of Life at Sea (SOLAS) regulations, and in the U.S. with Coastguard standards.
2. Liferafts that are intended for use in conjunction with leisure craft such as yachts, and which, because of cost and other considerations, may not be the equal of rafts made under category 1. However, they should certainly comply with either the standards set by the American Boat and Yacht Council (A.B.Y.C.) or those set by the Royal Ocean Racing Club (R.O.R.C.)

In other words, like so many other things related to sailing, the design and choice of a liferaft involves compromise. Donald Sharp put the matter frankly in a thoroughgoing article on liferafts, published in *Nautical Quarterly* – 'Whatever liferaft choice is made, the buyer will be weighing the perils of the deep against the depth of a pocket book.'

After the Fastnet

After the 1979 Fastnet a great deal of work was done by raft manufacturers and by the official committee and working party on the problems that had been revealed by that August storm. Valuable research was carried out in conjunction with the Icelandic Government, in whose waters many of the practical trials were made. Two of the questions that needed answering were: whether either water ballasting or the use of a sea-anchor – or both – improves the stability of a liferaft in heavy weather.

A vivid impression of the frightening experience it is to be inside a liferaft when it is capsized is given by Anthony Lealand: 'A crushing roar slammed us into numbness. The raft was very full of water, on its side and the door torn. We had just finished lashing the door shut when we were hit again. Again we bailed . . . and again we went over. This time the raft stayed upside-down, Annette did not know where she was and I was spluttering in the little air under the raft, trying to get my arm out of one of the rope handles.'

Ballasted Liferafts

It is probable that *Rushcutter*'s liferaft was unballasted, but self-filling ballast chambers were used on some liferafts before 1979, and they took two different forms – a number of small pockets arranged in a ring around the bottom of the raft, or a single large chamber suspended centrally like a bag beneath the raft. The former approach is typified by Avon, Beaufort, Lifeguard and Zodiac liferafts, and the latter by the American-made Givens Buoy liferaft, originally designed to withstand the capsizing effect of downdraft from a helicopter engaged in retrieving astronauts. Whatever type of ballast chamber is used, it must fill quickly and reliably, since the risk of capsizing can be very high during the time a crew are getting themselves and their emergency gear into the raft. To ensure this, some pockets are now weighted with small chains so that they fall away from the bottom of the raft and allow water to enter quickly through holes. From Gittelman's report it seems that the ballast chamber of a Givens raft also fills very quickly. But there any similarity ends, because the behaviour to be expected from a relatively lightly ballasted raft must be very different from that of a raft attached to a large ballast chamber holding a ton or more of water.

The crew of *Island Princess* had some trouble righting their liferaft after it inflated itself upside down, but as Gittelman says: 'Once the raft was free of the boat a wave crest immediately flipped it right side up and the ballast chamber filled.' This suggests that they were using a Givens raft with a single large ballast bag.

Some of the results of heavily ballasting a liferaft are evident from the subsequent experience of the crew as recalled by Matthew St Clair: 'Every time one of those thirty footers decided to collapse on us it would fill the raft with water and drive us so deep that our ears popped. At this point we would have to push down with our feet and up with our hands to make an air space at the top of the canopy. We were constantly up to our necks in water, and there were even fish swimming around inside the raft. The only thing that helped us to realise we were still alive was a little light glowing at the top of the canopy.' There is no risk that such a heavily ballasted raft would ever capsize, but the price of that assurance would seem to be extreme discomfort.

The ballasting arrangement preferred by most European liferaft manufacturers is to have a number of relatively small water ballast pockets attached beneath the circular or rectangular flotation tube, or tubes, of the raft. This disposition of ballast reduces the chance that the raft will be 'flipped' over by the wind while it is negotiating the crest of a wave.

Sea-anchors with Liferafts

Just as there are differences of opinion on the influence a sea-anchor will have on the behaviour of a yacht in heavy weather, so there are uncertainties about the value of a sea-anchor or drogue when attached to a liferaft. No firm conclusion can be reached from the statistical findings of the Fastnet Inquiry, since just as many respondents to the question 'Do you feel that a sea-anchor affected the behaviour of the raft?' felt that it did, as thought that it did not. On the other hand, one of the competitors who reported using a drogue as soon as the liferaft was launched, lost it within half an hour and extended his evidence by saying 'I am led to the conclusion that in storm conditions, if there is sufficient sea room, life is more comfortable and the raft less at risk if it is allowed to drift at the same rate as the waves.'

In moderate seas, and when it has been decided to reach land or rescue by blowing with the wind, a sea-anchor would obviously retard progress, and that was one of the reasons why the crew of *Guia III* hauled in their liferaft's sea-anchor 'and set off from the scene at about 2–2½ knots'; but George Marshall also added: 'The sea-anchor had made us decide to leave, as its violent snubbing was liable to damage the raft and we would sooner take our chance with a possible long trip than end up with a sinking liferaft.'

Improved Design of Sea-anchor

Tests carried out jointly by the National Maritime Institute, the National Physical Laboratory and the Icelandic Government showed that the snatch loads generated between a raft and its sea-anchor in 20 knots of wind, with seas of 3 to 5ft, can increase to 10 times the normal steady loading. Further work showed that the commonly used 'handkerchief' type of drogue offered too much resistance and should be replaced by a conical-shaped sea-anchor made from some strong net-like porous material so as to reduce loading to a more tolerable level. These recommendations have already been adopted by Avon, Beaufort, Zodiac and others for the drogues they now supply with yachtsmen's liferafts.

Being Seen

The chances of a liferaft being seen can be improved in a number of ways, the most obvious of which is for its canopy to be made of some brightly coloured orange or yellow material. A further improvement is claimed by Zodiac, who cover half the area of their canopies with a metallic reflecting material that is more likely to be detected by radar. Strips of retro-reflective material attached to the outside of the canopy can also provide additional aid to S.A.R. operations. At night a stroboscopic light based on the use of a xenon flash tube can be a life-saver because of the intensely bright intermittent flash it produces. The Guest Xenon Strobe Type 326 is automatically activated by contact with water and then will continue to flash for 36 hours. The Strobe-Ident Type STB-3 uses a xenon tube that is fed from a 3-volt lithium battery with a shelf life of 10 years, to produce about 60 flashes a minute over a period of 12 hours.

Under certain conditions and in daylight a dye-marker can be used to stain a large area of water a distinctive colour that will be easier to spot from the air than a tiny liferaft.

Search and Rescue Operations

The ways in which search and rescue operations are mounted, and how they usually involve several different disciplines, are well illustrated by the cases of *Mariah*, *Boatfile* and *Rushcutter*.

When the tanker *Navios Crusader heard Mariah*'s Mayday, she relayed it to the Cape May Coastguard 200 miles away in New Jersey, and within a short time the Coastguard had despatched an aircraft with a large emergency pump. The plane was a huge C-130 transport, and later it was to return with another pump. The Coastguard also despatched their cutter *Alert* as well as a helicopter which lifted two of *Mariah*'s crew from their Avon liferaft, before deciding to leave the others to be rescued by the *Alert*. The cutter, following the usual practice of the US Coastguard, launched a 19ft hard-keel Avon inflatable (similar to the R.N.L.I.'s 21ft Atlantic class) with two men on board to take the remaining five people off the sinking *Mariah*.

Rescue by Helicopter

The E.P.I.R.B. 121.5 MHz signal indicating the distress of the crew of *Boatfile* was picked up by a British Airways jumbo jet flying west across the Atlantic, but, as it happened, the simultaneous signal from the E.P.I.R.B. on 234 MHz was also received by an R.A.F. Nimrod on exercise that day. Before the Nimrod could locate *Boatfile*'s liferaft the plane ran low on fuel, and so another Nimrod was despatched from Kinloss in Scotland. Having found the liferaft, the crew of the Nimrod could see that it was only partly inflated, so they had to drop a series of liferafts, on parachutes, before the yachtsmen could secure one and climb aboard. While all this was going on, an R.A.F. Sea King helicopter of the 202 S.A.R. Squadron based at Brawdy in Wales proceeded first to Southern Ireland and then, after refuelling, out over the Atlantic in total darkness to pick up Hallam and Williams with the aid of parachute flares – altogether a remarkable operation lasting some 8 to 10 hours.

Rescue by Ship

Annette Wilde sent out a PAN-PAN call from *Rushcutter* saying that if they did not call up again within 24 hours, it should be presumed that they were in trouble; but it was the later signal from the E.P.I.R.B. they used after taking to the liferaft that alerted a R.N.Z.A.F. Orion plane. Having located them, the crew of the Orion marked the spot with smoke signals and a sonar buoy, and then guided a Japanese freighter, the *Toyu Maru*, back to the liferaft, to effect the rescue.

Getting Aboard Rescue Craft

Getting aboard a rescuing craft from a dinghy or a liferaft is never easy in a rough sea, but the difficulties are less when the rescuers are in a low-sided boat such as an R.N.L.I. lifeboat, a U.S. Coastguard hard-bottomed inflatable or even a small fishing vessel. In fact Michael Millar, who together with his grandson was picked up from their inflatable dinghy by a 'langoustier' off Brittany, makes it sound quite simple – 'the rolling of the ship made getting on board relatively easy; you step on the rubbing strake as it rolls down, then you are catapulted over the bulwarks as she goes back.' But it can be a very different story when the rescuing ship is a large freighter or tanker with her deck high above the water. In such cases it may be safer to carry out the rescue in two stages, as the captain of the *Hellenic Ideal* decided to do when he stopped his ship downwind of the crew of *Guia III* in their liferaft. George Marshall says: 'From round the stern a ship's lifeboat appeared; it was only when we saw it that we realised what size sea was running,' but they safely transferred to the lifeboat, taking all their kit with them, and soon they were alongside the *Hellenic Ideal* where 'we still had to manage ourselves up the ladder, but the deck officer in charge made us all tie a lifeline around us before allowing us to climb to the deck from the lifeboat. A very sensible precaution as it turned out. Not one of us after the climb was able to stand, and each of us collapsed against the bulkhead.'

Yachts Alongside Larger Vessels

Even greater difficulties arise when the yacht herself is still afloat but it has been decided to abandon her alongside a larger vessel. As can be seen from all the accounts describing such a manoeuvre, the yacht is invariably damaged and often sinks soon after being dropped astern of the vessel.

A graphic description of this kind of operation is given by Peter Combe of *Windstar*: 'As the steamer approached I yelled that we could not now steer or help in any way. A voice shouted back, "Do you want to come aboard?" – "Yes" I shrieked in amazement. A few moments later we struck her side head on, smashing in the stem and carrying away the forestay. I managed to secure a hawser around all the winches for'ard and it then seemed high time to leave. I had noticed the previous time, as the two vessels soared up and down alongside like a pair of demented elevators, that her deck rail for'ard came within reach now and again. For a pessimistic moment I wondered if I still had the strength to pull myself aboard; . . . I needn't have worried. When her deck ducked within reach I found myself up and over before I had time to think about making an effort.' Then Combe had to explain that his skipper, still aboard *Windstar*, 'could not be expected to do anything violent. "He's sick," I bellowed. Meanwhile they had thrown several lines down to him and were shouting to him to tie one round him. He seemed to make, as best he could, a sort of half-hitch with the end which none of us who were watching believed to be really secured.' Then the thing they feared most happened – 'Twice we nearly had his hands, and then as *Windstar* plunged down and away the lines jerked him overboard and he fell between the two hulls. It was a quite sickening moment, and I think I tried not to see. The gap, however, widened for a moment, and we eased in the line. There was a weight at the end and, expecting any moment to lose our prize, we pulled him aboard in about three heaves, and said, "Thank God – we never thought the rope was fast". He replied at once, "Nonsense, tied it myself."'

Damage while Alongside

After his primitive distress signal had been spotted by a 2,500-ton Norwegian tramp steamer proceeding northward in the Thames Estuary, the skipper of the *Un-named 5-tonner* decided to be towed from the end of the ship's bridge. Surprisingly, the skipper of the steamer agreed to do this, 'and we ran down under her stern, as far to loo'ard as it would be possible to heave a line . . . Events then followed with lightning-like rapidity. A handline came whirling down from the bridge, and with it we hauled aboard a hawser, which we quickly made fast round the bits. But before the steamship could get way on again, being in ballast and broadside on, she was down on top of us like an express train, and, being becalmed and helpless in the lee of her huge hull, in the twinkling of an eye we were sucked in under her stern and across her propeller aperture. There we stuck like a stick across a sluice, and with every sea one blade of her propeller caught us a glancing blow.' When it was quite clear that no efforts would save the little yacht, 'we reluctantly decided to abandon her while there was yet time . . . so by means of a Jacob's ladder, one by one we reached the tramp's deck, the climb something of an effort, one moment hanging far out over the ditch and the next crashing back against the ship's side. Finally, as I was about to leave . . . she got the first and only direct blow from the propeller. In a flash the whole port side was cut away from keelson to deck, and the waters of the North Sea closed around my sea boots as I sprang for the end of the ladder.'

Easting Down, too, suffered much damage while she was alongside the *Ossendrecht* in the North Sea: 'While we were abandoning, she dropped into a trough, pulling the bow rope taut and wrenching a mooring cleat from the foredeck. Then, as *Ossendrecht* got under way and started to leave the yacht, a big sea rolled *Easting Down* and her mainmast struck the ship's hull and broke.'

This is what will happen in almost every case, and the reasons are not hard to understand. A yachtsman requesting help from a merchant ship should always remember that although the captain of that ship is bound by maritime law to come to his assistance, he is not similarly bound to save the yacht – in fact by the very act of taking off the crew from alongside, the yacht will inevitably be damaged if there is any sea running. Peter Combe should not have been so surprised when one of the crew of the Norwegian ship *Alouette* shouted 'Do you want to come aboard?' since, for all he knew, *Windstar*'s immediate needs might have been served by the big ship standing by pending the arrival of an R.N.L.I. lifeboat or some other vessel. Now that VHF radio communication is so widely used, the intentions of both a yacht in distress and a potential rescuer can be much more easily made clear than was ever possible by shouting or signalling.

The skipper of a yacht in trouble will often be so relieved at seeing help on hand that his instinct may tell him to get alongside without delay, and the captain of the ship may do nothing to dissuade him. But from the bridge of a large freighter or tanker, perhaps 100ft above the water, a skipper may not be able to assess the danger that will arise as soon as the yacht is alongside; for one thing, if she is positioned to windward to provide a lee, nothing can stop the big ship from bearing down on the yacht. This then is the time when the skipper of the yacht must make his own decision – shall he go alongside and irrevocably commit himself and his crew to the hazardous task of getting aboard the ship, or should he steel himself to take some other action? If he has reason to believe that other help is on its way, then he could request the big ship to stand by. When no other help seems likely, and if he can talk to the big ship, the two skippers should weigh up the possibility of using a liferaft or one of the ship's lifeboats to transfer the crew of the yacht.

Once a decision has been made to get alongside, a hawser from the ship must be made fast to the strongest point on the foredeck of the yacht – and this may prove to be the first problem. Modern yachts are seldom fitted with substantial bitts or a samson post such as older wooden craft usually have, but if the mast is stepped through the deck it may serve to make the rope fast to the base of it. The yacht is now effectively at the mercy of the big ship and the crew of the yacht should realise this and waste no time trying to fend off; instead, they should concentrate on organising the safest possible means of evacuation. If the ship has a pilot's hoist, then it may be possible to use that, otherwise lifelines from the ship are essential; and instead of expecting each of the crew to bend the line round his body, they should be told to make the line fast to their safety harness – which they should all be wearing anyway.

DANGERS OF BEING TOWED

However tempting the opportunity may seem, a yachtsman should beware of being towed – except perhaps by an R.N.L.I. lifeboat. For, as the U.S. Coastguard says in a report on the subject, 'The towing of one vessel by another is an operation of apparent simplicity to those inexperienced in its execution. But it is an operation fraught with danger . . .' Claud Worth, in his classic *Yacht Cruising*, also warns: 'A small vessel cannot safely be towed in a heavy sea except at a speed low enough to allow her to rise to each wave.'

The hair-raising account of the brief attempt by a Lowestoft sailing trawler to tow the *Dragon*, as long ago as 1891, serves well to illustrate the disastrous results of towing a yacht at too high a speed. 'A great 70-ton trawler under reefed main and foresails . . . bore along close by us, her skipper asked if we would come aboard, we shouted would he tow us to Yarmouth? He hove a line and we hauled it in and found a strong wire rope attached; this we hastily secured to the bowsprit chocks and round the mast. Suddenly the rope they were paying out tightened, the trawler was dashing through the water at 9 knots, the strain was terrific, the bowsprit snapped off, carrying with it the forestay. Down came the mast, and now all the strain was amidships and over went the *Dragon* . . . we managed somehow to cling to her and scramble on her bottom.'

In much more recent times the little cutter *Odd Times* was lost in the North Atlantic while under tow from a tug at about 4 knots, the minimum speed at which the tug could keep adequate control. 'At 0655 the final disaster occurred. Either the bight of wire rope had come off the samson post, or else, under the enormous strain of being towed in the then heavy swell, the samson post had carried away; but, either way, the strain of the tow was taken directly on the mast, and before anyone on the tug could do anything about it *Odd Times* started sheering wildly and was pulled right over; she filled and sank. The master of the tug . . . had no option but to sever the tow line and proceed.' Something can be learned from this disaster. If it is necessary to take the strain of towing from the foot of the mast, the rope or wire must also be strongly stopped down to the stemhead by some means or other, or the yacht will surely sheer about unmanageably; particularly if her mast is stepped well back as is usually the case today.

Towing at Very Low Speed

R.N.L.I. coxswains and crews know about towing, and a splendid example of this understanding took place during the Fastnet storm, when the 47ft Watson-type R.N.L.I. lifeboat, the *Sir Samuel Kelly*, towed the rudderless yacht *Casse Tête V* for 12 hours at little more than 2 knots, to gain the safety of Courtmacsherry Harbour in SW Ireland, whence the lifeboat had been launched some 22 hours earlier.

COLLISION AT SEA

Peter Tangvald once did some research on the causes of yachts being lost or severely damaged, and out of 200 incidents he found that only four yachts had been run down by ships and none of the four was a total loss.

I was unaware of these findings when I commenced my search for the accounts needed for this book, and at that time I expected to discover numerous reports by people who had experienced the loss of a yacht after collision with some other vessel. This did not prove to be the case. It may be argued that the reason simply is that when such collisions do occur there are no survivors left to tell what happened, and the larger vessel may have known nothing of the accident. It is recognised that many famous yachtsmen have been lost at sea without explanation, and it does seem probable that some of them were victims of collisions. Furthermore, since I have chosen not to include reports of any incidents in which lives were lost, this too reduced the chance of my finding suitable accounts.

The Chances of Collision

Whether a yacht will ever have the misfortune to collide with another vessel while at sea must largely depend on where and how far she sails. The singlehander John Letcher has calculated that if he took no precautions whatsoever, he could expect to be run down once in a thousand voyages between Hawaii and Alaska. This statistic will provide little comfort for those of us who sail in busier waters, and neither does it tell us on which of the thousand voyages the one collision will occur. But singlehanders must be more vulnerable to collision than yachts with a crew to share the responsibility of keeping a look out, since it is generally accepted that a radar reflector does not guarantee that a yacht will be noticed. Whether a yacht is being sailed singlehanded or with a crew, the risk of collision will always be greater at night than during the day, except of course in fog. One way of improving the chances of being seen at night is to install *and use* the arrangement of masthead navigation lights now permitted by International Regulations.

The two accounts of collisions between vessels that have been included are about as different as could be imagined. One of them occurred more than a hundred years ago during a race on the Clyde in Scotland, and it conjures up a dramatic picture of both the helmsman and the skipper of the 117ft *Satanita* straining at the tiller in a desperate attempt to make her bear away. The other account describes the loss of the little *Tern* in the entrance to Poole Harbour, and it is a reminder that any yacht should give a wide berth to a passing ship.

Collision with Submerged Objects or Whales
Collisions with partially submerged objects appear to present a significant risk to yachtsmen, as the losses of *Dorothea* and *Easting Down* confirm; and, despite the impression sometimes given by conservationists, there still seems to be a large number of whales around in the south Atlantic. Both *Guia III* and *Pionier* were lost after colliding with whales while racing, and in 1972 and 1973 *Lucette* and *Auralyn* were lost after striking whales not far from the Galapagos Islands.

In the two latter cases, the survivors had a long time during which to reflect on their wisdom in deciding to take both a liferaft and an inflatable dinghy with them on their world voyaging.

FAULTY NAVIGATION

While my search for accounts of yachts lost by collision with other vessels yielded little, I had no difficulty in finding a great many cases of yachts being lost by collision with rocks or reefs. *Kelpie, Northern Light, Smew, Song* and *Quiver* were all victims of faulty navigation, and all came to grief for much the same reasons – darkness and fatigue.

Song was being sailed singlehanded among unlit islands and rocks when she was lost, and whereas it is possible to get some sleep while hove-to or under auto-pilot where there is sea room and no traffic, the problems of fatigue cannot be so easily solved when approaching land. George Harrod-

Eagles recalls his thoughts as he approached Fajardo on the east coast of Puerto Rico: 'The choice lay between finding a suitable anchorage – hazardous, in view of the uncertain weather, no information as to the holding quality of the bottom and the horrible consequences if we dragged – turning around and running back until there was enough sea room to stand off – the safest course, but one, it seemed, that would make pointless all the hours spent getting this far. Or else to continue sailing towards our destination . . . A decision had to be made, and, calculating all the factors, I chose to go on – a fateful and perhaps imprudent decision in view of the contrary winds and our slow progress up to then, but one prompted by . . . a desire to end this tiresome passage.' He continues, and reveals that the most likely cause of his fateful error was the disregard of local currents, about which he had no information. 'We were stowing sails and watching for white water; the echo-sounder was on, and registering thirty feet of water, and the lights from the complex on Isleta Marina were in plain view now way off to port. The depth shown on the echo sounder plunged to fifteen feet then up to twenty feet, the chart indicated a number of relatively shallow spots, and I thought to have a look at it, to see if I could relate our position to the depths indicated, when the depth shown on the echo-sounder plummeted to five feet and immediately the boat struck, crunching and bumping half a dozen times before coming to a stop. . . . I put her hard astern, hoping that she would come off: a forlorn hope, for the set which had by its invisible and unknown presence put us on the reef, was . . . forcing the bilge plates against and between great jagged coral heads, which were crunching and grinding in a horrifying way against the hull.'

Mistaken Lights

James Griffin and his wife Ann had invested in an automatic pilot for *Northern Light*, but one day out from Bermuda it had 'packed-in', so they had stood watch and watch about for the rest of their voyage across the Atlantic, and now they were within a hundred miles of Gibraltar: 'It had been so hazy that sights had been unreliable for the last two days, but the log was accurate and we were allowing for half a knot of current carrying us into the Straits – the charts and the Pilot Book said it was so . . . At 1930 we saw a lighthouse flashing twice every six seconds and went wild with delight . . . we had done it after 20 days at sea. We'd be in Gibraltar before dawn, God willing. We got to the lighthouse, but where was Tarifa light? Feeling very uneasy we put on the engine and hauled off. Shortly after we struck rock and stuck.' They found out later that there had been Force 6 and 7 easterlies in the Straits of Gibraltar, which had stopped the south-going current. The lighthouse had been the Santa Caterina, flashing twice every *seven seconds*.

Intuitive Feeling

Michael Millar was quite happy with the fix he obtained from Les Sept Iles light and the one on Les Roches Douvres, and so he altered *Quiver*'s course back to 240° Mag, and 'in due time picked up the light on Les Triagoz where expected, fine on the starboard bow'. They were then on a dead run and making 5 knots through the water, but their fixes indicated that they were making good only 3½ knots, 'which confirmed the rather meagre information gleaned from the charts and tidal stream atlas that there was a 1½-knot head tide. This tide was supposed to run until 0400, dropping to about one knot in the last hour.' By 0200 they were abreast of Les Sept Iles and Millar had a 'feeling' that they were being set to the south-east, 'towards the outlying dangers at the western end of that reef. I therefore altered course more westerly, until Les Triagoz light was just open to port . . . and until I was satisfied that we were well clear of Les Sept Iles. I then altered back about double the amount until Les Triagoz was well open in the starboard rigging; a quick check on the chart confirmed that at 3½ knots made good we could clear the eastern tip of the Les Triagoz reef by 1¼ miles, a comfortable margin. At about 0300, I was just contemplating resuming the compass course, when *Quiver*, with a resounding crash, stopped dead.'

Song, Northern Light and *Quiver* were all lost because of erroneous estimates of tidal currents. Such mistakes are much more likely to be made at night than during the day when, except in fog, there will be so much more visible evidence by which to assess drift or leeway.

Desire for Rest

On reflection after the loss of *Smew*, Edward Nott-Bower realised that 'a lack of resolution induced by strain and sleeplessness' had effectively sealed her fate. This is how it happened: the correct course for Dunmore was north-north-west but the best that *Smew* could sail unattended was north-west, which 'according to my reckoning, would take us to the westward of Dunmore, towards a part of the coast of which I had no charts. But, I argued to myself, my dead reckoning is so susceptible of error that for all I know north-west may be a better course; at least it will ensure that we do not miss the south-east corner of Ireland altogether and carry on into the Irish Sea. Anyway it was cold and wet in the cockpit, and I felt an overpowering desire for rest and inaction.'

All day they rolled on and on, until, at 2200, 'A light shows wide on the starboard bow. Another light shows on the port bow. If the latter showed a flash every three seconds it would be the Hook Head light off the Waterford entrance. But as we stood straining our eyes to detect a regular periodicity in the flashes our hopes gradually fell. More and more the light to starboard showed the three-second flash. The other was Mine Head far to the west. We could, I suppose, have set a reefed mainsail and embarked upon a heroic beat to the Waterford entrance. Had we had only one night out we should no doubt have done this, but this was our third night without sleep.' So, 'I alter course to west-south-west, a safe course to clear the coast beyond. I do not want to get too far out, otherwise we may have to beat into Youghal Harbour at dawn. I go below and turn to Youghal in the Pilot. I am on my way up to the cockpit again when there is a crash and a shudder.' Afterwards, Nott-Bower had this to say: 'I am still uncertain of the immediate cause of the accident; a shift of wind, a slip of the tiller lashing, or possibly a mistake in setting the course.' But the initial mistake must have been to sail on a north-west instead of a north-north-west course throughout the previous day.

That very experienced yachtsman, Conor O'Brien, was well aware of the risks a singlehander takes while proceeding at night; in fact his advise was 'that the prudent man does not go sailing alone, at least not in narrow and crowded waters'. During the passage from Oban to Limerick in *Kelpie*, he even wrote in his journal – 'in order that others might learn from my precept, if not from my example, that closehauled as I was then, I might hit seven different kinds of ships and be to blame for the collision: an overtaken vessel, a vessel to leeward holding a better wind, a vessel not under control, a vessel laying telegraph cables, a fisherman with his gear out, a vessel at anchor, and a light vessel; and then I must have dropped asleep, for I was next aware that I had hit an eighth thing which was the coast of Galloway. That damned alarm had failed.'

FAILURE OF GROUND TACKLE OR MOORING LINES

Of 200 accidents to yachts investigated by Peter Tangvald, 42 of the incidents were due to failure of anchor or cable, and 23 of those resulted in total loss. Such statistics serve well to emphasise the fact that it is the shore as much as the sea that destroys ships.

It is sometimes difficult to realise that even in harbour a yacht can still be at great risk if conditions change rapidly. One might think, as Clementina Gordon did, that inside the outer breakwater of Boulogne there would be safety and a chance to rest; but as she relates: 'When I came to, the wind had flown round . . . I now had the far side of the harbour in my lee, down Cap Gris Nez direction'. Her two anchors, one on a warp and the other on chain, held until just before 0300, 'when the west breakwater ceased to function and a heavy swell came in'. Soon after that, a bigger sea than the others came with a roar and turned the little Silhouette bow over stern.

Fortunately the dinghy was inflated, and although she was unable to get in she managed to hang on to it and be swept ashore beneath the esplanade.

Loss of Chain Cable

No doubt the 35lb C.Q.R. that Robin Gardiner-Hall was using on *Pentina II* was larger than the anchor on the Silhouette, and that it held in the shallow waters of the Elbe is clear from the fact that its cable sheared the port samson post off at deck level. Having then transferred the chain to the other samson post, Gardiner-Hall veered some extra cable to 'give a better catenary'. Half an hour later they were in heavy surf and pounding badly when 'the second samson post sheared in the same way as the first. The chain ran out and was lost; it parted the bitter end lashing in the chain locker, and the whipping end cut the lower starboard lifeline', a frightening reminder of the enormous snatch loads involved in rough weather. Perhaps a stronger lashing would have prevented the cable going overboard, but at least this incident should remind us to check that the bitter end of our chain is made fast with a long lashing that can reach the deck and be cut in an emergency, but is not likely to break.

Parted Chain

Even 'heavy three-eighths-of-an-inch chain from a big Whitstable smack' did not prevent *Thelma* from blowing ashore on Cocos Island. Bob Roberts had felt uneasy about anchoring in Chatham Bay: 'An open anchorage and no place for rough weather. It was one of those queer fancies of mine that made me dislike the place.' Roberts considered laying out a kedge as well as the bower anchor, but decided that since 'our two-inch tripping line had already chafed through on the jagged bottom in the matter of two hours, I felt it would be useless to use a kedge on a warp'. That was the danger signal, for if a warp could be chafed through in hours, even a chain might go the same way if left for days. In fact they left *Thelma* for five days while they went inland, and, when they returned to Chatham Bay, *Thelma* was on her beam ends among the rocks with the surf pounding over her. 'Trailing from her bow were many fathoms of anchor chain but no anchor. One of the links had been sawn clean through as if with a file.'

Just as Bob Roberts experienced a premonition that trouble would befall *Thelma* when she lay in Chatham Bay, Cocos Island, so Frank Mulville has never forgiven himself for not heeding the 'little voice' that told him it was a bad decision, that night in 1969, to moor *Girl Stella* in Porto Piqueran, just north of Santa Cruz on the Island of Flores.

'"We take you to Porto Piqueran. One mile up coast," the pilot said. "You OK there." "Don't let him do it," the voice said. "Shut up for Christ's sake, I can't tell him his job."'

Even when they had arrived in the 60ft-wide hurrican hole, Mulville remained uneasy. "'Pilot," he said, "suppose we have to get out quickly. Would it not be better to turn her round, so she'll face the sea?" "No," was the reply, "strong wind from the west – always face strong wind – best ropes forward." The little voice within Mulville persisted: "Make him turn her head round, you weak idiot – this may be a trap." "Stop your bloody nagging,"' was the outer Mulville's reply.

After spending most of the next day in Santa Cruz, the crew of *Girl Stella* returned to find her 'lying peacefully at her moorings. But the voice said "Watch it."'

Mulville and his mate, Dick Morris, carefully checked all the mooring lines and went to bed, but as Mulville so rightly observes, 'A boat is always there – you never stop worrying about her whether you are aboard or ashore'. During the night the wind came in from the east and freshened until it became obvious that they must leave. They made swift but careful preparations and 'were almost ready when there was a twang like someone plucking a violin string. I looked up and saw that the stern line on which we were relying had received one jerk too many. It had snapped in the middle and the inboard end was flying back towards the boat like a piece of elastic. I jumped into the cockpit, slammed the engine into reverse, gave her full throttle, and put the rudder hard to starboard. She began to pick up. "Good old girl," I muttered, "We'll get you out." Then the engine stopped – suddenly and irrevocably – the bare end of the broken line wound a dozen times round the propeller. "Now you're in trouble," the little voice said.

Change of Wind Direction

A sudden change in direction coupled with an increase in the strength of the wind has caused the loss of many yachts anchored close inshore. In December 1982, a large number of craft were lying at anchor in Cabo Harbour on the Baja Peninsula, Mexico, when a front moved in rapidly, caught them unawares, and 28 yachts were blown ashore – including Moitessier's *Joshua*. Of the 28, only four were considered to be salvageable.

LOSS BY FIRE, EXPLOSION OR LIGHTNING

Tangvald's informal survey indicated that about 5 per cent of total losses are due to yachts being burned out. As would be expected, the two major causes – about equally responsible – are petrol and bottle gas.

Risks from Petroleum Gas

Fewer petrol engines are being used in yachts now that small lightweight diesel units are available, and there must be very few boats indeed that still use a petrol/paraffin power unit, such as the one in *Ladybee*. These dual-fuel engines are designed to start on petrol and then continue to run on paraffin (kerosene) which was at one time much cheaper than petroleum. They tended to be troublesome, as James Houston found, and 'Despite regular attention by notable engineers, our engine had given trouble all spring. We were despondent to find that things were still not right, and that palliatives like stripping and cleaning the carburettors . . . made little or no difference.' James Houston's own explanation of the explosion that cost him his boat is given in a letter – 'After motoring out of Puillodobhrain and hoisting sail, we had a beat for a couple of hours towards Mull, during which time petrol from the carb, or somewhere, must have leaked into the bilge below the engine. The engine was enclosed in a watertight box in which the right mixture must have accumulated to be ignited by a spark from the new starter motor when we decided to restart it.'

Gas Detectors

Although petrol vapour and the propane or butane used for bottled gas all smell distinctively, they are all much heavier than air and will therefore tend to sink into the bilges of a yacht, where their presence may not be revealed by their smell. It is possible to detect such gases by other means, and one way is to install in the bilge a detector incorporating a semiconductor, the resistance of which will change according to the concentration of flammable gas that surrounds it. Such a device can be linked with an indicating meter and an alarm, but the siting of the detector is important because it must not be invaded by bilge water.

What happened immediately after *Ladybee* caught fire is instructive. With the engine surrounded by flames and the companion steps blown away, James Houston's first concern was to help his hurt wife out of the cabin and into the cockpit. He then remembered 'a fire extinguisher decorating a bulkhead at each end of our boat'. Houston discovered that the forehatch had been blown clean off and the forward extinguisher had fallen to the floor, whence he retrieved it, only to find that in use 'it was a bit of a disappointment, because the wind carried some of the white stuff into the sea and the remainder was soon exhausted; the jet seemed to choke a bit when directed towards the flames'.

Types of Extinguisher

It would seem that Houston was using a foam-type extinguisher, and because he had no choice but to work from the deck its effectiveness was negligible. Fire extinguishers project either a powder (usually sodium bicarbonate), a foam, CO_2, or some other oxygen-depriving gas. The purpose of all of them is to smother the fire by denying it oxygen, and it follows that to do this the blanketing substance, whether it be powder, foam or gas, must reach the root of the fire. But quite often, when fire breaks out in a small yacht, it quickly becomes impossible to stay below, and then the chances of aiming an extinguisher at the source of the fire are greatly reduced.

On balance, the best compromise for a yacht would seem to be to install at least two CO_2 extinguishers of not less than 3lb (1.3 kilos) each; one of them just inside the main hatch and easily reachable from the cockpit, and the other accessible through the forehatch.

Henry Irving met much the same problems as James Houston when fire broke out in the forecastle of *Strumpet*, although in Irving's case the earlier discomfort of his young son while down below did offer a warning. When Irving found that he couldn't get through the cabin to the source of the fire in the forecastle he knew that he should close the companion hatch to reduce the air flow into the boat, but the wash boards were stowed in the aft locker so he couldn't possibly fit them quickly enough. Instead he went forward on deck and opened the forehatch 'so that Barry could direct the extinguisher onto the source of the fire. Immediately a roar of black smoke and flame shot out of the hatch.'

Vulnerable Dinghies

There is another common factor in both of these incidents and the one to be considered next: an inflatable dinghy, whether lashed on deck or stowed in a locker, becomes very vulnerable when a yacht catches fire. *Ladybee*'s dinghy, already inflated, was on deck, but 'the lashings suddenly became fused to the rails . . . and we saw that the bow of the Avon had a great hole in it'. Fortunately the stern half of the dinghy remained fully inflated, so Houston and his wife were able to get ashore safely in half a dinghy. Henry Irving was less fortunate in *Strumpet*: 'I attempted to unfasten the inflated dinghy from the coach roof, but as I did so the forward section burst into flames, so I abandoned the attempt.' If their friend Peter in his yacht *Temptress* had not been on hand to take them off, the crew of *Strumpet* would have been forced to jump into the sea.

Advantages of Liferaft

A liferaft, packed in a glassfibre canister, would not catch fire as quickly as an unprotected dinghy made from neoprene or some similar material, and there would of course be no delay involved while inflating it. On the other hand, the need to get quickly away from a burning yacht must be borne in mind when considering how heavily ballasted the liferaft should be. A raft such as the Givens might take a fatally long time to paddle clear of danger.

Lightning Strike

The dinghy they had on board *Freedom To* was stowed in the cockpit locker when the yacht was struck by lightning in the English Channel. The dinghy didn't actually catch fire, but 'with Jim making a last desperate effort to free the inflatable . . . we yanked it clear, the rubber rather warm and sticky'. A very close call, and they yet had to inflate it without a pump, using their mouths instead. When they could stand the heat no longer they tossed the partially inflated dinghy into the water and followed it. Having no oars, they had to paddle with their hands to get clear of the yacht, which, with its tanks of diesel fuel and gas bottles, was likely to blow up at any moment.

The risk of a yacht being struck by lightning is very small indeed, but, as the story of *Freedom To* illustrates, when it does happen the result can be devastating and immediate. The crew of the Westerly Vulcan never knew where the fire started, but they did notice that after the strike their VHF antenna had disappeared, so it is possible that disconnecting it from the radio-telephone during the thunderstorm may have saved them. Generally, the initial damage caused by lightning striking a yacht is likely to be around the chain plates to which the mast shrouds are attached. When thunderstorms are around, some people attach a short length of chain to one of their topmast shrouds or the backstay and let it trail in the water.

EXHAUSTION OR ILLNESS

Several of the losses described in this book, especially those resulting from errors in navigation, can be attributed to faulty judgement, caused by exhaustion after long hours at the helm.

Gradual Onset of Fatigue

After he had lost *Smew*, Edward Nott-Bower realised how insidiously fatigue had crept over him, saying: 'It is difficult to trace the exact stages by which one is transmuted from a reasonably energetic and companionable person at sea to a silent, slow-moving being whose mind and muscles are clogged with heavy lassitude, and whose every thought and movement demand a conscious effort of will.'

Twenty-four hours in command of a yacht under difficult conditions are usually enough to reduce the ordinary yachtsman to a state of fatigue, and, if this period is extended to include two nights without sleep, then efficiency will drop off dramatically. Unfortunately, as Nott-Bower observed, there is never a point at which one becomes sharply aware of the change that has taken place in one's ability to deal with quite ordinary tasks such as identifying the characteristics of lights and appreciating their significance. Persuading oneself that a light is the one you so badly want to see while subconsciously ignoring the fact that its characteristic is not correct, would seem to be what James Griffin did as *Northern Light* approached the Straits of Gibraltar. 'At 1930 we saw a lighthouse flashing twice every six seconds and went wild with delight . . . we had done it, after 20 days at sea.' They took the light to be that of Tarifa, the characteristic of which is Gp Fl(3) 10 sec.

Short Spells of Sleep

Some singlehanders follow the example of Blondie Hasler and get their rest in short spells of half an hour or even less, depending entirely upon an alarm clock or timer to waken them. Bearing in mind the clock that let Conor O'Brien down, it would be safer to set two alarms.

Even the apparent protection of Boulogne's outer harbour proved unsafe for Clementina Gordon in her Silhouette. 'I dozed off, thinking myself perfectly secure. When I came to, the wind had flown round . . . Force 7.'

Seasickness and Serious Illness

Seasickness greatly accelerates the onset of exhaustion, and present-day yachtsmen are very fortunate in having drugs which will prevent most people from being sick without slowing up their reactions too seriously.

In 1967, before the days of Stugeron, Peter Rose thought he had been suffering from the side effects of a particular type of drug contained in some anti-seasickness tablets. So, before leaving Nova Scotia bound for England, he and his crew Paul 'jettisoned all anti-seasickness tablets'. But the pills were not the whole cause of Peter Rose's trouble, because 'as the days went on the fatigue increased and changed to exhaustion. During this period Paul handled the yacht by himself – either letting the boat self-steer when he needed rest or heaving-to when conditions were such that *Odd Times* would not hold a reasonable course.' But Rose knew, after a week of this, that the time had come to make a decision. 'There seemed to be three possibilities open to us. To carry on, to turn back towards Newfoundland or to seek assistance.' After weighing up these alternatives, he chose to look for help, which came in the form of a Spanish trawler whose radio facilities they then used to contact a tug bound for St John's. The crew of *Odd Times* were safely transferred to the tug, but the yacht was lost soon afterwards while under tow at too high a speed.

Peter Combe must have been constantly worried that the skipper of *Windstar* would succumb to the diabetes from which he was suffering and then not be able to help in any way. After all, Bertram Currie had only been allowed under protest by his doctors to 'take the trip' provided he did not 'overdo it'. In the event, Currie showed that he was a very remarkable man, who 'managed to give himself his daily injection of insulin – no mean feat in that weather'. However, that kind of resilience on the part of an invalid must not be expected of lesser men, for many of whom the experience in *Windstar* would have been a nightmare.

INSURANCE AND THEFT

Attitudes towards the insurance of yachts vary according to the philosophy of their owners, who are often influenced by the difficulties and very high cost of obtaining any insurance for boats making long voyages – particularly when the craft are old. It would seem that Robin Gardiner-Hill's insurance of *Pentina II* was in good order, because after losing her in the mouth of the Elbe on July 4th, 1979, he purchased another yacht in Hamburg and was on his way again by July 19th. *Northern Light* was also insured, yet as Ann Griffin sadly reflected, 'We were only insured for total loss, but we would have used our life's savings to get her back.'

'Bill' Tilman was less fortunate, and when in the dark he had dropped a note-case containing all his remaining money into the water half-filling *Mischief* as she was about to sink, he wryly remarked: 'Since she was not insured the "trifling sum of misery now added to the foot of the account" hardly mattered.' Tilman then explained that 'the premiums demanded for the sort of voyage *Mischief* undertook were always so high that it had never been worthwhile to insure her'. Bearing in mind Tilman's choice of cruising grounds, one can perhaps understand the insurance companies.

Theft and Vandalism
It is the duty of any skipper to salvage everything he can from a wrecked yacht, and this is doubly important when the loss occurs in some remote place where the native population may consider they are entitled to remove anything from a stranded vessel. George Harrod-Eagles was greatly saddened to find on his return to *Song* the morning after he had been wrecked on the Roncador Reef, off Puerto Rico, that 'The boat had been stripped of everything easily removable from on deck and from below. Sails, anchor, rope, were gone; lockers rifled, empty spaces where once had been the VHF radio, tape recorder, short-wave radio, camera, lenses, film, clothing and equipment. Saddest of all was the loss of my sextant and my log book, with its records of my grand venture. I think then I reached the depths of bitter despair, looking into the chaos and destruction wrought upon my boat.'

It took five days for James Griffin to get permission to return to *Northern Light* after she had been wrecked on rocks inside a prohibited area near Cadiz, and when he and his wife, Ann, finally got back to their yacht, 'vandals had been aboard, stripped her and even taken the bronze strips off her deadlights'.

Index

318

Index